Spirituality and Meaning Making in Chronic Illness

D1600937

SPIRITUALITY and MEANING MAKING in CHRONIC ILLNESS

How Spiritual Caregivers Can Help People
Navigate Long-term Health Conditions

KELLY ARORA

Jessica Kingsley Publishers
London and Philadelphia

First published in 2020
by Jessica Kingsley Publishers
73 Collier Street
London N1 9BE, UK
and
400 Market Street, Suite 400
Philadelphia, PA 19106, USA

www.jkp.com

Library of Congress Cataloging in Publication Data
A CIP catalog record for this book is available from the Library of Congress

British Library Cataloguing in Publication Data
A CIP catalogue record for this book is available from the British Library

ISBN 978 1 78450 996 5
eISBN 978 1 78592 658 7

Printed and bound in the United States

This book is written for everyone with a chronic health condition. May your stories be received with compassion, and may you find healing on your illness journey.

Disclaimer

The information contained in this book is not intended to replace the services of trained medical or behavioral health professionals or to be a substitute for medical advice. You are advised to consult a doctor on any matters relating to your health, and in particular on any matters that may require diagnosis or medical attention.

Contents

Acknowledgments

My family didn't volunteer for this illness journey, yet they are always loving, gracious, and dependable companions. Thank you, Nitu, for your deep reservoir of love and support as I find my way in life. Together, we've traveled an unexpected path that continues to unfold in front of us. I appreciate your careful review of the manuscript and recollection of the early days. Katie, you deserve a special shout-out for your work as Editor Extraordinaire on this manuscript. My work benefits from your careful eye and insightful questions, and my spirit benefits from your irreplaceable friendship. Alex, you always encourage me when I struggle: your hugs and humor are truly healing balms. Go Red Team!

Carrie Doehring, my life wouldn't be the same without you as friend and colleague. I treasure every conversation in which we dig deeply into the messiness and goodness of life. Debbie McCulliss, you inspire me every day to pursue my dreams. Linda Douty, I am forever grateful for your wise companionship on my spiritual journey. Sarah Norwood, you are a healer, a guide, and a light on my path. Thank you for inviting me into new worlds and revealing new possibilities for who and how I can be in this world.

Amos Bailey, Regina Fink, and Nancy Robertson: Thank you for ensuring I had the time needed to bring this book to life. It is a gift to know each of you and to work with you as a team. Mom, thank you for your unending support in all that I do. I also offer gratitude to the many friends, co-workers, students, and clients who helped form me as an academic, as a spiritual caregiver, and as a person. Emily Badger, editor at Jessica Kingsley Publishers, ensured that all the elements of the book came together.

Special thanks to the spirit of L. Frank Baum and the creative minds at Metro-Goldwyn-Mayer for bringing to life the rich story of *The Wizard of Oz*. I offer this book in gratitude for my trip on the Yellow Brick Road with rheumatoid arthritis, a demanding companion and wise teacher.

Last, but never least, I thank my spirit guides for creative insights and for encouraging me to be brave.

Namaste.

Introduction

I survived two powerful tornadoes in my lifetime. When I was 11 years old, a violent tornado devastated my hometown of Salina, Kansas. Ironically, our family lived in "tornado alley" in a small brick house without a basement or storm cellar.[1] When public sirens announced imminent danger of a tornado, we had to run through the storm, cross the main street in front of our house, and pound furiously on the front door of the elderly couple who offered us shelter in their basement. On that fateful night in 1973, our pajama-clad family ran out of our home into the greenish darkness of the severe storm, wind and rain spiraling around us, toward hoped-for safety on the other side. My palms still sweat when I recall the panic I felt as I banged my fists frantically on our neighbors' front door to wake them while my youngest brother screamed, "Don't let me die! Don't let me die!" Thankfully, we survived the storm and our home was spared damage, but the traumatic effects of this experience left me trembling for years at the mere prediction of rain within miles of where I lived.

The second tornado in my life appeared suddenly and incomprehensibly from clear blue skies when I first noticed piercing pain in my shoulder joints. But as the warning winds

---

1 "Tornado alley" refers to a geographic zone in the United States where tornados are common.

of this disease increased in velocity, damage began to appear: fingers so swollen I could not grip a toothbrush, feet that felt like the bones had been crushed with a sledgehammer, and pain that ricocheted from shoulder to knee to elbow as if my body was a pinball machine. After months of tests, treatments, and anxiety, the tempest was diagnosed as rheumatoid arthritis (RA), an incurable autoimmune disease characterized by systemic fatigue, chronic joint pain, and inflammation. Although the funnel cloud that heralded the diagnostic stage has long since passed, I continue to live with the after-effects of this life-altering tornado. What made the storm of RA, the *disease*, more challenging for me was the lack of psycho-spiritual support for my *illness* experience.[2] My intention in writing this book is to raise awareness of the psycho-spiritual dimensions of chronic illness so all types of spiritual caregivers can ease suffering and promote well-being for people living with long-term health conditions.

The Centers for Disease Control and Prevention (2019) tell us that "six in ten Americans live with at least one chronic disease." Numbers may be even higher in other parts of the world (e.g., Di Benedetto *et al.* 2014). Worldwide, billions of people live with incurable health conditions. Given these staggering numbers, it's critical for *all* care providers to understand how chronic health conditions affect body, mind, and spirit.

Many people describe chronic illness as "a spiritual event" (Balboni and Balboni 2018) because diagnosis with an incurable condition often generates spiritual struggles, beginning with the quintessential question of *Why?* Spiritual distress threatens our ability to cope with pain, to be resilient in the face of ongoing losses and uncertain prognoses, and to maintain a sense of well-being (Abu-Raiya, Pargament, and Exline 2015a). Spirituality comes to the forefront for most people during times of serious illness, and patients want to address spirituality as a part of their

---

2   I define illness, disease, and other key terms in Chapter 1. You can also find **bold** words and phrases in the Glossary.

health care (Kelly, May, and Maurer 2016; MacLean *et al.* 2003; Piderman *et al.* 2008).

Even though the healthcare community around the world recognizes the need for greater attention to patients' spirituality (e.g., Dyer 2011; Gijsberts *et al.* 2019b; Kruizinga *et al.* 2018; National Consensus Project for Quality Palliative Care 2018), numerous studies document the fact that the spiritual dimension of illness (and the chaplains who provide spiritual care) often remains marginalized or neglected in healthcare settings worldwide (Appleby, Wilson, and Swinton 2018b; Arora 2013; Balboni and Balboni 2018; Cheng *et al.* 2018; Franzen 2018; Hutch 2013; Timmins *et al.* 2018; VanderWeele, Balboni, and Koh 2017). Even faith-based healthcare institutions that profess a core value of providing spiritually integrated care may neglect patients' spirituality (Taylor *et al.* 2018). Most biomedical clinicians don't feel equipped or comfortable addressing spirituality (e.g., Appleby *et al.* 2018a; Badaracco 2007; Damen *et al.* 2018). Also problematic are spiritual caregivers[3] outside the healthcare arena (e.g., clergy, spiritual directors) who remain largely unaware of often-invisible chronic health conditions affecting people around them. This spiritual caregiver describes the status quo:

> We are prone to think of illness as a single acute crisis experience in which we are called to provide spiritual support, counsel, and encouragement. Like most other crises, we usually perceive illness as having a beginning, a turning point, and a conclusion. People either get better or they die, and for the most part we can handle that within our pastoral and theological grab-bag.

---

3   I use *spiritual care/caregivers* to reflect the broad definition of **spirituality** described in this book (see the Glossary and Chapter 1). *Pastoral theology* and *pastoral care* are most often associated with Christian theologies. These terms appear in some quotes and, in the context of this book, should be read as a placeholder for *spiritual care/caregivers*. Schuhmann and Damen (2018) and Anderson (2001) describe the way pastoral/spiritual caregivers continue to grapple with self-identity as the spiritual/religious landscape changes around them.

Chronic illness, however, has the power to alter all our predictable patterns of care and counsel. (Vander Zee 2002, p.181)

This book is for professional spiritual care providers, social workers, therapists, and healthcare professionals who care for people affected by incurable diseases. That said, **life-affirming** spiritual care comes from many sources. In fact, spiritual care is more often provided by the patient's family and friends than professional caregivers, and patient satisfaction with spiritual care does not necessarily depend on *who* provides care, but on addressing their spiritual needs (Hanson *et al.* 2008). With this in mind, I also hope this book will equip patients and their informal family caregivers to live well with chronic illness.

Methodology

Peer-reviewed research makes up the sacred canon of the Western healthcare system. Professional organizations that credential chaplains in the United States (e.g., the Association of Professional Chaplains and the Spiritual Care Association) recognize that chaplains need to be research literate in order for their profession to thrive in healthcare contexts (Fitchett *et al.* 2014; HealthCare Chaplaincy Network 2018). In the evidence-based and socially just approach to spiritual care presented in this book, I include studies about diverse illness experiences and spiritualities from around the world. Because evidence-based practice can privilege the voices of researchers over the voices of patients/participants, I also cite studies in support of my experiences, observations, and claims to bear witness to the patients'/participants' stories, "amplifying voices that would otherwise be silent, and connecting in solidarity voices that are otherwise isolated" (Frank 2017, p.6).

I use a critical correlation method (Graham, Walton, and Ward 2005) that brings the fields of spirituality, psychology, and medicine into dialogue about long-term illness experiences. I strive to honor "the distinctive norms and values of each 'conversation partner'" (Ramsay 2004, p.5).[4] I am mindful that the critical correlation method has been critiqued for its focus on the individual (e.g., Graham *et al.* 2005; Ramsay 2004). The use of my own story as a case study is also an individual experience of chronic illness. I address this concern by using an **intercultural spiritual care** approach (Doehring 2015, first published 2006) that considers how experiences are shaped by the familial, social, and cultural communities and systems that make up a person's **web of life** (Miller-McLemore 2008).[5]

The field of pastoral/spiritual theology and care has also been critiqued for privileging the Christian tradition (e.g., Mercadante 2012; Schneiders 2005). My personal spiritual history includes active membership in Lutheran, United Methodist, Episcopal, and Roman Catholic traditions. I am aware of and honor Christian values that remain embedded in my spiritual orienting system. However, today my *lived* spirituality aligns with Buddhist, Hindu, and core shamanic beliefs and practices.[6] Researchers might categorize me as a "**none**," "**unaffiliated**," or "**a religious resistor**" (Pew Research Center 2012, 2018). More generously, I might be

---

4   I am aware that tension between the biomedical goal of curing and the spiritual care goal to facilitate healing can complicate illness and death for patients and providers. Biopolitics is beyond the scope of this book. Coble (2017) provides a helpful exploration. I write with the assumption that biomedical professionals and spiritual caregivers share goals of well-being, quality of life, and a "good death," as defined by the patient.

5   Park (2014) notes that Miller-McLemore's shift from "living human web" to "living web" provides "more room to include different aspects of our lives such as the Internet and other technological developments as well as various non-human contexts such as the global environment and climate change" (p.3.2).

6   For years, I considered myself a Buddhist Christian. See Knitter (2009) for another example of this hybrid identity. In 1991, I married into a Hindu family and embraced aspects of Hindu spirituality. Goldberg (2010) would describe me as a practical Vedantist because I "view spirituality as a developmental process in which each person's spiritual path must be constantly adjusted to suit his or her temperament, circumstances, and ever-evolving needs" (p.23). Since 2013, I have been immersed in intensive education, training, and practice in core shamanism, which I describe in my illness narrative in this book.

described as "**spiritual but not religious**" (Mercadante 2012). For the purposes of this book, I will identify as **spiritually fluid**, a term coined by Bidwell (2018) to describe people who are:

> drawn to multiple traditions at different points in their lives, lured by Mystery itself (which some people, particularly those from a monotheistic stance, call G-d, or the ultimate, or the numinous, or the transcendent). These people are restless until they rest in a combination of spiritual thought and practice—a combination that speaks to and engages their entire being... their spirits adapt to or incorporate multiple experiences, communities, spiritual catalysts, and other circumstances that nourish and mold who they are at a given moment. (p.16)

Use of my personal narrative in this book is one limited way to share "stories seldom heard" from marginalized persons (Moschella 2018, p.20). As a "native informant" (Park 2014, p.3.11), I study, as well as report from, the lived experiences of these marginalized communities:

- Women, whose voices are heard in greater number today, but who remain socially disadvantaged and disempowered around the world (e.g., Gray 2018).

- People living with chronic diseases, whose invisibility is multiplied when their health condition is itself invisible to others. Women are even more disadvantaged as the primary group living with often-invisible chronic conditions (Hirsch 2018; Thorne, McCormick, and Carty 1997).

- People who are spiritually fluid, a group that remains "almost invisible outside academic conversations. They exist at the edges of spiritual and religious communities, erased from public view and rarely heard in public conversations about religion" (Bidwell 2018, p.19). More specifically, I represent people whose spiritual practices include direct engagement with the spiritual dimension (i.e., people who practice core shamanism), experiences that are often underreported for fear of stigma (Laird, Curtis, and Morgan 2017; Yaden *et al.* 2016).

Narrative framework

People make sense of their lives through narratives or stories (e.g., Grant, Sallaz, and Cain 2016). **Narrative approaches to spiritual care** view people as **living human documents**, explicitly and implicitly telling the stories of their lives (e.g., Cooper-White 2004; Gerkin 1984). People seek to reinforce the plots of their life stories *and* they are also able to create more life-affirming narratives when existing stories do not contribute to their well-being (e.g., Arora 2013; Carr, McCaffery, and Ortiz 2017; Neuger 2001; Risk 2013; White and Epston 1990). Narrative approaches view storytelling as a healing practice for both individuals and communities (Frank 2017). Narrative methods contribute "thick descriptions" (Geertz 1973) that help spiritual caregivers better understand the diversity of experiences, backgrounds, and contexts that affect the people in their care (Arora and McCulliss 2015; Moschella 2018).

The relatively new field of narrative medicine focuses on **illness narratives** to help healthcare providers "enter the worlds of their patients, if only imaginatively, and to see and interpret these worlds from the patients' point of view" (Charon 2006, p.9; see also Stanley and Hurst 2011). One healing professional said that "narrative medicine is to the management of suffering as biomedicine is to the management of disease" (Egnew 2018, p.163). Illness narratives are created by patients and the people in their **web of life** to make sense of illness and suffering from that person's particular vantage point. Illness narratives help people answer questions like *Why is this illness happening?* and *How will I cope with this illness and suffering that results from it?* Narratives around a particular illness experience influence each other and the ways in which people within the patient's web of life interact (Kalitzkus and Matthiessen 2009).

Many illness narratives are structured as restitution, chaos, or quest narratives (Frank 2013, first published 1995). In a restitution narrative, the person is healthy, becomes sick, and regains health. This story's happy ending is typically associated with acute illness experiences, and it's the most common type of illness narrative. Chronic illness is often told as a chaos narrative in which the person never gets better. In quest narratives, the person actively embraces the illness experience, often in the form of a journey, and gains from the illness experience.

The narrative framework in this book is provided by the story of Dorothy Gale, the protagonist in the beloved literary and film classic *The Wizard of Oz* (Baum 1899; Fleming and Vidor 1939). The original literary rendition of *The Wizard of Oz* has been read as a metaphor for topics such as political-historical commentary in the late 19th century (e.g., Liebhold 2016) and the spiritual journey in contemporary times (e.g., Houston 2012). Years ago, I discovered that *The Wizard of Oz* also rings true as a quest metaphor for the chronic illness journey. I expanded on Fetters' (2006) use of the story to teach medical students and have since used *The Wizard of Oz* to teach hundreds of spiritual caregivers, healthcare providers, undergraduate and graduate students, and adults learners about chronic illness experiences.

The cinematic version of *The Wizard of Oz* is oft-cited as one of the favorite films of all time (e.g., Shoard 2010). The story is familiar to millions of people across generations who have seen it broadcast regularly on television since 1956 (Library of Congress 2018). The film stands the test of time because Dorothy's tale is a **hero's journey**, an archetypal story in which people readily see themselves (Campbell 2008; see an example of using the hero's journey to understand work–life balance with multiple sclerosis in Vijayasingham 2018). Although *The Wizard of Oz* is not explicitly a story of chronic illness, this hero's journey aptly illustrates the liminal space inhabited by people with chronic health conditions who vacillate between **illness-in-the-foreground** (Dorothy in the Land of Oz) and **wellness-in-the-foreground** (Dorothy in Kansas).

I will use my personal quest narrative as a case study to help flesh out the archetypal experiences revealed in Dorothy's narrative. I write this book and share my story from the intersection of four distinct, yet overlapping, worlds:

- I am Co-Director and Assistant Clinical Professor of Spiritual Care for the Interdisciplinary Graduate Certificate and Master of Science in Palliative Care[7] degree programs at the University of Colorado Anschutz Medical Campus in Denver, Colorado. I teach spiritual care practices to palliative care providers around the world, including biomedical clinicians (physicians, nurses, physician assistants, pharmacists), social workers, psychologists, spiritual caregivers, and other allied health professionals.

- As the John Wesley Iliff Senior Adjunct Lecturer in Spiritual Care at the Iliff School of Theology in Denver, Colorado, I teach spiritual care to graduate and doctoral students who will support and help diverse people in varied contexts, with a special emphasis on people who are underserved or marginalized.

- As a spiritual director/companion for over two decades and as a healer using core shamanic practices,[8] I have provided spiritual care to many people who live with chronic health conditions.

- I am a person living with a chronic health condition. Over 20 years ago, I was diagnosed with rheumatoid arthritis, a chronic, invisible, incurable disease. I use my

---

7 **Palliative care** is specialized health care that eases physical, psychological, social, and spiritual suffering and improves quality of life for people and families living with serious and life-limiting illnesses.

8 I describe spiritual direction and core shamanic practices in Chapter 4.

story to provide contemporary and concrete examples of the spiritual dimensions of chronic illness. My story also offers glimpses into the potential for wholistic healing and well-being made possible by core shamanic practices that honor interconnections among mind, body, and spirit at energetic and spiritual levels.

Looking ahead

The chapters in this book follow Dorothy's journey from Kansas to Oz and back. Dorothy's tale has much to teach us about the journey of chronic illness. Following the tornadic experience of illness onset and diagnosis, our hero reluctantly begins to explore an unknown land where illness is in the foreground. As Dorothy and her companions follow the Yellow Brick Road in search of healing, we'll consider how their experiences can inform our practice of spiritual care for people with long-term health conditions.

Our hero/patient eventually returns to Kansas, the land of wellness-in-the-foreground. Because of her experiences in Oz, she can claim citizenship within both worlds of wellness and illness, highlighting the way many people with chronic illnesses must navigate shifts between these experiences. I use my own story to further illuminate practices of spiritual care that can ease suffering on the chronic illness journey. In each chapter, I offer guidelines and practical tools to help you integrate what you learn from this book into your own lives and practices of spiritual care.

Chapter 1 describes the unsettling threat and onset of a life-altering disease: the unwanted call to the hero's journey of chronic illness. This chapter also introduces important terms and concepts. In Chapter 2, I describe common ways people make meaning about the cause of illness. We focus on how people make meaning of chronic illness early in their experience, typically around diagnosis, illustrated by Dorothy in her conversation with Glinda, the Good Witch.

As our hero begins her journey on the Yellow Brick Road, the reality of long-term illness threatens Dorothy's well-being. Chapter 3 describes common psycho-spiritual concerns associated with chronic illness experiences. We consider losses, disenfranchised grief, anxiety, depression, demoralization, and the desire for hastened death. We also reflect on the burden family caregivers bear as part of their illness experience. In Chapter 4, Dorothy and her companions cope with the stress of illness in the chronic phase of their journeys. I identify common spiritual struggles associated with chronic illness, describe how people draw on spirituality to cope with stress, and recommend spiritual coping strategies that facilitate healing and well-being. Chapter 5 takes a closer look at the therapeutic relationship between patient and healer. We explore aspects of healing relationships and the importance of hope, using Professor Marvel and the Wizard of Oz as our case studies. In Chapter 6, the film ends as Dorothy shifts into a recovery phase and returns to wellness-in-the-foreground in Kansas. We return to the type of meaning making that typically occurs later in the chronic illness trajectory. We consider potential benefits and opportunities for post-traumatic growth from chronic health conditions. Finally, we consider how people ultimately negotiate a balance within and between the worlds of wellness-in-the-foreground and illness-in-the-foreground.

Although I write directly to spiritual caregivers, this book is for everyone affected by chronic health conditions. Perhaps you seek a better understanding of the spiritual dimensions of your own illness or wish to support someone you care for in some capacity. My hope is that immersion in Dorothy's story and my personal experiences will enhance your ability to care for people you know who live with chronic health conditions. Always keep in mind that illness experiences are unique for each person, and spiritual care must be specific to the person to help alleviate suffering. May these stories encourage you as you offer compassionate, authentic, and potentially transformative care for people with chronic health conditions. Whatever brings you to the Land of Oz, I invite you to join me now as we follow the Yellow Brick Road.

1

The Calm Before the Storm

WELLNESS-IN-THE-FOREGROUND

Once upon a time, our heroes' stories begin with normal, healthy lives. It's the calm before the storm of illness. This chapter describes the unsettling threat and onset of a life-altering disease for both Dorothy and me—our unwanted calls to the **hero's journey** of chronic illness. But before we step into these worlds, we need to pack our bags for the journey with shared understandings of key terms, basic skills for offering spiritual care to people who have chronic illnesses, and a map of the Yellow Brick Road.

Our natural inclination is to assume that other people think the way we do. Unfortunately, this belief can lead to misunderstandings and even disastrous outcomes (Briggs 2016). For example, the vast majority of adults in the United States believe that miracles are possible today (Association of Religion Data Archives 2012), but it's not always clear what people mean when they "hope for a miracle" during a health crisis. Researchers found that hope for a miracle may be a literal appeal for divine intervention, a symbolic hope for recovery, an expression of shaken faith, or a strategic way to wield power over family members or healthcare providers (Shinall, Stahl, and Bibler 2018). Another study shows a broad range of what people mean when they say they want healthcare providers to "do everything" for them in a health crisis (Quill, Arnold, and Back 2009). Different meanings of terms and understandings of illness require different responses from healthcare *and* spiritual care providers. As I describe in greater detail later in this chapter, attention to often-subtle differences in values, beliefs, practices, and meanings between caregiver and care receiver is a critical skill in both intercultural spiritual care (Greider 2018) and health care (Kørup *et al.* 2018). You likely have thoughtfully considered understandings of the terms I use in this book, but I don't want to assume you know what *I* mean when I use these terms. Refer to the Glossary for definitions of these and other bold terms used in this book.

Definitions

To many people, **disease** and **illness** mean the same thing: a person is sick or unhealthy. However, the subtle difference between these terms is quite important. Where health care is dominated by biomedicine, people often think of disease and illness as physical conditions,[1] distinct from psychological, social, and spiritual experiences. *All* healthcare providers address disease, a medically defined condition in which physiological structure and/or function are impaired (Cassell 2004, first published 1991). *Some* healthcare providers address illness.

Illness encompasses all dimensions of the person: physical, mental, psychological, spiritual, and social. Illness is a person's subjective experience of disease and their response to the diagnosis and multi-dimensional effects of living with the disease (Kleinman 1988). While only one person has the disease, that person *and* members of that person's web of life have **illness experiences** related to the disease (e.g., Mehta and Cohen 2009).

---

1   As Miller (2010) indicates, understandings of mental illness are also increasingly rooted in the body.

We always want to keep in mind that illness experiences affect each person differently:

> For example, two people living with lung cancer may have markedly different symptoms, functional limitations, and psychosocial [and spiritual] responses to the illness. Even in describing chronic illness, there is no limit to the factors or combination that make every individual's experience unique. (Nichols and Hunt 2011, p.53)

Chronic illness is an ongoing experience related to incurable diseases (Larsen 2016). Chronic illness is often experienced as a **liminal** state in which the patient[2] exists on a continuum between illness and wellness. The description of this woman illustrates the challenge of living in a liminal state:

> "I can't say I'm healthy anymore," but she also resists describing herself as being ill... Caught in the "between"—the expanse between being healthy and being acutely ill—[she] reveals how language fails to account for the experience of chronic illness. Rather, she searches for a "new way" or a "new word" to describe herself. (Ironside *et al.* 2003, p.179)

Chronic health conditions can affect a patient's web of life for many years, particularly affecting the inner circle of the web that includes the person's family system (Baider 2012). The **family system** is made up of every person considered family by the patient (Dale and Smith 2013, first published 2003). In addition to blood relations, a family system may include spouses/partners, foster parents, stepparents, former partners, and advisors or friends who are so close emotionally or so important to the patient's well-being that they are part of the inner circle.

Wellness-in-the-foreground (WITF) and **illness-in-the-foreground** (IITF) describe a person's relative location within the

---

2   I use *patient* and *person* living with chronic illness interchangeably for variety. In some cases, *person* may refer other members of a patient's web of life, and this should be clear from the context in which I use these terms.

liminal reality of chronic illness (Paterson 2001). During periods of WITF, pain and other symptoms are well managed, illness is not the person's focus (although it may still require attention), and the person experiences a sense of control and stability. During IITF, pain and suffering return the focus of attention to the illness. Life may feel chaotic, uncertain, and unstable.

Because this book is about chronic illness, I won't often refer to **curing**—the eradication of disease. Within the context of spiritual care for people living with incurable diseases, we'll focus on healing, using a definition that comes directly from patients: **healing** is a dynamic and ongoing process of seeking, restoring, and experiencing wholeness and well-being (Scott *et al.* 2017). People can experience healing without a change in health status. People who have chronic diseases may not think of themselves as healthy, per se, although they may experience periods of relatively good health (i.e., WITF) (Brody 2015; Huber *et al.* 2011).

Wholeness and **wholistic care**[3] describe the inclusion and integration of all dimensions of a person's life that influence well-being: physical, psychological, spiritual, and social (Dyer 2011; Kirmayer 2004; Thomas *et al.* 2018). **Well-being** is a person's subjective experience of life satisfaction or contentment, even in the midst of stressful experiences, such as chronic illness (Baldacchino 2003; Freeman 1998). Like healing, well-being is also a dynamic state of being. Signs of spiritual well-being include a sense of inner peace, a sense of hope, and feelings of self-worth (Schultz *et al.* 2017). People who experience spiritual well-being are able to share emotions, make meaning of their experiences, and engage in spiritual practices that help maintain an overall state of well-being (Murray *et al.* 2004).

People with chronic illnesses may find it particularly challenging to experience well-being when they're coping with pain. The International Association for the Study of Pain defines

---

3   *Wholistic* care is sometimes written as *holistic*. I use *wholistic* to emphasize the importance of mind–body–spirit *whole*ness. See Ziebarth (2016).

pain as "an unpleasant sensory and emotional experience associated with actual or potential tissue damage, or described in terms of such damage" (2018). The working definition most often used in health care is: "pain is whatever the experiencing person says it is, existing whenever the experiencing person says it does" (Margo McCaffery cited by Pirschel 2018). These definitions reveal that pain has both an objective quality (it is a physiological phenomenon) and a subjective quality (the person's response to these sensations).[4] **Suffering** describes a person's response to pain and other physical, psychological, social, and spiritual distress related to chronic illness.

Scholars in psychology, medicine, and spirituality have been grappling for years with definitions of **spirituality** and **religion** (e.g., Anderson 2001; Coruh *et al.* 2005; Pargament 2007; Zinnbauer *et al.* 1997). It's difficult to translate the complex ways these terms have been understood within religious and theological settings in ways that are relevant and compelling to healthcare professionals today. Changes in popular usage of these terms over time also complicate definitions (Bregman 2004). However, there is growing consensus that *spirituality* is the more inclusive term and is more appropriate for use within caregiving relationships (e.g., Hall, Meador, and Koenig 2008; Puchalski *et al.* 2014).

Since 2009, national experts from diverse fields have met a number of times to discuss how to integrate spirituality into health care (Puchalski *et al.* 2014). We'll use their consensus definition of **spirituality** as "the aspect of humanity that refers to the way individuals seek and express meaning and purpose and the way they experience their connectedness to the moment, to self, to others, to nature, and to the significant or sacred" (Puchalski *et al.* 2014, p.643).[5] **The sacred** is a term coined by Pargament (1997;

---

4   See Cohen (2016), Faraj (2019), and Taylor (2010) for patient and clinician reflections on how challenging it is to reliably describe and quantify pain.
5   Gijsberts *et al.* (2019a) note that this definition is nearly identical to the definition used by the European Association for Palliative Care (EAPC).

Pargament *et al.* 2017) for the myriad ways people talk about what is of ultimate importance to them. We'll use *the sacred* in this book as a placeholder for the diverse terms you'll encounter in spiritual care relationships. The sacred is something greater than the person, with qualities of boundlessness and infinitude. What a person holds sacred may change with time and experience (Pargament 2007). These definitions of spirituality and the sacred do not require belief in God (also known as Allah, Yahweh, Spirit, Brahma, etc.) or other divine beings. People who identify as atheist or agnostic[6] still hold worldviews that help them "*ask* and *reflect on* 'big questions'…e.g., what exists? how should we live?" (Taves, Asprem, and Ihm 2018, p.207; emphasis in original).

The sacred is at the core of each person's unique **spiritual orienting system** (SOS): the set of values, beliefs, meanings, and practices that guide behaviors and decision making and help people understand who they are and their purpose in the world. A spiritual orienting system is like a GPS—a global positioning system—that orients us, provides a sense of coherence, and offers guidance or direction. If spirituality is like a *global* positioning system, religion is like a *localized* orienting system. **Religion** refers to an established set of values, beliefs, practices, meanings, and relationships shared among people who are part of public and/or private organizations that focus on the big questions of life (e.g., the Church of Jesus Christ of Latter-day Saints, Hinduism, Jediism) (Pargament 2007; Zinnbauer *et al.* 1997). A person's global SOS may include a localized orienting system(s) that orients them to a particular religious tradition(s).

Spiritual struggles are conflicts related to some aspect(s) of a person's spiritual orienting system (Pargament 2007). Spiritual conflicts may be *intra*personal (Abu-Raiya *et al.* 2015a; Roze des Ordons *et al.* 2018). For example, a person might resist a new way of thinking, or a family member might feel challenged to live out

---

6   The diverse categories of atheist and agnostic are further described in Hafiz (2013) and Lipka (2013).

a core value of independence while caring for someone who is ill. People also experience *inter*personal spiritual struggles (Abu-Raiya *et al.* 2015a; Roze des Ordons *et al.* 2018). An interpersonal struggle might refer to conflict between family members about the cause or meaning of an illness. People may also have conflicts with the sacred (Abu-Raiya *et al.* 2015a; Roze des Ordons *et al.* 2018). This struggle often takes the form of questions about why the illness is happening. To complicate matters, people can experience multiple spiritual struggles at the same time.

Spiritual struggles are experienced as **spiritual distress** (Schultz *et al.* 2017). Spiritual distress is *not* the opposite of spiritual well-being. People can experience spiritual distress *and* spiritual well-being at the same time. Spiritual distress is like having day-to-day conflicts with someone you love. Even in conflict, you still love and feel loved by this person, and, overall, your relationship isn't threatened as you experience these struggles. We can also think of spiritual struggles as ripples in the larger ocean of spiritual well-being. As spiritual care providers, we want to prevent these ripples from becoming waves that overwhelm people living with chronic illness. When this happens, struggles can develop into **spiritual crises**, events that severely undermine or destroy the person's relationship with what is sacred or their ability to make meaning of life experiences.

These key definitions will guide our conversation throughout the book. There are two more topics that deserve our attention before we begin our journey. First, I introduce intercultural spiritual care. Then, I explain how *The Wizard of Oz* serves as a metaphor for the chronic illness journey.

Intercultural spiritual care

Until relatively recently, most spiritual care relationships took place between people with shared religious orienting systems. Today, people have easy access to information through the internet, and they are exposed to diverse belief systems from all parts of the world. A multitude of beliefs, values, practices, and meanings now have the potential to inform people's spiritual orienting systems, depending on a person's curiosity and openness to change (e.g., Bidwell 2018; Gecewicz 2018). SOSs are simply too diverse, and people are too unique for caregivers to make assumptions about shared values, beliefs, and meanings, even when they share a religious identity with the other person. For example, today *Christian* is an incredibly diverse category that includes numerous denominations and non-denominational identities that are further complexified by localized congregational, as well as personal, interpretations and lived practices. Other religious and non-religious spiritual traditions and identities present the same challenges. In light of this reality, I consider *every* spiritual care conversation to be **interspiritual dialogue**, dialogue between people with unique spiritual orienting systems.

The intercultural approach to spiritual care used in this book was first described by Lartey (2003) "to push spiritual caregivers beyond recognition of diverse cultures to a critical awareness and engagement with that which is 'other' in careseekers" (p.2).[7] Doehring (2010, 2013) further describes **intercultural spiritual care** as an approach that explicitly recognizes diversity in spiritual beliefs and practices (see also Clegg 2014). Intercultural spiritual care emphasizes the caregiver's self-awareness, values the unique qualities and attributes of each person, and respects the person as the expert on his or her SOS and life experiences. Intercultural spiritual care also facilitates collaborative meaning making (Doehring 2013), an important practice to help people living with chronic illnesses to experience healing and well-being.

I find it helpful to think about spiritual care conversations as if we're entering another person's spiritual home.[8] When we visit

---

someone's physical home for the first time, we enter a relatively public area, often a living room or other family space. Only after we develop a relationship of trust with this person is it likely that we'll be invited into more private areas, such as bedrooms. Let's take this analogy a bit further. When we enter someone's home, we don't typically walk in and rearrange their furniture because *we* like to have a lamp in the corner, or *we* would prefer the chair by a window. Rather, we respect the way they have arranged and decorated their space.

This respectful behavior is also appropriate when we enter someone's *spiritual* home. Instead of trying to recreate our own comfort zone through assumed values, beliefs, meanings, and practices, we want to remain curious and pay attention to how this person's spiritual home is different from our SOS. We should also focus our attention within a person's spiritual home as we would in their physical home. For example, most people's homes include chairs for sitting. When we enter someone's physical home, we wouldn't typically comment on the fact that they have a chair, unless that chair is particularly unusual. Instead, we're more likely to notice and comment on personal items that express who this person is, such as artwork or family photos. Focusing on similarities (e.g., having a place to sit) in the care receiver's spiritual home can be helpful, but it also can lure us into making assumptions about what else we have in common. When we notice what makes this person's spiritual home special and different from our SOS (e.g., artwork, family photos), we gain deeper insight into the other person's spiritual life. Our curiosity about these differences builds trust with the person and improves our chances of being invited deeper into their spiritual home/SOS.

SNAP is an easy-to-remember mnemonic I created to teach healthcare professionals how to practice intercultural spiritual care with patients: **S**elf-awareness, stay in the **N**ow, **A**sk questions, and let the other **P**erson guide the conversation. SNAP will also help you remember the key skills in intercultural care with people living with chronic illness.

SNAP: Self-awareness

Respect for the other person requires an ongoing practice of Self-awareness so we don't make assumptions or unintentionally impose our own values, beliefs, and meanings on that person (i.e., so we don't rearrange the furniture in the other person's spiritual home) (Doehring 2013). Our spiritual values, beliefs, and meanings are of ultimate importance to us. When these aspects of our SOS feel threatened, we can respond in emotionally charged ways, such as becoming defensive about our own beliefs; imposing our ideas on the other person; expressing judgment through words, tone of voice, or body language; or withdrawing from the other person to avoid conflict. Self-awareness makes it less likely that we'll respond in these ways and endanger the spiritual care relationship.

It's the caregiver's responsibility to monitor the power dynamics of the caregiving relationship. We need to maintain balance between being in control of the conversation to gain important information (e.g., *Are you thinking about taking your life?*) and being receptive so that care receivers lead the conversation deeper into their spiritual worlds (Doehring 2015, first published 2006). Self-awareness includes an ongoing practice of reflecting on caregiving experiences in order to enhance our spiritual care practice going forward (Skinner and Mitchell 2016). At the end of this section, I provide an exercise to help enhance your self-awareness.

SNAP: Stay in the Now

Spiritual caregivers create and nurture relationships in which people feel safe enough to be vulnerable about their spiritual questions and concerns (White 2006). We facilitate these relationships by being a compassionate and healing presence (Connell and Beardsley 2014). Compassion differs from *sympathy*, which is motivated by pity, and *empathy*, which demonstrates our effort to understand another person's position.

Compassion "requires action and is motivated by virtues such as love, kindness, and genuineness, thereby rendering it more dynamic and distinct" than sympathy or empathy (Sinclair *et al.* 2018, p.2). We look deeper into these aspects of healing relationships in Chapter 5.

Contemplative practices (e.g., meditation and mindfulness practices) help prepare spiritual caregivers to go beyond "invitational silences" that encourage people to say more. Contemplative practices equip spiritual care providers to offer "compassionate silences" during care conversations. In these silences, compassion is:

> transmitted through a quality of mind that requires active intentional mental processes—it is the opposite of passive, receptive activity. These compassionate silences arise spontaneously from the [provider] who has developed the mental capacities of stable attention, emotional balance, along with prosocial mental qualities, such as naturally arising empathy and compassion. (Back *et al.* 2009, p.1114)

Contemplative practices help us continually to bring ourselves back to the present moment and stay in the Now during spiritual care conversations. Our commitment to a "contemplative stance" makes it more likely we'll be invited into more private spaces within the other person's spiritual home (Clayton 2013).

SNAP: **A**sk questions and let the other **P**erson guide the conversation

People may be reluctant to talk about spirituality explicitly. A 2018 survey shows that:

> a range of internal conflicts is driving Americans from God-talk. Some said these types of conversations create tension or arguments (28 percent); others feel put off by how religion has been politicized (17 percent); others still report not wanting to

appear religious (7 percent), sound weird (6 percent) or seem extremist (5 percent). (Merritt 2018)

When people do talk about spirituality, they may not be fluent in the vocabulary that spiritual care providers are comfortable using in their personal or professional lives (e.g., Schmohl 2017). People are often more inclined to talk about *core* values, beliefs, and meanings without explicitly connecting them to the idea of a spiritual orienting system (e.g., Antonio *et al.* 2014; Molzahn *et al.* 2012). This may be particularly true with teens and younger adults (Barton *et al.* 2018). Spiritual caregivers should follow the other person's lead with regard to vocabulary used to talk about what is sacred or of ultimate importance to them. If the other person refers to the sacred as *God*, we should use *God*. If the other person uses *Higher Truth*, that's the term we should use. This rule applies to all spiritually oriented vocabulary. Using the other person's choice of words demonstrates that you are attentive to and respectful of the unique elements in that person's spiritual home.

Even as we use the other person's terms, it's important to maintain a posture of humility and not assume we know what the other person means by these terms (Stanley and Hurst 2011). This includes the way the other person describes the sacred (e.g., God, Allah, Yahweh, Hashem, the Divine, a Higher Power, Ultimate Truth, Ultimate Reality, Vishnu, Krishna, Buddha, a Moral Compass, the Greater Good, Nature, or the Highest Self, to name but a few examples). Caregivers need to remain curious, with an attitude of "not-knowing" about the other person's experiences and SOS (Arora 2011).

Staying humble and curious means we might literally **A**sk questions like *What does atheist mean to you?* or *How would you describe the way the Holy Spirit works today?* We might also express curiosity in the form of a statement: *I'd like to understand what you mean when you say you "deserve cancer as punishment."* Or we might offer an invitation: *Please say more about how* *you're suffering today.* When we remain curious and use their vocabulary, the other **Person** stays in the lead and may guide us deeper into their SOS. The **A** and **P** steps of SNAP also relieve the pressure some caregivers feel to be knowledgeable about all belief systems they might encounter in practice—a truly impossible task. People are spiritually diverse and unique. We can and must trust them to be the experts on their spiritual orienting systems. Now you have the opportunity to practice the first skill in SNAP: Self-awareness.

Integration: Self-awareness exercise

This self-reflection exercise will help you become more aware of your embedded values and beliefs related to health and illness.

Imagine you are a tree. The roots of your tree represent deeply held or embedded core values and beliefs that make up your spiritual orienting system. These embedded values and beliefs came from family, society, and culture as you were growing up. The deepest roots, from our earliest years of life, are not necessarily the thickest or strongest roots, but they anchor us in a shared system that can be challenging to change. As you grew older, you took on values and beliefs from new life experiences. These values and beliefs are often represented by stronger, thicker portions of the root system because you chose them for yourself, rather than inheriting them from others. It's often easier to see our embedded values and beliefs in the ways our parents or other primary caregivers lived out this shared root system.

- Think about the people who took care of you when you were growing up, and make a list of your embedded values and beliefs about health and illness. Consider these questions:

  - How were you explicitly and implicitly taught to care for your body (e.g., consider exercise, diet, and sexual activity)?

- Where did your family seek health care when someone was sick (e.g., home remedies, folk healers, spiritual healers, biomedical providers, or some combination of healers)?

- How were sick family members expected to behave (e.g., keep working despite pain or illness, take time off to recuperate, or use illness as a means of gaining extra attention)?

- How were you taught to care for people who were ill or dying (e.g., avoid them until the illness passed or wait on their every need)?

- Which of the embedded values and beliefs lived out in your family (or societal or cultural context) do you still claim as core values and beliefs today?

Your embedded values are below ground in the root structure, and your *lived* values are visible as the branches and fruit of the tree, expressed through your words and actions. Lived values may include or replace embedded childhood values. For example, generations of my family have raised cattle. Our family values the farming/ranching way of life and the place of animal protein in the human diet. However, as an adult, I have been vegetarian or have eaten a primarily vegetable-based diet for many years.

- Now make a list of the values and beliefs about health and illness that you live out today.

When we can live out our core values, we experience well-being. If I work in a setting where I can express my core value of helping people heal from spiritual struggles, I feel aligned with my purpose in life. However, when I'm in a setting that focuses on administrative tasks, I can feel dissatisfied or distressed because I am not living out this core value of relationship building. In times of stress (e.g., someone challenges our value system, or an embedded value feels threatened by current circumstances), values and beliefs from childhood and youth may surprise us and rise to the surface. We have the potential to become protective—even defensive—about them. We may impose our values/beliefs on the other person or withdraw from the person to avoid further conflict.

- Think of a time when you experienced a core values conflict. How did you respond (withdrew, became defensive, imposed your values/beliefs on the other person, expressed judgment through words, tone, or body language)?

- How do you wish you had responded in this situation?

- We often become aware of our emotions through our bodies. Think about how your body responds to stress (e.g., clenched jaw, tight fists, shallow breathing, upset stomach, etc.). Use physical signs to remain self-aware when you experience conflicts in spiritual care conversations with people who have chronic health conditions so you can respond in ways that nurture healing relationships.[9]

The hero's journey

People have used metaphors for centuries to better understand and describe the complexities and ineffable qualities of illness experiences (e.g., Duval 1984; Kistner 1998; Kralik 2002). Some scholars have challenged the usefulness and ramifications of using metaphors in relation to illness experiences (Clow 2001; Kirmayer 2004; Klass 2014; Sontag 2001, first published 1978). However, using culturally significant metaphors can support public acknowledgment and validation of illness experiences, reducing the chance that these experiences will become disenfranchised (Glucklich 2001). Metaphors also provide an

---

9   Arora (2011) provides an extensive exercise in self-awareness across all dimensions of social identity.

accessible way to explore stories that are challenging to articulate (Camus 2009) and to make meaning of life experiences (Baldwin, Landau, and Swanson 2018).

In this book, we'll explore chronic illness experiences using the monomyth the **hero's journey** (Campbell 2008). This is a classic tale in which a person is—often reluctantly—called to an adventure. This is the case for people diagnosed with chronic health conditions. The adventure is characterized by trials and tribulations, as well as encounters with guides and helpers. The hero overcomes the challenges of the journey and returns home transformed (Campbell 2008). Dorothy Gale's journey from Kansas to the Land of Oz and back represents a hero's journey.

Dorothy is the patient-hero in *The Wizard of Oz* illness narrative. We meet her in Kansas, the familiar world in which Dorothy is healthy and enjoys **wellness-in-the-foreground** (WITF) life experiences. In the 1939 film, the world of WITF is portrayed in black and white. When disease interrupts her life as a tornadic event, Dorothy is reluctantly called to an adventure in the Land of Oz. This is a new world marked by **illness-in-the-foreground** (IITF) experiences, where disease asserts itself. Now Dorothy must attend to pain, suffering, loss, and other symptoms associated with her illness experience (Paterson 2001). The film dramatically illustrates Dorothy's shift from the world of WITF to the world of IITF by changing to full color when Dorothy opens the door of the farmhouse and steps into the Land of Oz.

On Dorothy's journey, illness is initially personified by Miss Gulch (Kansas), a character who later transforms into the Wicked Witch of the West (Oz). Dorothy's **spiritual orienting system** (SOS) is represented by Glinda the Good Witch. Three farmhands (Kansas) are reimagined as fellow patients (Oz) and become Dorothy's allies: Hickory/Scarecrow, Hunk/Tin Man, and Zeke/Cowardly Lion. Other members of Dorothy's family system—Aunt Em and Uncle Henry—are noticeably absent during the extended period of IITF in Oz.

On her journey, Dorothy faces numerous challenges (e.g., the haunted forest, the quest for the Wicked Witch's broom), engages spiritual coping strategies (e.g., teaming up with her companions on a shared mission), and places her faith in a biomedical healer (the Wizard of Oz) before learning to trust Glinda/her SOS. When Dorothy experiences healing, she returns to Kansas/WITF, signified by the film's return to black and white. Dorothy's return home represents another shift in perspective within the liminal experience of chronic illness. Forever changed by her illness experiences, Dorothy must negotiate a **new normal** or way of living with chronic illness. In the coming chapters, we'll unpack each aspect of this journey to Oz and back. I invite you to view the 1939 film (readily available through streaming services) as a companion to this book. Let's begin at the beginning.

The storm of illness

In the opening scene of *The Wizard of Oz* (rendered in black and white, signaling a WITF perspective), Dorothy and her dog Toto run to the safety of the family farm after an encounter with Miss Gulch, a cantankerous woman who represents the initial signs of Dorothy's impending illness. Dorothy is upset because Miss Gulch threatens to take Toto from her. The dog's name comes from the Latin *totum* for wholeness/well-being. Once they land in Oz, Toto also represents Dorothy's hope for well-being and a return to wellness-in-the-foreground. This beloved companion is only absent when Miss Gulch/the Wicked Witch/illness takes him from Dorothy.

Dorothy is the only person alarmed by these early signs of illness. When she attempts to tell her aunt and uncle about her symptoms (i.e., the encounter with Miss Gulch), they brush her off, focused on their own concerns with the farm. Family members and patients often fail to respond to early warning signs, and only mobilize support when real disaster strikes and illness seriously threatens life as they know it (Eriksson and

Svedlund 2005). People also find it challenging to respond to symptoms they cannot see, and many chronic health conditions are invisible to the outside world (e.g., autoimmune conditions and diabetes) (Charmaz 1995; Defenbaugh 2013). Sometimes people don't know how to respond compassionately to illness. They may feel "embarrassed, revolted, shocked, silenced, sorry; they may change the subject; they may withdraw" (Barrett 1995, p.161). Family members typically respond to serious or life-limiting illness as they've responded to other life challenges. Some people easily cope with change and uncertainty, and they may be quick to rally in support of each other. Other people focus on their own stress about this situation, leading them to lash out at, fight with, or even abandon the patient. A 20-year-old cancer patient reported that "one of the hardest things about cancer—the last thing you expect to face at college—was dealing with her friends' inability to process her illness. 'No one spoke to me because they didn't know what to say'" (Griffiths 2016).

Ironically, my illness narrative also begins with a young woman living in Kansas. I first experienced a piercing pain in my left shoulder. The pain was intense enough for me to wonder if I had fractured my collarbone, although nothing had happened to me to suggest this was even possible. Two days later, the pain had moved to my right shoulder. A few days after that, the pain was localized in one knee. For days, excruciating pain appeared randomly in my body, moving from joint to joint. Then the fingers on both hands became so swollen I couldn't grip a toothbrush or use a fork. When I consulted our family physician, he was mystified. He scheduled a battery of tests, trying to diagnose by a process of elimination. Did I have multiple sclerosis? Was there a brain tumor? The intense pain, swelling in my hands and feet, and questions about what was happening to me were practically and emotionally challenging. I was 32 years old with an infant and a toddler. My husband traveled frequently for work. I had no choice but to carry on with my life, even though everyday tasks reduced me to tears.

Most of my extended family lived at a distance. Via email and phone calls, they acknowledged my symptoms with emotional support. Not all my friends knew how to respond. My best friend was particularly challenged. When I started medical tests to determine the cause of my symptoms, I tearfully shared the news with our Bible study group. I'll never forget that night because my friend stopped speaking to me. She abandoned me in my greatest time of need, without a word of explanation. I was devastated by her response and grieved the loss of this relationship for years. We spoke about it once, but she was unable to explain her behavior. Today, I feel compassion for her and can attribute her extreme reaction to a number of plausible causes. She may have felt betrayed by a broken "relationship contract" that assumed I would remain healthy and available to her (Lyons and Sullivan 1998). She may have been overwhelmed by her own emotional response to my experiences, she may have perceived my illness as a threat to her own health, or she may have found my mysterious condition unexplainable by her SOS, leading to her own spiritual crisis (Byczkowski 2013; Southwood 2018). As Barrett (1995) observes, uneasiness about a prognosis can elicit strong reactions from the people in the patient's **web of life**.

In Dorothy's world, Aunt Em dismisses Dorothy as a worrier, and farmhand Hunk suggests Dorothy is to blame for her symptoms/conflict with Miss Gulch. Zeke suggests Dorothy's problems can be remedied with a courageous or positive-thinking mindset (Hilbert 1984). These common responses discount Dorothy as the expert on her body and negate her experiences until a conclusive diagnosis validates their reality (Kralik, Brown, and Koch 2001; Russell, White, and White 2006). In some cases, patients are unable to claim "a socially understood sick role" that allows them to better manage their symptoms through rest and extra support (Rebman *et al.* 2017, p.542).

I was also limited in my ability to benefit from the sick role because I didn't receive needed support from family to help me on a day-to-day basis. Friends occasionally provided much-needed relief. My physician took my complaints seriously enough to order tests, but he also prescribed an anti-depressant "just in case" it helped. With this act, he sent the message that he wasn't sure if my pain was physiological or psychosomatic in origin. Biomedical professionals hold so much authority that patients' experiences of their bodies can be diminished or outright denied. Patients participate in this socially supported power dynamic:

> With chronic illness comes the definition of self as "patient" and the culture of patienthood that situates "the patient" in relation to healthcare providers as knowers and experts on the patient's body. The body known, the body lived with, becomes estranged, as we rely upon the experts to interpret for us the workings of our own bodies, and biomedical tests to dictate the parameters of everyday activities hitherto taken for granted: what to eat, what to drink, when to eat, etc. ... In chronic illness, the patient's loss of autonomy, and the medicalization of the body, is not a temporary phenomenon, but is part and parcel of the everyday. (Tang and Anderson 1999, pp.84, 86)

When responses disavow or diminish a person's experiences, these experiences become *disenfranchised* and privatized (Wendell 1996). I'll say more about disenfranchised experiences in Chapter 3.

Symptoms escalate for Dorothy as Miss Gulch arrives at the farm, determined to seize Toto. Dorothy pleads with her aunt and uncle for support, but Miss Gulch threatens their livelihood, concretizing the potential ramifications of illness on the family system. When Miss Gulch presents legal papers (medical tests) that authorize her to take Toto, Aunt Em and Uncle Henry merely glance at the paperwork before they acquiesce and relinquish Toto/well-being to the demanding Miss Gulch/illness. This exchange illustrates how a lack of health literacy may lead people to unquestioningly accept expert healthcare opinions. Another interpretation of these interactions is that some people readily surrender to illness as fate.

Miss Gulch leaves the farm with the dog, but Toto escapes and finds his way back to Dorothy. She recognizes that the reprieve from symptoms and return of her well-being are likely short-lived. This is a fork in the road on Dorothy's burgeoning illness journey: she can take control of her life in ways that preserve her well-being, or she can surrender—as her aunt and uncle have done—to the unwanted illness that has intruded on their lives (Eriksson and Svedlund 2005). Because the illness is so frightening, and her family does not provide the support she needs, Dorothy chooses to act and runs away.

Dorothy soon crosses paths with Professor Marvel. His character represents therapists and non-biomedical healers (e.g., folk, complementary, alternative, and faith healers). In Chapter 5, we'll explore this interaction and compare Professor Marvel to the Wizard of Oz, a stereotypical biomedical healer. After talking with the Professor, Dorothy decides to return to the family farm.

As Dorothy and Toto head back, the wind picks up, and we see a tornado on the horizon. This is the crisis of illness onset that takes over Dorothy and her web of life in a painful, scary, dark, chaotic, messy, out-of-control experience. No one is safe because the tornado of incurable disease has the potential to destroy home and family life. Although her family is worried and wants to ensure Dorothy's safety, they're unable to connect with her in the midst of the storm. Their need for self-preservation eventually becomes the priority, and they scramble to relative safety in the storm cellar. Dorothy and Toto are alone in the terrifying storm. No matter how near (physically or emotionally) family members may be, no matter how much they may want to shelter the patient from the storm of illness, the force and depth of this tornadic event can threaten them beyond their abilities to cope. A woman whose son was diagnosed with muscular dystrophy also uses a storm metaphor to describe her experience:

> I live for a time in a blurred dark universe, one in which real feelings fuel my dreams but the day-world is meaningless... I am in the middle of a whirlwind, and all I can do is hang on...

> I am aware of [my husband] as compatriot, but we lie separately, emotionally apart, because we have to preserve our strength and our own resources. (Wolfson 2003, p.41)

Dorothy finds her way into the farmhouse and is knocked unconscious. When she regains consciousness, the tornado of disease is still raging. She helplessly watches from the bed as her family swirls past her, engaged in normal life activities. They smile and wave, but she is unable to participate or even communicate with them. They are separated by the impenetrable wall of her illness experience, leaving Dorothy isolated from her support system. She can only watch in fear.

The experience of isolation is common, described by a couple in their twenties coping with cancer: "the pair realized that while their lives had morphed into a blur of hospital visits and chemotherapy, the outside world was still moving along as normal" (Griffiths 2016). People with chronic health conditions may be physically or emotionally isolated because they live far from family, they no longer have living family members, or they have strained relationships with family members. Some patients experience isolation imposed during hospital stays or exacerbated by relocation to long-term care or palliative care settings. The need for breathing tubes or other medical support can limit the person's ability to communicate effectively. Dorothy is knocked unconscious by flying debris, reminding us that disease symptoms, as well as side effects of medications and treatments, can cause overwhelming fatigue. Patients may sleep more than usual, limiting opportunities and energy needed to be in relationship with loved ones. Some patients are literally unconscious due to surgical procedures or comas (induced and natural). Emotional isolation also results when family members and friends are unable to be fully present with the patient during experiences of uncertainty and suffering (as my friend demonstrated).

Like Dorothy, people in the pre-diagnosis phase of chronic illness feel threatened by troubling physical symptoms, confusing medical terminology, stressful tests/surgeries, potential treatments to control symptoms, and worst-case scenarios (Doka 2014, first published 2009). One man said this about cancer: "There is nothing linear about having a terminal illness. There are stops and starts, pulls and pushes, detours and dead ends. Recognizing the chaotic and oftentimes unpredictable nature of a terminal illness is crucial" (Kaufman 2018).

The event of diagnosis occurs for Dorothy when she sees Miss Gulch transform into the Wicked Witch of the West, riding the tornadic winds on her broomstick. Dorothy screams in response to this evil manifestation of disease, an apt illustration of the intense emotional reaction many people have to diagnosis. After the storm deposits the farmhouse on the ground, an uncertain and shocked Dorothy opens the door to her future, leaving behind the known world of wellness-in-the-foreground.

Integration: Spiritual care in the storm

How can you offer spiritual care to people during the onset and diagnosis of chronic illness? Doka (2014, first published 2009) names common psycho-social tasks people address as chronic illness progresses. As we move through the book, we'll look at these tasks and identify spiritual concerns that may also arise during each phase of chronic illness. We'll consider how spiritual care providers are uniquely prepared to help alleviate suffering associated with these tasks and concerns (Adams 2018b).

The early phase of chronic illness can be relatively brief or continue for weeks, months, or even years of tests, surgeries, and treatments to bring symptoms under control. Patients and/or family members may be consumed with learning all they can about these aspects of the illness experience and theorizing on the culprit. Once they have a diagnosis, they may be consumed by learning about the disease and considering how to manage it (Doka 2014, first published 2009). These activities can provide a helpful focus for the patient and family, affording them time to acknowledge the reality of their situation (Doka 2014, first published 2009). A common spiritual concern with symptom onset and diagnosis is addressing the question of *Why?* We'll explore this important topic in the next chapter.

Beyond understanding why illness is happening, patients and families may not feel they have spiritual concerns or be able to articulate concerns at this time. Often, they just need to lament. Offer spiritual support by acknowledging the patient's/family's experiences and emotions. Pay attention to any desire you have to quickly "fix" what troubles them. Stay focused on the needs of the person and family. Affirm that you're with them in their uncertainty. It can be a great support to have someone share the hope that their concerns will be happily and quickly resolved, but take care not to offer false hope by assuring them that all their wishes will be realized (Cooper *et al.* 2014) (more on hope in Chapter 5).

You may also support the patient/family with another important task in this phase: addressing how the illness has affected and will affect their relationships (Doka 2014, first published 2009). Families react in various ways to stressors brought on by chronic illness, depending on the unique dynamics within the family system and the influence of their unique social and cultural contexts (Baider 2012). Some patients and families readily come together in stressful situations and take on tasks with confidence and vigor. Other families are overwhelmed by medical decisions, coping with lifestyle changes, and threatening prognoses. Families vary in their willingness to receive outside support (Mehta and Cohen 2009). You can affirm positive dynamics that relieve stress within the family system. Thoughtfully consider how you might address or refer the family to experts for help with relational dynamics that exacerbate stress.

As Dorothy's and my narratives attest, people may come and go from the patient's life, for many reasons. People who remain at a distance from the patient—geographically and/or emotionally—can cause the patient great concern. The patient may want to reconnect with distant family or friends in times of crisis. You may be able to help facilitate connection and potentially reconciliation, if that's desired. Some people prefer to find peace on their own, without direct contact with the other person. As a spiritual caregiver, you can be a stable source of support in the midst of relational upheaval. Your regular presence can help alleviate feelings of isolation. Stay mindful of your responsibility to establish and maintain appropriate boundaries within these caregiving relationships (Doehring 2015, first published 2006).

Dorothy survived the tornadic onset of chronic illness. She now finds herself in the Land of Oz, where illness asserts itself. Let's join her there to explore the diagnosis phase of illness and how she makes meaning of this strange new world.

2

The Wicked Witch of the West

ILLNESS AND MEANING MAKING

When the storm ends, Dorothy opens the farmhouse door to survey the tornado's damage. With this move, she crosses the threshold from the world of **wellness-in-the-foreground** (Kansas) to a new world of **illness-in-the-foreground** (the Land of Oz). In Oz, illness affects every aspect of Dorothy's experience, a shift highlighted by the 1939 film's transition from black and white to color. Encountering this foreign world, Dorothy tries to make sense of her experience.

Embedded meaning making

If Dorothy had a cold or appendicitis, she would expect to be cured and back in Kansas after a brief visit to Oz. She might even enjoy her illness for a few days as a break from responsibilities on the farm. Acute illnesses like these are commonplace and have minimal long-term repercussions, so they don't often challenge our assumptions about the way the world works. However, diagnosis with an incurable health condition threatens our assumptive world and can lead to a "crisis of meaning" for both adults and children (Agrimson and Taft 2008; Cassell 2004, first published 1991; Gall and Grant 2005; Pakenham 2008; Pattison 1989, p.34).

Meaning making is the process of making sense of our experiences in the context of our **spiritual orienting system** (SOS) (DeAngelis 2018; Harris and Winokuer 2016). All members of the patient's **web of life** may participate in meaning making about the illness, both individually and collectively. The most common meaning-making question for both adults and children during the diagnosis stage of chronic illness is *Why?* (Ferrell *et al.* 2016). If the person's SOS can explain what's happening, they retain a coherent understanding of the world. For example, older adults who expect to have chronic health conditions as they age may make sense of a diagnosis more readily than younger people and their families who are surprised by disease onset (Hannum *et al.* 2016; Maiko *et al.* 2019; Saunders 2017). Experiences that don't align with a person's SOS can lead to **spiritual struggles**, a topic we examine in Chapter 4.

The initial shock of diagnosis may postpone meaning making, as described by this patient:

> For many people, including myself, the idea of chronicity does not fully register in the first conversation. It seems to be happening in another place and in someone else's circumstances; it surely does not relate to me... The message of permanency resounds at a fundamental level where logic and rationality appear less relevant. Full and conscious acceptance of the news will require time before it can be taken on board. (Adams 2016, p.50)

Other people begin to make meaning immediately. This woman describes how well-intentioned people in her web of life imposed their initial meaning making on her:

> I have been shocked by how often people feel like they have to rush in with an explanation for what I'm going through. It's got to be my family. It's got to be what I ate. It's got to be some habit, or I deserve it in some way. The theological reasons just come out like gangbusters. (Faith & Leadership 2018)

Because the diagnostic phase of chronic illness is often a time of crisis and high stress, most people in this early stage of chronic illness answer the *Why?* question in a passive, automatic way by relying on meanings deeply embedded in their SOS (Attig 2001; Hunt, Jordan, and Irwin 1989). These meanings are typically acquired from and reinforced by familial, societal, and cultural contexts (Goodman *et al.* 2005; Hunt *et al.* 1989; Kirmayer and Sartorius 2007; Kralik *et al.* 2001; Van Gorp and Vercruysse 2012). More active and reflective meaning making usually takes place after the crisis/diagnosis phase subsides, when people can consider the helpfulness of embedded meanings, contemplate the effects of the illness experience over time, and construct new ways to understand these experiences. We'll explore this reflective meaning-making process in Chapter 6.

A growing body of evidence from around the world shows that the way people understand their illnesses affects physical health, psychological health, and well-being (e.g., Bernard *et al.* 2017; Carney and Park 2018; Fitchett *et al.* 2004; Graves *et al.* 2009; Ironside *et al.* 2003; Petrie and Weinman 2012; Sherman and Simonton 2012; Sterba *et al.* 2008). Biomedical professionals typically aren't equipped to help patients make meaning beyond scientific understandings of disease (Charon 2006). Patients can "feel self-conscious about the relatively unsophisticated, foolish, or even superstitious nature of their beliefs about illness when confronted by a doctor and may therefore be loath to disclose them" (Furnham 1994, pp.715–716). People with chronic health conditions need spiritual caregivers who create and nurture healing relationships with narrative competence and compassionate presence to help facilitate ongoing meaning making of illness experiences.

Common models of understanding the cause of illness

In the remainder of this chapter, we'll focus on how people answer the question *Why?* Based on my extensive review of literature in the fields of religion/spirituality, pastoral theology and care, sociology, disability studies, psychology, and medicine, I've identified four common models people use to understand why they have a chronic illness. I call these understandings the **moral model**, the **biomedical model**, the **social model**, and the **energy body model**. No model is better or worse than another model. What is **life-affirming** for one person may be **life-limiting** for another person, or even problematic for this person at another point in the illness trajectory.

Healthcare providers often assume that patients understand the cause of their illness the same way the provider understands it (Frosch and Elwyn 2010; Street and Haidet 2010; Wittink *et al.* 2009). The way patients make meaning of their illness affects their choice of providers, adherence to treatment plans, and the effectiveness of these relationships and interventions (Chen, Tsai, and Chou 2011; Lyketsos and Chisolm 2009; Moskowitz and Wrubel 2005). Unfortunately, most healthcare providers are so encultured in a biomedical belief system that it can be challenging for them to engage alternate understandings of illness. One physician says:

> I was not taught in medical school to make the connection between a person's spirituality or that which is held sacred, and their health outcomes... I have learned to speak the language that my patients understand. This language is through the voice of spirituality, purpose and meaning. (Sethi 2016)

I've changed healthcare providers because of mismatched beliefs about illness. A physician once asked me, "What could spirituality possibly have to do with illness?" If this doctor had asked the question out of genuine interest in a reply, it could have enhanced our healing relationship. Unfortunately, the tone of this question/statement conveyed judgment about any belief in a relationship between health and spirituality. I didn't respond to the physician, and neither of us pursued the topic further. Today my healthcare team includes a rheumatologist who values wholistic beliefs about illness and supports my non-biomedical approaches to symptom management.

I'm certainly not the only person who's felt judged for a particular understanding of illness, as this patient's comments affirm (model-of-illness identifiers added for clarity):

> In our competitive society, chronic infirmity or illness is viewed as a personal failing [moral model] rather than the random stroke of fate that it is [biomedical model]. If my pain and disability were temporary, I would get sympathy and accommodation, but incurable suffering makes most people uncomfortable. They become impatient and distant, and I detect an undercurrent of belief that I must have done something to deserve this [moral model]—something they can avoid doing. (Byczkowski 2013)

Experiences like these underscore the need for spiritual caregivers to be aware of different meanings ascribed to chronic illness. This is part of your self-awareness, and it will help you identify how meaning making may affect the people you care for in life-affirming and life-limiting ways. I'll describe each model independently for clarity. However, meaning making is often complex, and people—individually and communally—often use more than one model to make sense of illness (e.g., Leavey, Loewenthal, and King 2016; Van Gorp and Vercruysse 2012).

Moral model

The essential belief of the moral model is that a healthy body reflects a healthy soul (Betcher 2001). For thousands of years, people didn't have the ability to look *inside* the human body to understand the cause of illness; instead, they looked *outward* to the supernatural agents they believed were in control of their lives.

Illness was the result of spirits, demons, and gods who sought to punish, teach, bestow favor, or amuse themselves, so shamans—intermediaries between the physical world and the spirit world—served as community healers *and* priests (Ahaddour and Broeckaert 2018; Beck 2007; Koenig and McCullough 2012, first published 2001; Pattison 1989; Sajja and Puchalski 2017). The healer-priest paradigm continued with the growth of Western civilization. For centuries, clergy-operated monasteries were the primary institutions of healing and medical education (Kinsley 1996). It wasn't until the early 19th century that priests and physicians became separate professions (Koenig 2000). Contemporary shamans still offer healing from and in the spirit world, a topic I'll say more about in Chapter 4.

The moral model remains the most used paradigm for understanding illness around the world, regardless of spiritual identity (Christians and atheists: Gall and Kafi 2014; diverse spiritual beliefs: Haug *et al.* 2016; agnostics: Kutz 2000; Muslims: Nabolsi and Carson 2011; Jews: Sharabi 2014). People use the moral model today when they attribute illness to sin, the power of their thoughts, karmic justice, "God's plan," fate, divine favor, a life lesson, or an opportunity for personal growth and transformation (Arabiat *et al.* 2013; Dose and Rhudy 2018; Dumit, Magilvy, and Afifi 2016; Fadiman 1997; Krippner 2012; Nelson 2003; Ngyuyen, Yamada, and Dinh 2012; Pakenham 2008; Russell *et al.* 2006; Taïeb *et al.* 2010; Yodchai *et al.* 2017). In some cultures, witchcraft, demonic possession, or the "evil eye"[1] are also common moral-model causes of illness (Arabiat *et al.* 2013; Berger 2013; Johnsdotter *et al.* 2011; Metta *et al.* 2015; Monaghan and Gabe 2015; Taïeb *et al.* 2010).

These patients illustrate moral-model understandings:

---

1   Arabiat *et al.* (2013) explain: "In the Arab culture, pain and illness are believed to be the harmful effect of the evil eye when admiring a child without mentioning the name of God" (p.249).

Look, I don't question the Lord, I don't ask... He knows why and that's good enough for me. (Williams 1984, p.193)

I know I behaved badly with my parents and my brothers. They suffered a lot; maybe that's why it all happened to me. (Araten-Bergman *et al.* 2016, p.1151)

I never thought I would have kidney disease. I was unhappy I had it. I tried to accept it and thought people were born to pay for what they did in their past lives [bad karma]. I don't know in which life I did something wrong so I have to pay for bad deeds in this life. (Yodchai *et al.* 2017, p.362)

I'm not really spiritual, but I've had a religious background... I've always wondered why the hell I was being put through all the crap that was going on in my life, and I seem to believe now that maybe [fate] is why. (Unantenne *et al.* 2013, p.1152)

I blamed myself for writing a book on death. I blamed myself for going to the doctor so late. I blamed myself for being arrogant and not budgeting for something like this from the beginning. I blamed myself for daring to have a wish list. (Southwood 2018, p.89)

[I was] put into a wheelchair for a reason, [I was] being knocked down to size. (Irvine *et al.* 2009, p.604)

Illness is a test from Allah where God examines the believers, if they tolerate the suffering this means they pass the test and God will forgive him for his sins, so I am a believer I do not complain I thank my God and pray to him to support me to be patient and to cure me as I am also now looking after my health. (Nabolsi and Carson 2011, p.720)

People benefit from moral-model understandings when these beliefs prompt them to make healthy choices. In Buddhism, for example, personal accountability for health aligns with religious teachings: "Good deeds (e.g., regular exercise, proper nutrition, etc.) lead to good health, whereas bad deeds (e.g., poor living habits, abusing the body and the mind) in this and previous lives bring illness" (Ratanakul 2008). Illness experiences can lead to positive spiritual growth or stronger relationships with the sacred. On the other hand, the moral model can be problematic when people experience spiritual struggles, such as questioning how a loving God can be responsible for their suffering (Carney and Park 2018; Nelson 2003; Orsi 2005), or when people feel judged and experience shame for hidden sins (Eiesland 1994; Smart and Smart 2006). When illness is seen as a test of faith or will, people may also feel undue pressure to be martyrs or inspirational heroes (Harnett 2017; Wong 2019).

Biomedical model

The biomedical model is the second-most common understanding of illness around the world (e.g., Arabiat *et al.* 2013). Even highly religious people make meaning of illness using scientific understandings of disease. This is particularly true for people living in Westernized cultures where biomedicine is the dominant path to healing disease (Hale-Smith, Park, and Edmondson 2012; Leavey *et al.* 2016). In the biomedical model, chronic illness is the result of poor health habits, genetics, aging, germs, viruses, accidents, environmental toxins, and random acts of nature (e.g., Pakenham 2008; Taïeb *et al.* 2010). For example, this person attributes illness to genetics:

> For many years, my grandmother's illness was kept secret; nobody talked about it…then I got sick. Once I heard my father saying to my mother: "It's all because of your mother." Now I know what he meant. (Araten-Bergman *et al.* 2016, p.1152)

This modern, scientific understanding of disease views the human body as a machine, and healthcare providers as the mechanics who fix physical and biological defects (Harrington 2008; Hutch 2013; Kurapati 2018; Leng 2013; Smart and Smart 2006; Zhang 2018). This mechanistic perspective is life-limiting when patients feel dehumanized and disconnected from healthcare providers. Technology continues to reinforce this limitation, as we see in this physician's description of his experience as a patient:

> The electronic record of my three-hour stay would have looked perfect, showing close monitoring, even though to me as a patient it lacked a human dimension... [P]ast admissions, the details of surgeries undergone, every consultant's opinion, every drug given over every encounter, thousands of blood tests and so many CT scans, M.R.I.'s and ultrasound images reside in there. This computer record creates what I call an "iPatient"—and this iPatient threatens to become the real focus of our attention, while the real patient in the bed often feels neglected, a mere placeholder for the virtual record. (Verghese 2011)

The biomedical model is clearly helpful when patients feel supported by treatment options, pharmaceuticals, and biomechanical aids that improve their quality of life. However, the exponential growth of medical advances has also led to the "medicalization of suffering," the belief there's "a pill" to eliminate every form of suffering (Badaracco 2007; Hanson 1999; Swinton 2007). People can become angry or feel betrayed when the healthcare system fails them by not providing a cure on demand. Biomedical explanations for illness can help alleviate shame or stigma when illness is attributed to something beyond the person's control (e.g., genetics or a virus). However, people often still feel judged for poor health, with one study finding that "over half of patients experience guilt or shame when they leave a doctor's office" (Beck 2014; see also Miller-McLemore 1988; Salwitz 2013; Thagard 2018; Whiteman 2014).

Social model

A social model[2] of understanding disability emerged in the United States in the 1960s (Jette and Keysor 2003). This model of framing disability also works well for many chronic health conditions, and the terms are sometimes combined in literature as CID, for "chronic illness and disability" (Grue 2016; Livneh 2001). Social-model understandings are at work when people believe illness is caused by systemic, communal, and cultural factors, such as "poverty, unemployment, poor housing, migration, experiences of racism and discrimination... modernity...secularism and loss of religious identity" (Leavey *et al.* 2016, p.1611; see also Southwood 2018).

The social model suggests that every person experiences health limitations in some way, so chronic illness is a normal experience (Thomas 2004). Variations in health and physical ability limit people to different degrees, depending on the particular social setting (Avert 2018; Jette and Keysor 2003; Smart and Smart 2006). For example, if ramps are available, people who use wheelchairs are no more restricted from access to a building than a person who can walk up the front steps. The social model builds on scientific understandings of disease found in the biomedical model, but the social model takes the moral stance that responsibility for chronic health conditions falls on society rather than on the individual (Swain and French 2000). Society might address chronic health conditions by supporting research for a cure or by educating the public about disease prevention. Society might also attend to the way aspects of social identity negatively affect health (also known as **social determinants of health**). There is growing recognition around the world of the need for socially just decision making to improve global health and well-being (e.g., Bichell 2017; Metta *et al.* 2015).

---

2   The social model is also known as the functional, environmental, socio-political, or minority model.

Social-model understandings are beneficial when they prompt individuals and communities to address embedded values about health limitations. The value industrialized societies place on a person's ability to produce or contribute to the societal machine, for example, can lead to judgment and ostracization of people with limiting health conditions (Arora 2009; Byczkowski 2013; Crislip 2005). A limitation of the social model is that practical support and compassion for individuals who suffer can get lost when efforts focus on systemic solutions (Pattison 1989). As society imposes limits that lead to or exacerbate chronic health conditions, secular and faith-based communities of care often provide safe spaces for people to lament, share hopes for future cures, and work together for social advances that reduce or remove limits.

Energy body model

The fourth common model of understanding chronic illness is the energy body model, which asserts that every person is made up of layers of energy (Desy 2019). Vital life force energy is also known as *chi/qi* in China, *ki* in Japan and Korea, and *prana* in India. Life force energy is associated with specific vibrations, sounds, colors, pathways (meridians), and locations in the body known as *chakras* (e.g., Blinne 2012; Burden, Herron-Marx, and Clifford 2005; Ngyuyen *et al.* 2012). Health is a transient state of energetic harmony. Illness is the result of general mental and spiritual imbalances or of more specific imbalances, blockages, or disharmony in life force energy. Healing is an ongoing process of restoring energetic balance and can be facilitated by the person who is ill or with the help of energy healers (e.g., James 2002, first published 1994; Kirmayer 2004; Unantenne *et al.* 2013).

Energy body ideas are informed by Hindu and Buddhist teachings, the mind-cure movement, and positive psychology (Cousins 1979; Goldberg 2010; Harrington 2008; Peale 2003, first published 1952; Seligman and Csikszentmihalyi 2000).

Energy body understandings are foundational to meditation and mindfulness practices (Benson and Klipper 1975; Kabat-Zinn 1990), which are promoted as pathways to health and well-being for people with a wide variety of chronic health conditions (Buchholz 2015; Polusny *et al.* 2015). Likewise, energy body understandings undergird a growing corpus of studies exploring how spiritual beliefs and practices affect health (see Koenig and McCullough 2012, first published 2001, for the most comprehensive compilation). Energy body beliefs are also affirmed in popular media (e.g., Melnick 2017) and self-help books (e.g., Hay 2004, first published 1984).

Because the energy body model emphasizes balance, this model can motivate people to make healthier lifestyle and behavioral choices. However, changes needed to restore life balance may feel overwhelming to some people, like actor-director Woody Allen, who said: "You know I can't express emotions. I internalize, I grow a tumor" (Harrington 2008, p.67). Because stress and imbalance are impossible to avoid, the energy body model can help normalize illness. That said, some people may feel ashamed that their inability to adapt leads to health issues. For example, this woman with an autoimmune condition attributes her physical illness to psycho-spiritual imbalance: "It is ironic that one of my most salient personality characteristics is to be critical of myself and metaphorically to beat myself up and that I have a disease in which my cells literally beat up my own cells!" (Maggio 2007, p.577). People using the energy body model may feel that "negative" feelings should be privatized, and they can feel shamed if they don't heal despite positive thinking, as seen in this quotation from a well-known positive thinker: "There are no incurable diseases, only incurable patients" (Siegel 1998, first published 1986, p.99).

Energy body understandings can promote spiritual growth if people are attentive to their inner selves and seek balance in life. However, these views can also cause people to feel the need to address psycho-spiritual healing on their own before or in lieu of seeking helpful diagnoses or treatments for mental and physical ailments. Because energy body views are not well understood or accepted by many biomedical providers, patients may hesitate to share their beliefs, and the lack of communication can affect their commitment to a biomedical treatment plan.

To summarize, I have described four common ways people understand the cause of chronic illness. People may use more than one model to make meaning of an illness experience. The primary model used depends on how the person's family explained illness, their cultural background, and the person's experiences with spirituality and health care. Each model has benefits and challenges, which vary by person and situation. You'll have the opportunity to practice identifying meaning-making models in a case study at the end of this chapter. First, we return to Dorothy's story and my story of early meaning making about our diagnoses.

Crossing the threshold: Dorothy and Kelly make meaning of illness

When we left Dorothy, she had just opened the door of her Kansas farmhouse to the new, colorful world of illness-in-the-foreground (IITF). When she was still on the farm and experiencing mysterious symptoms, Dorothy wished she was already "somewhere over the rainbow," with uncertainty behind her. She didn't realize there was a long journey still ahead, just as this patient describes: "I wish I'd known that being diagnosed wasn't the answer to it all. It was the start of the question, 'How do I live now?'" (Jacqueline 2018, p.19).

Dorothy's experience represents the way many people experience diagnosis with a chronic health condition. In her memoir about a serious eye condition, Gallagher (2013) describes her introduction to IITF this way:

Like crossing a border from one country to another in a second.
This is what I wrote down when I got home... I dropped out of
the world I lived in, where I thought I knew about disease and
vulnerability and death and *all that*, and entered another country.
It was a spooky familiar world, same streets, same buildings,
same people—a sci-fi version of my streets, my buildings, my
people—but it was as if the furniture were slightly rearranged,
the people not quite right. It was not *like* another place; it *was*
another country. It was falling into Oz. I walked right over the
border without knowing I was crossing it. It had no border
patrol. I did no planning. I had no map. Dr. Lowe handed me
the passport. I had it in my hands before I knew what it was. My
ideas about illness and medicine and then "God" would soon be
revealed for what they were: tickets on a train that had left the
station. (p.6; emphasis in original)

When I was in the early diagnosis phase, I felt like a tourist
unprepared for a visit to a foreign country. I experienced a lack
of proficiency in the native tongue when I was bombarded with
unfamiliar medical terminology, including acronyms, medical
jargon, and the cumbersome names of pharmaceuticals.
Like many tourists, I was also unaware of local customs (e.g.,
what constitutes an emergency health situation) and had to
become adept at using the local currency (health insurance
and other means of financial support for health care, such as
pharmaceutical company programs to offset patient costs). My
lack of mental preparation exacerbated an already physically
challenging experience.

Dorothy steps out of the farmhouse and into a world that
resembles Kansas/wellness-in-the-foreground but is clearly
different. At first, she quietly takes in her new surroundings. Like
many people at diagnosis, she may be in a state of shock, only
able to passively absorb what is happening to and around her.
When the rheumatologist delivered my diagnosis, she observed

that I was "quite stoic." I, too, needed to process the moment of "You have an incurable disease."

As Dorothy acclimates, she calls on her **spiritual orienting system** (SOS) for initial **meaning making**. Glinda the Good Witch personifies Dorothy's SOS/the sacred. Glinda arrives as a mystical, glowing orb of energy that manifests into a woman who projects calm, safety, and beauty. Her butterfly necklace subtly reinforces her role as spiritual guide/orienting system.[3] Glinda asks Dorothy to explain how she landed in Oz (i.e., the cause of her illness), and we are invited into Dorothy's initial meaning-making process. Dorothy begins by rejecting the moral-model understanding that she is responsible for the storm that brought her to Oz.

I also rejected moral meaning making when I was diagnosed with rheumatoid arthritis (RA). I didn't blame my sins/shortcomings, God, or other supernatural forces for my illness. I believed in a benevolent God/higher power present in all life experiences. Our family was actively involved at a local United Methodist church during this time, and I drew on my spiritual resources to cope with both uncertainty (pre-diagnosis) and knowing (diagnosis). My embedded meaning making was rooted in the biomedical model where disease was an amoral event that simply reflected the condition of my body, but not the state of my soul. I focused on learning all I could about potential biological and environmental triggers (the cause of RA is still unclear today) and on understanding the biomedical treatment options available to me. It was years before I thought differently about illness and healing.

My embedded meaning making reflected understandings of health and illness constructed within the family/social/cultural context of lower-to-middle-class Germanic, Midwestern,

---

3   Edwards (2018) notes that "many cultures associate the butterfly with our souls. The Christian religion sees the butterfly as a symbol of resurrection. Around the world, people view the butterfly as representing endurance, change, hope, and life."

Lutheran farmers and cattle ranchers.[4] Because of their livelihood, my relatives repeatedly experienced the birth-to-death cycle of animals and people. My family developed pragmatic ways to understand and cope with losses of livestock, other farm animals, semi-feral cats, adults who succumbed to disease and accidental death, and infants who died young in an often-unforgiving environment. I was implicitly and explicitly taught that illness and death are normal, expected parts of life that do not warrant overly dramatic responses.

My meaning making was also greatly influenced by a close relationship with my maternal grandmother. She lived with multiple chronic health conditions and endured dozens of surgeries in 88 years. I observed family members express compassion for my grandmother's physical challenges. But I also observed family members treat her chronic health conditions in a matter-of-fact way with the implicit expectation that she would carry on with her work unless confined to the hospital. By the time I was diagnosed with RA, I was well trained to respond to health crises with the stoicism I exhibited in the rheumatologist's office. In the days ahead, I generally kept my emotional responses to diagnosis private as I carried on with my responsibilities.

Back in Oz, another instance of early meaning making occurs when Dorothy and Glinda discover the legs of the Wicked Witch of the East sticking out from under Dorothy's transplanted farmhouse. This Witch also represents illness. The celebratory reaction of the Munchkins (other patients) suggests that Dorothy has avoided another harmful diagnosis, or perhaps she has been quickly cured of a secondary infection. Glinda calls this healing episode miraculous. The Munchkins also invoke moral meaning making as they sing about the dead Witch, saying she now resides with goblins in a lower world. Their song suggests that this potential illness was the result of demonic forces that have

---

4   I describe my mother's side of the family, which was the primary influence on my embedded SOS. My father's family was largely absent from my life.

now been exorcized. Dorothy rejects all imposed moral meaning making, opting for a biomedical understanding that her arrival in Oz and the death of the Wicked Witch of the East are the result of nature randomly dropping the farmhouse in this location.

When the Wicked Witch of the West suddenly arrives to view her sister's body, Dorothy comes face to face with her illness incarnate. Dorothy leans into Glinda, seeking safety and comfort from her SOS. Glinda cleverly gives the dead Witch's ruby slippers to Dorothy as a symbol of Dorothy's life force. The Wicked Witch of the West/illness desperately wants to claim the ruby slippers/life force, and she threatens to destroy Dorothy's SOS as she achieves her goal. Dorothy stands strong in the face of illness here, but the Wicked Witch of the West departs with the threat that she will return to attack Dorothy and her sense of hope/well-being (Toto) again.

Dorothy recognizes that she cannot return the way she came—her diagnosis cannot be reversed. With a referral to see the Wizard of Oz, a renowned specialist in a faraway city, Dorothy is ready to begin a new journey toward healing. The Munchkins share her optimism that the path will lead her to wellness. Even though Dorothy is surrounded by this initial support network, our patient sets out alone. The beginning of Dorothy's path, the origin of the Yellow Brick Road, is represented by a tight spiral that illustrates the way patients often feel they travel in circles from provider to provider, appointment to appointment, test to test, before their path finally lies out more directly in front of them. The Munchkins bid Dorothy goodbye, and her marathon journey of chronic illness begins.

Integration: A case study in meaning making

Emily Wick (2015) posted her illness narrative on Buzzfeed.[5] Her story illustrates how people seek to understand illness, and they often use more than one model of understanding to do so. Emily's story also reveals how meaning making can change over time, a topic we explore in Chapter 6. I share selected quotes from Emily's narrative and describe my observations about the ways Emily, her boyfriend, and her healthcare provider make meaning of this illness experience. I encourage you to consider how you would describe the meaning making that takes place in this narrative.

When Emily shares her diagnosis of rheumatoid arthritis with her boyfriend, he responds out of embedded understandings from his family of origin. His grandmother had ongoing arthritic complaints, likely due to osteoarthritis. While osteoarthritis is also a chronic health condition, it doesn't affect a person systemically like RA, which is an autoimmune disease. His family viewed his grandmother's health condition as an inconvenience, and he assesses Emily's RA diagnosis as a similar threat: "It's not like you're not dying. Still want to go grab that beer?" In this response, Emily's boyfriend expresses social-model meaning making. He minimizes Emily's illness experience as a normal part of the human life cycle in which we're all in the process of eventually dying. In addition, because Emily has an invisible disease (i.e., she *looks* fine to him), he doesn't see the need to limit their normal activities, like getting a beer together. Although Emily initially accepts his meaning making, the question *Why?* still nags at her.

At Emily's first post-diagnosis visit to the rheumatologist, her physician is focused on treatments and side effects. Emily confronts the physician with her meaning-making struggle: "What does this mean for my life?" When the provider responds

---

5   Review Wick's narrative in its entirety at www.buzzfeed.com/emilywick/ how-to-keep-living-when-your-body-turns-on-you.

that Emily "can still have children," we see another instance of social meaning making. The physician doesn't view this chronic illness as a limitation for what she assumes Emily wants in life. Dissatisfied, Emily remains caught in spiritual struggle, saying, "My doctors didn't spend much time trying to figure out the why of my illness, but I wanted something to blame."

Over time, Emily explores potential causes for her auto-immune condition. She considers a variety of biomedical causes (genetics, the environment, hormones). She examines energy body understandings: "I wondered if my tendency to criticize my body and to stuff my 'unfeminine' emotions like anger and frustration deep into the caverns of myself made me more likely to become ill." She considers a moral-model approach: "Did I do something to deserve this? … I was in pain: I wanted it to have a purpose." Emily also explores the use of metaphors related to illness, including illness as enemy, companion, and the love of her life. She ends her narrative lamenting current and future losses and limitations. The question *Why?* remains unanswered as Emily continues to grapple with social-model understandings:

> I can say its name aloud in public and not have anyone shrink away in fear or disgust. Perhaps it will one day rob me of my able-bodied privilege, and maybe it is misunderstood as the creaky disease of age, but for now the ascribed meaning, the useless metaphors, the judgment, come only from me.

Emily would benefit from a spiritual caregiver who could help her with ongoing meaning making now and as her illness progresses.

Integration: Self-reflection on meaning making

Because we don't want to impose our meaning making on other people, it's important for you to be aware of how you understand the cause of illness.

- Think of an example of how you or your family made meaning of illness when you were younger. Which of the four common models of understanding illness can you identify in your/your family's meaning making?

- How would you make meaning of that illness experience today?

- Which model(s) of understanding illness do you resonate with most today?

- Identify ways you have the *potential* to judge people or withdraw from people who do not make meaning of illness as you do. For example, *I might judge someone who believes mental illness is a sign of demonic possession*, or *I might withdraw from someone who only makes meaning using a biomedical approach without considering psycho-spiritual contributors to physical illness.*

Integration: Guidelines for spiritual care in initial meaning making

- From a place of genuine curiosity, ask people living with chronic illness how *they* understand the cause of their health conditions. Use the **SNAP** skills you learned in Chapter 1.

- Notice which model(s) people use to make meaning of illness. Is their understanding comforting to them, or does it cause them stress? Remember that in the diagnosis stage patients and family members will most likely rely on embedded meanings, even if these meanings are ultimately life-limiting.

- Ask if meaning making is consistent throughout the patient's web of life. If so, this layer of support may be a source of comfort for the patient and family members.

If meaning making varies considerably across the patient's web of life, you may notice conflicts that limit the patient's quality of life.

- Acknowledge meaning making and lament without imposing your own meanings on the patient or family members. Be especially aware of imposing the assumption that chronic illness will ultimately be a life-affirming experience for the other person. Imposing this belief is easy to do if we're uncomfortable talking about pain, loss, or struggle; if we hold redemptive beliefs about suffering (see Nelson 2003); or if we want to "fix" spiritual struggles.

- When offering spiritual care to people in the diagnosis phase, respond to *Why?* questions by assuring the person there will be time to consider these questions later. Help people focus on meaningful spiritual practices as they make decisions about and adjust to the diagnosis and initial treatment plans.

With Dorothy's diagnosis confirmed, we shift into the chronic phase of illness. First, we'll look at common losses and people's responses to them. In later chapters, we'll examine other aspects of chronic illness.

3

The Yellow Brick Road

LOSSES AND GRIEF ON THE ILLNESS JOURNEY

Diagnosis behind her, Dorothy is now in the chronic phase of illness. This phase may last for years or alternate with periods of recovery (Doka 2014, first published 2009). The spiralized beginning of Dorothy's solo journey on the Yellow Brick Road foreshadows the often isolating and circular experiences of ongoing losses and grief associated with an incurable health condition. In this chapter, I highlight common losses and responses to them that affect spiritual well-being for people living with chronic illness, including anxiety, depression, demoralization, and a desire for hastened death (e.g., Kuluski *et al.* 2014; Mahon, O'Brien, and O'Conor 2014).

We don't see Dorothy's family again until she returns to Kansas/**wellness-in-the-foreground**. Family caregivers often feel invisible within the context of an illness experience. I will also describe signs of caregiver burden so you can help alleviate this form of suffering.

Losses with chronic illness

If a person can fill in the blank to one of these sentences, they have experienced a **loss**:

- I no longer can ____.

- I no longer have ____.

- I no longer am ____.

With a chronic illness, the **primary loss** is one's health. Losses that result from the primary loss of health are **secondary losses** (Webster 2018). Secondary physical losses are often troubling (e.g., the person can no longer bathe without help), but losses in psychological, social, and spiritual dimensions also dramatically affect quality of life and may cause patients even greater distress (Jakoby 2012; Schellinger *et al.* 2018). A **tertiary loss** is an illness-related loss experienced by another person in the patient's web of life (Worzer, Kishino, and Gatchel 2009). For example, a patient's family may lose their home (tertiary loss) because the patient is unemployed (secondary loss) due to their illness (primary loss).

Chronic health conditions unleash a cascade of ongoing losses that can affect everyday activities and completely alter a person's life trajectory. All losses accrue over time and profoundly affect a person's illness experience (Gubar 2014; Harris and Winokuer 2016; Larsson and Grassman 2012; Roos and Neimeyer 2007). This woman laments a number of everyday losses: "The ability to be spontaneous... Variety... Being actively involved in the life of my family... Socializing... Time in nature... The ability to pursue my former interests... Health not being the topic of conversation" (Bernhard 2013). Another woman living with cancer observes: "My losses, like those of most people, vary in scope... The smaller losses of my hair and of not being able to feel my feet sometimes loom larger than they should" (Gubar 2014). Although you might expect that repeatedly coping with losses would dull their impact, the effects of loss may even increase with years of chronic illness experience (Larsson and Grassman 2012).

In this chapter, I highlight four common secondary losses associated with chronic illness and describe a range of emotional responses to them. Spiritual caregivers should be familiar with these often-invisible aspects of the chronic illness experience so that you can acknowledge losses and help people get specialized support for **life-limiting** psycho-spiritual responses to illness.

Secondary loss: Control

People with chronic health conditions often feel out of control of bodies taken over by healthcare providers, treatment protocols, and the disease itself (Charmaz 1995; Rebman *et al.* 2017; Tang and Anderson 1999). These feelings can spread to other areas of life that now feel uncertain due to illness symptoms, progression, and prognosis (Giffords 2003; Williams and Koocher 1998). These patients describe their loss of control:

> I wanted to control everything. I wanted to control my husband. I wanted to control the way my kids were raised. I wanted everything to be perfect and you cannot do that. I mean that's not human…you have to let go of things. (Mount, Boston, and Cohen 2007, p.381)

> How do you live without control? How do you surf the chaos that's going on around you and under you? It's like, you know, you're riding on a wave on a hypothetical surfboard…and you're sitting at the peak of the whole convergence of forces that you have nothing to do with really and you're just lucky to be up there able to keep your balance on all this stuff going on… that elusive balance that keeps slipping away at the top of the wave. Yeah, it keeps slipping away or it keeps coming back. (Whittemore and Dixon 2008, p.184)

Patients also lose control over their illness narratives. They may struggle to describe or validate illness experiences, particularly invisible symptoms of pain and fatigue (Rebman *et al.* 2017). Patients may also feel pressure to conform to narratives imposed by healthcare providers (Jurecic 2012). For example, a woman recovering from breast cancer was chastised by the office nurse for not wearing a prosthesis to her appointment. The patient had chosen *not* to wear a prosthesis as an act of reclaiming her body as her own. The nurse told her: "You will feel so much better with it on… And besides, we really like you to wear something, at least when you come in. Otherwise it's bad for the morale of the office" (Frank 2016, p.11).

Patients may also experience loss of control if members of their support network create a double-bind situation with messages that imply the patient should "be independent…and be active in your care; *but* when you have a serious exacerbation, place yourself submissively in our hands, and we will blame you for what you did or failed to do to worsen your disorder" (Kleinman 1988, p.170, emphasis in original; see also Holmes 2017a).

Secondary loss: Identity

Chronic illness is a catalyst for identity loss, including the person's current identity and potential future selves (Bourland, Neville, and Pickens 2011; Doka 2014, first published 2009; Frazier, Cotrell, and Hooker 2003; Irvine *et al.* 2009; Larsson and Grassman 2012). Bury's classic article (1982) describes chronic illness as a **biographical disruption**, a "fundamental re-thinking of the person's biography and self-concept" (p.169). A woman with multiple sclerosis describes it this way: "What [I] used to be is not there anymore. I have to find a new way of describing myself. I can't say I'm healthy anymore… I have to find a whole new way of looking at myself" (Ironside *et al.* 2003, p.178).

Health care that is embedded in a biomedical culture contributes to identity loss when providers dehumanize people, viewing them as "an intricate machine with faulty parts that needed to be fixed" (Kurapati 2018). Technology further challenges patients' identities as human beings worthy of person-centered care, as Verghese (2011) noted when his emergency room experience found him competing with the "iPatient" of his electronic health record for the provider's attention.

Loss of self-image is also prompted by disfigured joints, wounds that don't heal, the need for assistive devices (e.g., a cane, wheelchair, or arm splint), skin issues (e.g., rashes, scarring), hair loss, weight changes, tracheotomies, and ostomies (Giffords 2003; Seawell and Danoff-Burg 2005). Visible changes are more distressing and stigmatizing than changes a person can hide (Lempp, Scott, and Kingsley 2006; Vickers 2000). This woman describes her struggles with disfigurement:

> It is my hands, the shifting of the fingers. That's what made me start to feel arthritic. For years, I could always keep them straight when I wanted to. Now, I can't. Some things I can hide, like I can wear long dresses to hide knees and shoes to cover my toes. But you can't hide your hands. (Plach, Stevens, and Moss 2004a, p.147)

Changes in physical appearance and sexual health also affect a person's identity as a spouse, partner, or lover (Leonardi-Warren, Wenger, and Fink 2016; Matzo 2015; Redelman 2008; Seawell and Danoff-Burg 2005). Women may also experience identity loss related to their ability to conceive or carry a pregnancy (Cassell and Rose 2003; Graffigna *et al.* 2017).

Identity is often strongly associated with a person's purpose in life and the ability to work in/out of the home, contribute to society, earn a living, and engage in other important social interactions (Kayser and Sormanti 2002; Kristiansen *et al.* 2014; Lempp *et al.* 2006; Vassilev *et al.* 2014; Vijayasingham 2018). A person's professional work identity and/or sense of purpose is often deeply embedded and socially reinforced:

> The messages I received from my family were clear: Self-sacrifice and hard work are of the utmost importance. These messages also come from the larger cultural views of women as caretakers and nurturers as opposed to dependents. For example, instead of acknowledging the fatigue that often accompanies lupus, I am quick to view it as laziness or lack of motivation. (Maggio 2007, p.579)

This woman's comments also reveal how challenging it can be for people with chronic health conditions to claim time off from work and other social commitments. The **sick role** is a social agreement in which people who are ill are relieved of their responsibilities at work and/or home in exchange for managing their condition without taking undue advantage of illness for attention, financial gain (e.g., disability pay), social support, or other benefits (Frank 2016). People who have visible signs of illness typically find greater acceptance when they claim the sick role. However, they may be hesitant to claim the sick role because increased visibility of illness can also lead to greater social stigma and rejection (Perry 2011).

Secondary loss: Social support and relationships

People living with chronic illness often worry about loss of social support and relationships (Fong, Finlayson, and Peacock 2006; McCaffrey *et al.* 2016; O'Neill and Morrow 2001). Unfortunately, I've discovered firsthand, with the loss of my best friend during the pre-diagnosis phase, that some relationships can't withstand the challenges of chronic illness (Griffiths 2016; Jacqueline 2018; Maiko *et al.* 2019). Members of the patient's web of life will change over time, but the ability of the support network to meet the patient's and family's needs (i.e., quality) is more important than the number of people within the support network (i.e., quantity) (Fong *et al.* 2006).

Couples/partners can experience the loss of established roles when one partner becomes the primary caregiver for the other person. Illness can disrupt healthy boundaries, especially if the relationship becomes overly focused on the illness. Rolland (1994) notes that "chronic disorders have an insidious tendency to become embedded in even the healthiest relationship" (p.330). One physician even observed that "many marriages fall apart the minute somebody gets unwell—it can expose whatever weakness there is. I've seen people walk out on their spouse while they were getting a bone-marrow transplant" (Tsoulis-Reay 2016).

Friendships may collapse because of the patient's limited energy to engage with other people, preoccupation with illness, or withdrawal from people who don't meet their emotional needs (Griffiths 2016; Plach, Stevens, and Moss 2004b; Rebman *et al.* 2017). Even relationship changes that are ultimately **life-affirming** for the person can have negative secondary effects. For example, one woman with a chronic health condition stopped drinking and using drugs with her friends. Although she experienced health benefits from this change in behavior, she sacrificed these friendships (Barrett 1995).

Co-workers, colleagues, group/club members, customers/clients, and neighbors may only be loosely connected to the patient. They may not learn of the person's illness or act on this information when they do find out. Patients may feel the loss of these acquaintances more deeply than you might expect; peripheral relationships can symbolize connections to the person's broader web of life. Patients who live in long-term care facilities also lose relationships when other residents leave or die. Healthcare providers in these facilities can become habituated to the ongoing loss of residents, and their diminished responses to these losses can disenfranchise grief for the surviving residents (Djivre *et al.* 2012).

Secondary loss: Spiritual losses

People experience spiritual losses when values, beliefs, meanings, practices, and their understandings of the sacred can't support them in the context of an incurable health condition (Adams 2016; Balboni and Balboni 2018; Delgado-Guay *et al.* 2012; Doka and Aber 2002; Gall and Cornblat 2002; Gall and Grant 2005; Puchalski 2006; Rowe and Allen 2004). Spiritual losses are the most likely type of loss to be unacknowledged because spirituality is marginalized within the chronic illness experience. We'll examine spiritual losses and struggles in Chapter 4.

Grief

Grief describes a broad range of normal human responses to loss (Harris and Winokuer 2016). Traditionally, **mourning** is used to describe shared or public expressions of grief (e.g., rituals such as funerals or memorial services). Today **mourning** and **grieving** are often used interchangeably. We most often think of grief as sadness, but it can include numbness, heartache, regret, anger, loneliness, irritability, and shame. Other signs of grief include changes in appetite and digestion, sighing, tightness in the throat, changes in energy or activity levels, sleep changes, isolation, unclear thinking, and increased daydreaming (Romm 2014; Widera and Block 2012). People vary in how they express grief: some struggle, some are more emotional, others are more action-oriented (Doka 2016).

In Western popular culture, Kübler-Ross's classic text on death and dying (1969) is an oft-cited description of how people should grieve: they should move from denial to anger, bargaining, depression, and acceptance. Unfortunately, this progression misinterprets Kübler-Ross's work and suggests that people should grieve in linear fashion. As a result, people who don't follow these steps can feel judged for grieving the "wrong" way, or they can feel confused when their grief trajectory doesn't fit the expected model. People may also feel shame for not quickly "fixing the problem" of grief.

I find it helpful to think of grief as a wave-like experience (Widera and Block 2012). Feelings of grief come and go over time, sometimes (metaphorically) knocking people off their feet, but eventually diminishing to gentle waves or a quiet ocean. This woman's description bears out the usefulness of this metaphor:

> Sometimes you have to allow yourself to go back and go through one or more of the emotions again and again, however long it

takes for you to deal with it yourself…and to allow yourself the right to do that. The right to be unhappy, the right to feel all the different things. (Reynolds and Prior 2003b, p.1234)

Worden (2002) describes grieving as a set of tasks people eventually need to complete to avoid long-term psychological problems such as complicated grief. The person who grieves is an active agent who completes these tasks in any order, sometimes more than once. The tasks include accepting that the loss is real, processing the pain without avoiding challenging emotions, adjusting to life with loss, and (in the case of death) finding a way to remain connected to the person who has died. Doka (2014, first published 2009) added an additional task of reconstructing the spiritual orienting system, a process we'll explore in Chapter 4.

When responses to loss are not acknowledged, either by the person who experienced the loss or by other people, grief is disenfranchised. There are many reasons why **disenfranchised grief** is common with chronic illness. Most cultures lack shared guidelines for grieving chronic illness (Wendell 1996). Invisible losses are easy to discount, and people (patients included) often trivialize the everyday losses that are common with chronic illness (Doka and Martin 2002; Miles 2009; Sapey 2004). Caregivers may experience compassion fatigue as they tire of listening to a litany of losses over time, so losses that occur later in the disease trajectory are at greater risk of being disenfranchised (Cassell 2004, first published 1991). People may assume that once the patient adjusts to life with illness, losses will be accepted without grief. People who are uncomfortable with grief or the patient's way of grieving may discourage or disengage from the patient.

Integration: Addressing loss and grief

As a spiritual caregiver, you can help people experiencing loss and grief related to chronic illness. Invite people to share their illness narratives as a way for them to regain control of these stories (Charon 2006). Reassure them that ongoing losses are normal with chronic illness. Ask people about new losses since the last time you connected. Compassionately acknowledge all losses, big and small. You can acknowledge loss using words and/or body language, but be aware of your tendencies to respond in the same way each time someone shares a loss. Varied responses help communicate an authentic acknowledgment of each loss, reassuring the other person that you are fully present to *this* loss at *this* time with *this* person.

Encourage people to express grief in whatever way is comfortable for them and assure them that the way they grieve is normal. Use the wave metaphor to help people understand how grief is ongoing but dissipates with time. Dispel the myth that grieving is a linear process.

Anxiety, depression, and demoralization

Anxiety is worry, concern, or fear about what might happen, with feelings that range from unpleasant to catastrophic. Anxiety is common with the ongoing health crises of chronic illness (e.g., diagnoses, tests, side effects, symptoms, surgeries, and new losses) (Stoklosa *et al.* 2011; Traeger *et al.* 2012). Even when things are going well, patients and families may worry about what the next crisis will be and when it will happen. In relatively quiet moments, people also have more time to think about their fears (Doka 2014, first published 2009).

Anxiety can be challenging to identify because it's often experienced and described in subtle ways. People may feel jittery, apprehensive, tense, or dizzy. They may have an insatiable need for information, or they may experience sleeplessness, restlessness, heart palpitations, vague pain, or stomach upset (McGlensey 2015; Miller 2014; Quinn 2018; Stoklosa *et al.* 2011; Traeger *et al.* 2012). Anxiety can be life-affirming when it prompts patients to follow treatment plans or make changes that improve their quality of life. Spiritual caregivers should refer people to behavioral health professionals if they become overwhelmed by anxiety (Gaudette and Jankowski 2013; Strada 2016; Traeger *et al.* 2012).

People living with chronic health conditions may have a heightened awareness of mortality that leads to **death anxiety**: feelings of dread, apprehension, and fear when thinking about the process of dying or ceasing to exist (for themselves or someone close to them) (Gaudette and Jankowski 2013). Some cultures don't encourage talking about death with patients, but open and direct conversations can help ease this form of anxiety (Doka 2014, first published 2009; Nyatanga 2016).

As many as 82 percent of people with chronic health conditions experience **depression** related to their illness (Breitbart and Dickerman 2018; Caruso *et al.* 2017; Di Benedetto *et al.* 2014; Strada 2016). The risk for depression increases as physical symptoms worsen, people lose function, and losses accumulate (Caruso *et al.* 2017). Sadness that doesn't go away is the number one sign of depression. Normally, waves of grief diminish with time. Depression feels more like the person is sinking deeper and deeper into an ocean of distressing feelings that do not improve. One patient described the all-pervasiveness of depression this way:

> I can be talking to you normal and the next minute I sink into such despair that all I see around me is just clawing up a mud pit… I wake up with the black dog and I go to bed stroking the black dog and it's been the bane of my life. I can be as happy as a pig in a poke but it still comes… I've not been able to cope with it. I've hid it, I've put it to one side, but the black dog has always been there. He will always come out and no matter what medication I take; it will always raise its ugly muzzle. (Vassilev *et al.* 2014, pp.284–285)

People with depression lose interest and no longer find pleasure in activities they once enjoyed. They may have a flat affect, feel worthless, and withdraw from relationships. They may think about death or suicide, but not always with a specific plan in mind. In contrast, after the intense early stage of normal grief, people usually still feel good about themselves. Even when they feel sad, they can take pleasure in life and maintain a sense of hope (Noorani and Montagnini 2007; Widera and Block 2012).

Anxiety and depression are often disenfranchised experiences: people may assume that someone living with chronic illness would naturally be worried or feel sad about their condition. Stigma around mental illness leads people to dismiss symptoms, and some people aren't comfortable sharing their feelings with healthcare providers (Noorani and Montagnini 2007; Strada 2016). It's also challenging to differentiate anxiety and depression from grief, spiritual distress, illness symptoms, and side effects of treatment (Breitbart and Dickerman 2018).

A minority of people (e.g., 13–18 percent of cancer and palliative care patients) may experience **demoralization syndrome** in which they feel helpless, hopeless, or bereft of meaning (Robinson *et al.* 2016). **Helplessness** includes feeling trapped, lacking control, or feeling like a failure (Grassi and Nanni 2016). **Hopelessness** is the feeling that life will never get better. This feeling may begin when people aren't able to cope effectively with illness (Grassi and Nanni 2016). A third sign of demoralization syndrome is loss of meaning or purpose (e.g., *What's the point of living?*). The risk of demoralization increases with loss of dignity as people are unable to care for themselves (e.g., independently managing toileting and feeding needs) (Vehling and Mehnert 2014).

Integration: Addressing anxiety, depression, and demoralization

Spiritual caregivers should know how to recognize signs of anxiety, depression, and demoralization (e.g., Kroenke *et al.* 2010; Quinn 2018, see www.mentalhealthfirstaid.org for training). The general guideline for depression is someone who feels sad and has lost interest in life for more than two weeks.

If you suspect a person is depressed, you should be direct and ask: *Are you feeling depressed?* and/or *You seem sad; have you lost interest in activities you enjoy?* Patients often know when they feel more sadness than usual (Robinson and Crawford 2005). Know how to find behavioral healthcare professionals you can refer to when needed (e.g., see www.psychologytoday.com for listings of therapists worldwide).

It can be challenging to differentiate between depression and demoralization. With depression, distress often feels as if it comes from inside the person. With demoralization, the person usually views the source of their distress as something that happened *to* them (Grassi and Nanni 2016). The **visitor test** may also help you determine what a person is feeling. Think about how this person would likely respond to news of an upcoming visit from a loved one. When people are demoralized, they would say this visit would make them happy, but it would be too much for them at this time. People who are depressed won't have interest in the visit or may not even believe the visit could make them happy. People who are demoralized question their beliefs about themselves and the world, feel disconnected from the past and to the person they once were, and may feel unsure about the future. When people are depressed, they have a sense of future, even if it's not a future they want. People with demoralization also don't usually feel guilty or think they're bad people because they're unable to manage their current situation (Grassi and Nanni 2016). People can be both demoralized and depressed (Noorani and Montagnini 2007).

You can help ease mild anxiety. People living with chronic illness worry about very real concerns, such as major life changes, finances, pain, and dying. Reassuring them that everything will be fine is *not* as helpful as inviting them to talk about specific concerns. As they describe their concerns, you can help normalize their experiences, dispel myths, provide perspective on perceived threats, and help them accept what can't be changed (Traeger *et al.* 2012).

Simple relaxation exercises can also help people who feel anxious. Familiarize yourself with the following exercises and explore online resources you can share with others. For example, there are many YouTube videos about these and other helpful practices:

- Diaphragmatic breathing: Breathe slowly and deeply in and out of the lower abdomen. This practice counteracts shallow chest breathing that can lead to increased heart rate, dizziness, and muscle tension—physical responses that reinforce anxious feelings (instructions on diaphragmatic breathing: Ankrom 2019).

- Progressive muscle relaxation: Momentarily tighten and release muscles from one end of the body to the other. This practice helps divert attention from sources of anxiety, and it gives the person a sense of control over their body (instructions: Anxiety Canada 2018).

- Guided imagery: Imagine the self in a relaxing place and state of mind (e.g., on a beach). You can guide people through this practice spontaneously or using a script. Speak slowly in a soothing tone. It's helpful to engage all five senses to enhance the reality of the experience. You can also recommend online resources for private use (e.g., guided imagery podcasts are available at Michigan Medicine 2018).

Spiritual caregivers may be concerned about taking away hope by talking realistically about chronic illness. We also don't want to offer false hope that ignores the patient's reality. However, it's important that we show support for the person's broad hopes with simple affirmations: *I also want to see you return to the person you were*, or *I, too, hope for a cure soon*. Balance these broad hopes by helping people identify realistic, more narrowly defined hopes that the patient or family can realize in the next day, week, or month (e.g., talking with a friend who lives out of town, attending an important event, or creating a lasting gift for loved ones).

Of course, spiritual caregivers should always address **spiritual struggles**. Spiritual struggles can lead to psychological suffering and/or exacerbate these feelings. Anxiety and depression are less likely when people experience spiritual well-being, so helping a person maintain a **well-integrated spirituality** can help prevent other forms of suffering (Abu-Raiya *et al.* 2015b; Alradaydeh and Khalil 2018; Breitbart and Dickerman 2018; Chaar *et al.* 2018; Seo *et al.* 2015). In Chapter 4, you'll learn more about spiritual struggles and spiritual coping strategies.

Desire for hastened death

Some people with chronic illnesses have a desire to die sooner than death will naturally occur (Douglas, Windsor, and Wollin 2008). In the extreme, the **desire for hastened death** leads to thinking about or attempting suicide. However, what appears to be a desire for hastened death is not always an actual wish to die. Patients may talk about hastened death because they'd like to control how death happens to them. They may be expressing sadness and despair about their situation. Talking about hastened death may be a way to solicit attention, or it may help patients learn how other people feel about their illness and prognosis (Branigan 2015; Nissim, Gagliese, and Rodin 2009). The desire for hastened death may be a response to isolation, as this widow describes: "There are medications for my diabetes, my blood pressure, my kidneys. There's no medication for feeling alone. I don't even want to take my meds anymore. I just want to be reunited with my [late] husband" (Ahmadmehrabi 2018). It's a myth that talking about suicide will make people more likely to think about ending their life. In fact, talking about a desire for hastened death can be a relief as people learn that these feelings are common and normal with serious illness.

A person's desire for hastened death may change with the course of their illness. One day, it might be just a passing wish. Another day, a patient might actively request information about medical aid in dying or refuse medical interventions (Wilson *et al.* 2007). Risk factors for a desire for hastened death include depression, feeling one is a burden on one's family, hopelessness, a personal or family history of mental illness (especially with a history of suicidal behavior), financial concerns, relationship issues, loss of control, and spiritual distress (Rodin *et al.* 2009). Actress Sarah Hyland presents a recent example:

> [Her] failing kidney left Hyland feeling "very depressed" and questioning her own self-worth… "For a long time, I was contemplating suicide, because I didn't want to fail my little brother like I failed my dad," she continued. "I had gone through (my whole life) of always being a burden, of always having to be looked after, having to be cared for." (Delbyck 2018)

Laws in some parts of the United States and in some countries around the world allow mentally capable and terminally ill adults who are suffering to request and receive a prescription for medication they can take to bring about a peaceful death. Wilson and colleagues (2007) found that only 10 percent of patients would consider medical aid in dying if it was legally available to them. Studies like this remind us that it's important to ask questions about what patients really mean when they talk about hastened death. Spiritual caregivers should reflect on their personal values about hastened death to be able to engage effectively in these important, but emotionally fraught, conversations with patients, family members, and healthcare professionals (MacLeod, Wilson, and Phillipa 2012).

Integration: Addressing desire for hastened death

If you suspect someone has a desire for hastened death, be direct: *Are you thinking about killing yourself?* or *Are you thinking about ending your life?* If the answer is yes, you should ask: *Do you have a plan to kill yourself?* or *Have you done anything recently to prepare to end your life?* (For example, have they collected medications, bought a gun, cut themselves?) If the person is actively thinking about hastened death, ask: *On a scale of 1 to 5, where 1 is not at all likely and 5 is very likely, how likely are you to kill yourself today?* If they respond 4 or 5, seek help immediately from a suicide hotline or other resource.

Desire is not the same as the ability to act on that wish. That said, a person may be able to act in more passive ways, like this man: "I've been in a very dark place... I didn't take my medicines because I didn't wish to live" (Michlig *et al.* 2018, p.513). Obviously, people who have both the desire and the capability are at the highest risk for suicide. If you feel uncomfortable in any way about the person acting on a desire for hastened death, seek help from a suicide hotline or other behavioral health professionals. Spiritual well-being buffers against the desire for hastened death, so we want to address spiritual struggles and help people find life-affirming ways to cope with chronic illness (see Chapter 4) (Wang and Lin 2016).

Caregiver burden

I want to call attention to family caregivers who—like Dorothy's family in *The Wizard of Oz*—are often invisible as the illness narrative naturally focuses on the patient (Williams, Morrison, and Robinson 2014). **Informal family caregivers** (i.e., not paid care providers) are part of a system of **reciprocal suffering** in which everyone experiences distress related to the illness (Möllerberg *et al.* 2017; Piburn 1999; Rolland 1994; Wittenberg-Lyles *et al.* 2011). Caregiver suffering is called **caregiver burden**.

Many factors contribute to caregiver burden: the patient's physical, emotional, and spiritual needs; financial stress; employment issues; the number of other people the caregiver supports; other health concerns within the family; cultural expectations about care; and the quality of the caregivers' support network (Adelman *et al.* 2014; Goldstein *et al.* 2006; Grytten and Mäseide 2005; Kim *et al.* 2018; Kim *et al.* 2015; Nissen *et al.* 2016; Shukla *et al.* 2018). Informal caregivers often experience losses related to their roles in the family and workplace, privacy, personal freedom, future plans, spirituality, and control (Gall and Kafi 2014; Irvine *et al.* 2009; Munck, Fridlund, and Mårtensson 2008). Spouses/partners may lose the patient as an important source of their own emotional support, friendship, and intimacy (Bernhard 2014b; Eriksson and Svedlund 2005). Informal caregivers are at high risk for anxiety and depression due to losses and other stressors associated with caregiver burden (Trevino, Prigerson, and Maciejewski 2017).

Coping is challenging for caregivers who neglect self-care, find it difficult to share responsibilities with other people, or don't feel supported. They may also experience **compassion fatigue**, a feeling of indifference to the patient's needs because the caregiver has already given so much of themselves. Caregivers may also resent the patient (Mann 1982; Williams *et al.* 2014, pp.602–603). One daughter said this about her mother: "I think she uses [the] breast cancer card a bit too much sometimes which is really annoying" (Gall and Kafi 2014, p.124). Feelings of inadequacy are common:

> The thing is that I always feel guilty: If I am not paying her enough attention, I feel guilty. If I chat and don't get the things done that I need to do to support her, I feel guilty. If I occasionally lose it and feel angry, or fed up with the situation, I feel guilty. It's a lose-lose situation. (Middleton-Green and Chatterjee 2017, p.99)

Not all caregivers feel burdened by their role (Roth, Fredman, and Haley 2015). This woman reflected on caring for her late husband: "Some days were more difficult than others, but there were moments of joy, laughter, tenderness in every day—if I was willing to look hard enough" (Grant 2016). That said, spiritual caregivers should be aware of signs of distress in the informal caregiver because their well-being affects both themselves and the quality of care they provide for the patient (Cubukcu 2018; Hashemi, Irajpour, and Taleghani 2018).

Integration: Alleviating caregiver burden

Notice when family caregivers appear angry, resentful, stressed, afraid, overwhelmed, or uncomfortable providing care. Provide a safe space for them to lament, especially if you sense they feel embarrassed or ashamed of their feelings. Refer caregivers to behavioral health professionals if needed.

You can validate the importance of the informal caregiver role *and* remind informal caregivers that they're not superheroes (Bernhard 2014b). Without imposing a "grin and bear it" approach, highlight potential benefits of being a caregiver: feeling needed, having a sense of meaning or purpose, building stronger relationships, increasing their activity level, learning new skills, and even living longer than people who don't care for someone else (Roth *et al.* 2015; Tarlow *et al.* 2004). One caregiver described her experience this way: "I will never again be as good a person as I was when I cared for Bill. I will never again have that high a purpose" (Grant 2016).

Support a caregiver's self-care practices, particularly life-affirming spiritual coping strategies that enhance spiritual well-being (see Chapter 4). Encourage caregivers to address family communication issues (Applebaum and Breitbart 2013). Patients want mutually supportive relationships, so they also need to be aware of their caregiver's concerns (Bernhard 2014b). Silk and Goldman (2013) suggest this practice to decrease stress in the family system: ask family and friends to offer "comfort in" to the center of the patient's web of life (the patient and primary caregiver[s]) and share "complaining out" to people who are not as intimately involved with the patient. Some families may also be open to group spiritual direction (described in Chapter 4), which has been helpful for families living with Alzheimer's disease (Mahdavi *et al.* 2017).

Dorothy and Kelly: Losses on the journey

We can only imagine what Dorothy's family experiences after the storm passes in Kansas because they don't appear again until the end of the film. We can assume they're bereft when they discover that the Dorothy they've known and loved for years is nowhere to be found. My maternal grandmother often looked deep into my eyes and said I had "lost the sparkle" I had before I was diagnosed. We both mourned the loss of that Kelly.

My husband has been the unseen primary caregiver in my illness narrative. His greatest burden is financial. As his career progressed, he changed companies several times. These moves benefited our family in the long run, but they also raised concerns about health insurance coverage for the expensive medications (thousands of dollars each month) needed to control my pain and fatigue. When we've waited weeks for a new insurance carrier to approve my medications, I've experienced debilitating disease flare-ups before resuming my treatment protocol—which also often took weeks to bring symptoms under control. My husband has borne the emotional weight of putting me in this unavoidable predicament. Our relationship has also been affected by physical limitations associated with RA. Not infrequently, we postpone, reschedule, or cancel activities because I lack energy or don't feel well. I am not the person he hoped I would be when we married.

Both Dorothy and I experienced the loss of people in our lives. When Glinda the Good Witch drifts away, Dorothy observes that people move in and out of her life when illness is in the foreground. Healthcare providers, other patients, and peripheral acquaintances may appear only briefly to offer information, advice, or support. These fluid relationships can be both helpful and challenging, depending on the circumstances of departure.

I also experienced loss of support that I expected from family members. My mother has encouraged me through frequent emails, but she didn't help with the physical realities of caring for my home and children when I was incapacitated by pain, fatigue, and inflammation. This was particularly frustrating because during this time she expected and received my full support when her husband was ill. I frequently offered our home as a makeshift hospital suite when they visited the regional medical center. When my mother diminishes the challenges of living with RA by saying the disease made me who I am today, the reality of my pain and suffering is further disenfranchised. My brother rarely acknowledges my reports of disease flare-ups. I know they care about me, but the boundaries they set on physical and emotional support have exacerbated isolation and suffering in my illness experience.

In *The Wizard of Oz*, the most prominent loss for Dorothy is her sense of identity, represented by her desire to return "home." Identity is also the critical experience of loss for Dorothy's traveling companions, the Scarecrow, the Tin Man, and the Cowardly Lion. When Dorothy first meets the Scarecrow, he is paralyzed in the sick role/on a pole. The Scarecrow's identity is tied to his ability to work in the fields, but he is no longer able to scare crows. The Scarecrow believes that curing his brain condition will give his life purpose again.

The immobilized Tin Man is similarly locked into his illness identity. His desire for a heart may represent a congenital heart condition (the tinsmith left out this important component when he was built), or it may be a chronic mental health issue (he bemoans a lack of emotional responsiveness). The Tin Man's rusted condition also represents arthritis and/or age-related stiffness, conditions that flare up occasionally on the journey to Oz. When properly medicated/oiled, he can speak and move, albeit with balance issues. However, his missing heart prevents wholistic healing, and he joins the group in search of a cure for this primary condition.

In contrast to the amiable Scarecrow and Tin Man, the Cowardly Lion greets the group with a threatening demeanor. This behavior masks his lack of courage, which he blames on lack of sleep and chronic suffering. Fear and fatigue may indicate anxiety and/or depression. The Lion is also aware of stigma associated with his condition and notes that the group may not want to be seen with him. The Lion seeks healing and a return to his true identity as courageous King of the Beasts. All three of Dorothy's new friends are discovered alone, suggesting they have also experienced social or relational losses. They are eager to join forces to seek cures from the Wizard of Oz.

The companions recognize that diminished health for any member of the group puts their journey at risk. The Wicked Witch/disease threatens the groups with flare-ups. She lights the Scarecrow on fire and her monkeys remove his stuffing. Tears and rain rust the Tin Man. Dorothy and the Lion are lulled to sleep in the poppy field by their reaction to toxic medication. The Witch also threatens their tenuous web of life by isolating Dorothy in the Witch's castle and stealing Toto, their symbol of hope and well-being.

I lost my identity as someone who "could do it all" and moved through life like a sprinter. It's been challenging to become a long-distance runner/walker (speed depends on the day!) to conserve energy. I didn't give up my role as primary caregiver in our family, partially out of necessity with a husband who traveled frequently, and partially as a way of maintaining my identity and a sense of control over my life. I was home with my children when they were young. When I returned to the workforce, I discovered that systemic fatigue and negative side effects of medications curtailed my ability to work full-time. Thankfully, I have flourished in academia, which supports a flexible schedule and the ability to work from home. At home I can balance periods of activity and rest.

In the past two decades, I have experienced many other losses that most people would find meaningless, such as the ability to stand on my head in yoga practice (too risky for my cervical spine) or staying up late (sleep is critical for pain management). I have not experienced depression, demoralization, or the desire for hastened death. I have grieved and coped with manageable anxiety. Dorothy and I have both had spiritual losses. We'll describe our spiritual struggles and the spiritual coping strategies we've used for healing in the next chapter.

4

Scarecrow, Tin Man, and Lion

SPIRITUAL STRUGGLES AND SPIRITUAL COPING

Dorothy and Toto join forces with the Scarecrow, Tin Man, and Cowardly Lion—other patients living with chronic health conditions—for the long trek to the Emerald City. As they progress on this **hero's journey**, the group is tested, and they struggle with threats to their **spiritual orienting systems** (SOSs) (Campbell 2008). Dorothy is missing home/identity. The Scarecrow seeks a brain/knowledge/meaning. The Tin Man desires a heart/emotions/compassion, and the Lion lacks courage/hope. The group must learn, individually and collectively, how to access spiritual resources to cope with these threats to their health and well-being. In this chapter, we'll identify common spiritual struggles associated with chronic illness, determine when spiritual distress becomes a spiritual crisis, and consider spiritual coping strategies that support well-being for people living with chronic illness.

Spiritual struggles

In Chapter 1, I defined **spiritual struggles** as conflicts related to a person's spiritual orienting system. People experience spiritual struggles[1] within themselves, with other people, and with the sacred. In a survey of hundreds of cancer patients with varying commitments to spirituality, nearly two-thirds had at least one spiritual struggle (Balboni and Balboni 2018). Other studies show spiritual struggles in 15 to 50 percent of patients with a variety of chronic health conditions (Ellis *et al.* 2013; Fitchett *et al.* 2004; King *et al.* 2017a, 2017b). Even people who appear to have well-developed spiritual orienting systems experience spiritual distress (Pargament *et al.* 2005b, p.252), as we see in these comments from a theologian diagnosed with cancer:

> I thought that the gospel requires us to surrender everything, and when I really thought through what that meant, I thought it was actually impossible and unfair. The easy stuff? Fine. Smoking? Whatever. Not committing adultery? Great. But don't ask me to give up my toddler. Only a monster would ask me that. (Faith & Leadership 2018)

Of course, spiritual struggles aren't all bad. Like butterflies fighting to emerge from their cocoons, people with chronic illness experiences can undergo positive transformation through struggle. Some religious traditions believe spiritual challenges are a necessary part of spiritual growth (e.g., "dark night of the soul" experiences described in St. John of the Cross 2003, first translated 1959). That said, in an important two-year longitudinal study, Pargament and colleagues (2004) found that people who "get stuck" in chronic struggles experience poor health outcomes and diminished well-being.

Chronic illness jeopardizes well-being and puts all aspects of the spiritual orienting system at risk (Abu-Raiya *et al.* 2015b; Aburub *et al.* 2018; Cummings and Pargament 2010; Gordon *et al.* 2002; McConnell and Pargament 2006; Selman *et al.* 2011). This person describes how chronic illness can shatter a person's SOS:

---

1   Boston and Mount (2006) note similarities between existential and spiritual struggles/distress. I use **spiritual struggles/distress** in this book as an inclusive term for these conditions.

[When I got cancer, I felt] total isolation and no connection with anything. I really think that was probably the saddest feeling I could ever have, because that meant there was no god, no nature, no animals I care about. There are no people. There are only nothings. It's a black hole. No spirit, no soul, nothing left. [It was like being] a robot woman—just a body that breathes, functions, eats. The battery died. There was no spark. (Mount *et al.* 2007, p.377)

As I described in Chapter 2, the most common spiritual struggle is coming to terms with *why* the illness is happening (Balboni and Balboni 2018). As people consider this question, they wrestle with understandings of the sacred, suffering, illness, health, the meaning of life, purpose, and justice (Doka and Aber 2002; Sakellariou, Boniface, and Brown 2013). The meanings embedded in their SOS may not be as broad or deep as they need to cope well with an incurable disease (Pargament 2007).

People may struggle when they can't blame someone/thing for the illness (Cassell 2004, first published 1991). They may feel abandoned or punished by God/a higher power (Balboni and Balboni 2018). They may exhibit a sense of "spiritual entitlement" and be angry with God/a higher power for inflicting or not responding to their suffering (Grubbs *et al.* 2018). They may feel personal shame if they feel they lack the faith to heal (Gall 2003; Smart and Smart 2006). Chronic illness brings mortality into focus (Boston, Bruce, and Schreiber 2011). People may struggle with their desire to live, challenging spiritual beliefs about who/what controls death and how much suffering a person can bear (e.g., Larsson and Grassman 2012).

Social/cultural pressure for patients to maintain a positive mindset and fight disease is often **life-limiting** for patients (can lead to shame) or caregivers (can feel let down by the patient) (Holmes 2017b; Southwood 2018; Wong 2019). A professor of behavioral medicine described the burden these expectations place on patients in a *New York Times* editorial:

> If people are insufficiently upbeat after a cancer diagnosis or
> inadequately "spiritual" after a diagnosis of AIDS, are we to
> assume they have wilfully placed their health at risk? And if they
> fail to recover, is it really their fault? ... It is difficult enough to
> be injured or gravely ill. To add to this the burden of guilt over
> a supposed failure to have the right attitude toward one's illness
> is unconscionable. (Sloan 2011)

Physical symptoms and changes challenge spiritual values and
beliefs about independence and self-worth (Mann 1982; Roze
des Ordons *et al.* 2018). Chronic pain is particularly troubling
because it reinforces and is worsened by spiritual distress (Harris
et al. 2018; Hilbert 1984; Wachholtz, Pearce, and Koenig 2007).
One patient said: "The inside physical pain binds up really
deep with the spiritual self because of the pain being so deep.
Sometimes you can't tell the difference where you're actually
hurting" (Haozous and Knobf 2013, p.1055).

Deeply meaningful relationships may be threatened by
conflicts about the meaning of the illness (Rolland 1994).
Changing roles in the **web of life** challenge understandings of
the self and one's purpose in life. Another source of spiritual
struggle comes from the isolating effects of chronic illness on
relationships with the sacred, people, and animals/pets. People
also experience spiritual struggles when they feel guilt, shame,
or regret for things done and not done (e.g., becoming a burden
on family, broken relationships).

Chronic illness can threaten private or communal spiritual
practices. People may not be able to travel to a place of worship,
or they may be unable to fully participate in spiritually oriented
activities such as volunteer work, fasting, prayer vigils, or
ceremonies (e.g., Haozous and Knobf 2013; Patel *et al.* 2014).
Personal practices may no longer offer comfort if the person's
relationship with the sacred is disrupted, as this woman describes:

> The doctors can measure the changes in my sight and my hearing,
> but only I can measure the part of my faith I lost. You will find

me in church on Sundays, but not in the pew. Instead, I sit with a few others in a small chapel to the side of the main sanctuary in a twenty-minute meditation between services… Through the walls I can hear the choir practicing various familiar hymns. It is the right metaphor for me: I hear them but only through the walls. I am in a different but related room. I am glad to be freed from saying words that have ceased to be mine. The loss of old words has left space for new ones, here, written down. I went into exile and came out with something else; I am reimagining the nature of faith or, at least, of my faith. (Gallagher 2013, p.202)

Spiritual struggles in Oz and Kansas

Dorothy's primary spiritual struggle is lack of belief that she can experience—even deserves—well-being while living with a chronic health condition. This struggle plays out when Dorothy is regularly challenged to hold on to her life force/the ruby slippers and her well-being/Toto when threatened by the Wicked Witch of the West. The Witch is relentless, demanding Dorothy surrender to illness and forcing Dorothy to watch her life blood drip away in the form of an hourglass filled with blood-red sand. The Wizard also challenges Dorothy to prove her commitment to healing and well-being by bringing him the Witch's broom. We also see Dorothy struggle with self-blame for causing Aunt Em to suffer in her absence and for her own isolation from family. Even after Dorothy returns to Kansas, she encounters relational struggles when the family's understanding of her illness experience (it was a nightmare) conflicts with her own experiences of reality.

Dorothy and her companions constantly have their will to live tested (e.g., angry apple trees pelt them with fruit, the Witch's army of monkeys harasses them, toxic poppies overwhelm them with fatigue). On their way to the Emerald City, they must pass through a haunted forest, a metaphor for dark and threatening obstacles to healing. Its entrance is even marked with a sign that warns people not to enter.

Although they are not the primary patient in this narrative, we also gain insights into the spiritual struggles that Dorothy's companions experience. The Scarecrow's desire for a brain represents spiritual struggles with meaning making. The Tin Man bemoans his lack of emotion/compassion. The Lion longs for hope/courage.

During the diagnostic phase, I had few spiritual struggles. My SOS provided a coherent understanding of what was happening, I felt connected to the sacred (which I called God at that time), and my spiritual beliefs and practices were **life-affirming**. As I described in Chapter 3, my greatest source of spiritual struggle was the lack of a mutually supportive relationship with my mother. I felt abandoned when physical symptoms and uncertainty were at their worst. This experience reignited emotional and spiritual distress from childhood and youth, when I also felt my needs were disenfranchised within the family system.

It was several years before my SOS was seriously challenged. The disease itself didn't prompt these struggles. Rather, I opened the door to spiritual challenges when I chose to reflect on the meaning of illness (in general, as well as the meaning of my own illness) while completing my doctoral work. I say more about these struggles later in this chapter.

Spiritual distress and spiritual crisis

Signs of **spiritual distress**[2] include lack of peace, the inability to accept what is happening, loss of meaning, and relationship struggles (King *et al.* 2017a; Schultz *et al.* 2017). Chaplains may use tools (e.g., checklists of questions) to assess spiritual distress, but currently there is no single accepted tool. The simplest and most

---

2   Boston, Bruce and Schreiber (2011) and other researchers also refer to spiritual distress as *spiritual pain*.

direct assessment is to ask the person: *Are you at peace with this situation or experience?* or *Are you struggling with meaning in your life?* or *Do you have what you would describe as spiritual struggles?* (King *et al.* 2017a; Lopez *et al.* 2019; Steinhauser *et al.* 2000).

People naturally try to maintain spiritual equilibrium (a calm ocean) by integrating new experiences, such as chronic illness, into their spiritual orienting systems. But they can't always resolve spiritual distress on their own (Pargament 2007). Without help, ripples of spiritual distress can escalate to overwhelming waves of **spiritual crisis**, where people struggle with profound loss, an incoherent worldview, and questions of meaning (Agrimson and Taft 2008). The relative severity of the person's illness (e.g., autoimmune disease vs. cancer) does not predict the magnitude of spiritual distress (Adams 2016).

In order for people to resolve spiritual distress, they need relationships of trust in which they can address difficult topics with people who will respect their spiritual beliefs (Roze des Ordons *et al.* 2018). Do these characteristics sound familiar? They should—these relationships embody the **SNAP** communications skills described in this book. Spiritual caregivers who embody SNAP skills can help people connect with life-affirming ways to cope with chronic illness and avoid spiritual crises.

Spiritual coping

Coping describes people's attempts to manage stressful or threatening experiences. Worldwide, people of all ages and spiritual identities rely on spirituality to help them cope with a diverse array of chronic diseases (e.g., Anderson and Asnani 2013; Arabiat *et al.* 2013; Cruz *et al.* 2017; Daly, Fahey-McCarthy, and Timmins 2019; Ellis *et al.* 2013; Esmaeili *et al.* 2015; Gall 2003; Pérez and Smith 2015; Reynolds, Mrug, and Guion 2013; Reynolds *et al.* 2014; Roze des Ordons *et al.* 2018; Sharif *et al.* 2018; Tan, Wutthilert, and O'Connor 2011; Unantenne *et al.* 2013; Wachholtz *et al.* 2007; Whittemore and Dixon 2008;

Yodchai *et al.* 2017). People are more likely to rely on spirituality to cope when they have limited access to other resources (e.g., financial means or practical support) (Cruz *et al.* 2017; Keefe *et al.* 2002; Pargament 1997; Smith *et al.* 2008).

A wealth of empirical evidence links spirituality[3] with positive physical and mental health outcomes (see Koenig and McCullough 2012, first published 2001, for a comprehensive catalogue of studies). However, spirituality can also hinder a person's ability to cope. For example, people who have had negative (even traumatic) spiritual experiences and people who use **negative spiritual coping** (described later in this chapter) may find spiritual coping problematic (e.g., Gordon *et al.* 2002; Harrison *et al.* 2001; Keefe *et al.* 2001; Pargament 1997; Pargament *et al.* 1998; Pargament, Koenig, and Perez 2000; Vitorino *et al.* 2018).

Most research on spiritual coping focuses on North America and Europe with a Protestant Christian bias (Cummings and Pargament 2010; Pargament *et al.* 1988). Researchers are addressing this bias by focusing research on and including participants from other religious traditions, as well as people who identify as spiritually fluid, atheist, and agnostic (e.g., Muslim: Kahn and Watson 2006; Jewish: Keshet and Liberman 2014; Buddhist: Phillips *et al.* 2012; Hindu: Tarakeshwar, Pargament, and Mahoney 2003; diverse traditions: Van Laarhoven *et al.* 2010).

Spirituality is most helpful when it's integrated throughout a person's life, enabling the person to live out core values (Pargament 1997; Pérez and Smith 2015). A **well-integrated spirituality** is flexible (adaptable to cope with changing circumstances), complex (able to support meaning making about suffering), liberative (supports freedom in the person's life), and grounded in benevolent views and experiences of life and **the sacred** (Doehring 2015, first published 2006; Pargament 1997).

---

3   Research often uses *religious coping* because studies examine activities associated with religion, such as worship service attendance and prayer practices. I use the more inclusive term **spiritual coping**.

This person illustrates the characteristics of a well-integrated spirituality:

> [Spirituality] helps in accepting, "well this is something I've got and I've got to learn to live with it. Let's use it or live with it in the best way I can" [*flexible and complex*]...my personal faith that God is in control and knows what's happening, and [I] have that relationship with God and that gives support and comfort and strength and all those sort of things [*grounded in a benevolent view of the sacred and liberative*]. It's a bit hard to clarify or define, but it's just an overriding part of who I am in my life [*integrated*]. (Unantenne *et al.* 2013, p.1154; comments added in italics)

Meaning making, hope, peace, self-efficacy, support, and connection to others/the sacred are important elements of life-affirming spiritual coping (Garssen, Uwland-Sikkema, and Visser 2014; Greer *et al.* 2017; Kristofferzon, Engström, and Nilsson 2018; Lucette *et al.* 2016; Park 2007; Pérez and Smith 2015; Rafferty, Billig, and Mosack 2015; Rowe and Allen 2004; Thauvoye *et al.* 2018; Thomsen, Hansen, and Wagner 2011; Unantenne *et al.* 2013). This man illustrates the impact life-affirming spiritual coping can have:

> If it weren't for my faith, I don't know how I would have kept my equilibrium through this. It is definitely through grace. My natural state of anxiety and manic nature would have spiralled out of control... It is profound. (Balboni and Balboni 2018, p.820)

Styles of spiritual coping

There are four primary styles of spiritual coping. People using a **self-directing style** try to manage stress on their own. Self-reliance does not mean they don't have a relationship with the sacred: "[God] gives you a problem. You need to solve it... My way of solving it is go to the doctor and take your doggone medicine" (Harvey 2009, p.213). This style works best when the person can control the stressful situation. Because so many aspects of chronic illness are beyond personal control, self-directing coping is not the most life-affirming strategy (Ano and Vasconcelles 2005).

At the other end of the spectrum, people may use a **deferring style of spiritual coping** where they give control of their illness experience to God/a higher power:

> This illness has just made my faith stronger because it's forced me to pray more. Who do I want to be in charge? I love Dr. Q——, and I really let him believe that he is in charge, but he's not. God is the one that's in control of all of those things. (Maiko *et al.* 2019, p.581)

> When I get pains and soreness—soreness and pain or aches or whatever, I pray to God… I can take all the medicine that's in the pharmacy, and if He doesn't want me healed, I won't get healed. It's up to Him to make the medication work, to heal me. (Harvey and Silverman 2007, p.208)

This more passive style *is* helpful for some people, but the *most* life-affirming strategy is collaborative spiritual coping (Ano and Vasconcelles 2005; Pargament *et al.* 2004; Pérez and Smith 2015). With the **collaborative style of spiritual coping**, the person shares responsibility with God/a higher power: "In addition to seeking support from friends and engaging in her life, the daughter talked to God as a means of calming herself" (Gall and Kafi 2014, p.117). People with well-integrated spiritualities tend to use collaborative coping (Pérez and Smith 2015). This man describes how he collaborates with God:

> I think God works through man… He guides you through His divine wisdom. He just some kind of way moves you by some spiritual forces. He directed me to a good doctor… I take their medicine like they say…that is spiritual because if God hadn't sent a man down here with wisdom, where would we have been?

God gave them the wisdom of being a doctor... I had faith in
God. (Harvey 2009, p.208)

Muslims profess Allah's ultimate control over a person's state
of health and illness. Although this may sound like deferring
coping, this belief can support collaborative spiritual coping:

> Illness is also planned from Allah that is to test the patience and
> the strengths of our belief in God's Will. Facing illness or death
> the faithful Muslim should accept it without questioning and
> look for cure and ask for the help of Allah by prayer, but this
> does not free the person from the responsibility to take care of
> his health. (Nabolsi and Carson 2011, p.719)

The fourth style of spiritual coping, **surrender**, is also associated
with spiritual well-being (Wong-McDonald and Gorsuch 2000).
The surrender style is similar to collaborative coping in that both
the person and God/a higher power are active in the coping
process. When using a surrender style, the person seeks the will
of God/a higher power, and acquiesces to that path, even though
the person may have other—even preferred—options available.
One person described surrender this way: "[Illness] is giving me
meaning in my life. If I don't see [the purpose of things]...I leave
it to God's will to do whatever he thinks is best for me" (Mount
et al. 2007, p.380).

Researchers also describe spiritual coping strategies as
positive or negative. **Positive spiritual coping** strategies include
believing in a loving God/higher power, being spiritually
connected to other people, using a collaborative coping style, and
feeling supported by spiritual practices or a spiritual community
(Pargament 1997; Pargament, Ano, and Wachholtz 2005a).
Positive spiritual coping is generally associated with improved
health (Pargament *et al.* 2004; Reynolds *et al.* 2016).

Negative spiritual coping tends to be life-limiting (Gall and
Bilodeau 2017). It includes experiencing spiritual struggles and
doubts, believing in a punishing God/higher power, and believing

that demonic forces are responsible for illness (Cummings and Pargament 2010; Pargament 1997; Pargament *et al.* 1998; Pargament *et al.* 2005).

Integration: Spiritual coping strategies for chronic illness

In this section, I provide an *overview* of common spiritual coping strategies that enhance well-being and help people adjust to life with chronic illness. Spiritual coping strategies most often accompany biomedical care for chronic illness. Many patients are reluctant to tell biomedical providers about spiritual coping practices for fear of disapproval, but providers often support these practices, as long as they don't interfere with biomedical care (Jou and Johnson 2016).

I encourage you to explore these and other spiritual coping strategies in greater depth on your own and with people in your care. There may be several variations of a practice (e.g., prayer and yoga). People with chronic illness may have one or more life-affirming spiritual practices, and/or they may be open to new practices (Anderson and Asnani 2013; Sirois, Molnar, and Hirsch 2015; Tatsumura *et al.* 2003).

Prayer and meditation

Prayer is the most frequently used spiritual coping practice (Balboni and Balboni 2018; Jors *et al.* 2015; Reyes-Ortiz, Rodriguez, and Markides 2009). Almost 80 percent of participants in the Baylor Religion Survey (United States) said they prayed for their own healing, and nearly 90 percent have prayed for other people's healing (Levin 2016). Even people who don't identify as spiritual pray in health crises: "I was a pure atheist before my mom's breast cancer. My mom got diagnosed and I was like, 'Oh, my God'... So I started praying which was very weird because I don't pray to God" (Gall and Kafi 2014, p.121). Prayer helps people cope by reinforcing their connection to the sacred, providing a distraction from suffering, and generating feelings of peace that contribute to well-being (e.g., Wachholtz and Keefe 2006).

There are many forms of prayer: recitation of traditional religious prayers (e.g., the Muslim salat, the Christian Lord's Prayer/Our Father), repetitive chanting (Gao *et al.* 2017; Saniotis 2018), and meditative/silent prayer (e.g., Centering Prayer, as described in Bourgeault 2004), to name just a few. Studies document healing as a result of prayer for self and others (Dossey 1996, 1997; Robinson 2016). This woman is one example:

> There have been moments when I've had severe palpitations, shortness of breath, and pain. And I have just simply prayed and asked God to alleviate the situation and to change the situation. What makes me believe in it so much is that I found that the physical ailment just merely went away. (Harvey and Silverman 2007, p.209)

There is also a growing body of research on many types of meditation and mindfulness practices that help people cope with stress, manage pain, and experience greater well-being (e.g., Chan and Larson 2015; Chisea and Serretti 2011; Davidson and Kaszniak 2015; Fortney and Taylor 2010; Jacob 2016; Melnick 2017; Morone *et al.* 2008; Thomas Jefferson University 2012). Meditation practices include focused attention on thoughts or sensations, repetition of a mantra/phrase, guided relaxation, non-judgmental awareness of one's thoughts, compassion for self and others, and reception of love/energy/insight from higher powers (Chan and Larson 2015; Doehring 2011; Folk 2013).

Some types of meditation (e.g., vipassana or Zen practices) remain deeply embedded in religious tradition (Burke 2012; Wijesinghe and Parshall 2016). Other types of meditation, as well as mindfulness practices (focused awareness on the present moment), have been adapted to appeal to the general public (Chan and Larson 2015; Kabat-Zinn 1990). Prayer and meditative practices that use gentle movements are also beneficial for many people with chronic health conditions (e.g., prayer walking, yoga, Tai Chi, and Qi Gong) (Burke 2012; Deshpande 2018; Hanh and Anh-Huong 2006; Jyotsna *et al.* 2012; Scholl 2014; Sun, Buys, and Jayasinghe 2014).

It can take time for people to find a meditation or mindfulness practice that suits them, so encourage exploration (Folk 2013; Villines 2017). Even the most basic (and easy-to-teach) practice of focusing the attention on the breath or on a mantra/word/phrase can improve well-being (Chan and Larson 2015).

Reflective reading and writing

Reading sacred scriptures (e.g., the Torah, the Bible, the Koran, the Vedas) helps people with chronic illness find comfort and connect with the sacred (e.g., Daly *et al.* 2019; Hamilton *et al.* 2013; Krause and Pargament 2018). People can also benefit from reading contemporary spiritual reflections, such as *The Tao of Healing* (Jampolsky 1993) and memoirs by people living with chronic health conditions (e.g., Bernhard 2010 and Cohen 2000, both written from a Buddhist perspective; Jaquad 2015, an online blog about living with cancer).

There is significant research on the health benefits of reflective writing (Abercrombie 2002; Burton and King 2010; Lu *et al.* 2019; Pennebaker 1997a, 1997b; Ryan 2006; Willig 2009). Writing gives voice to what might otherwise be disenfranchised. In this man's case, writing literally gave him a voice after losing the ability to speak:

> My life is certainly unusual now: no real speech, no breathing, no eating, and no running toward the sky, orange trees, dogs and kids. But I can still think, for good or for ill, and I can communicate the results of this thinking, thanks to some astounding computer magic. (Ryan 2006, p.432)

Helping people share their stories has been described as "the most significant" aspect of spiritual care (Graham *et al.* 2005, p.67).

Storytelling through any medium (e.g., poetry, video) empowers people to take control of lives disrupted by illness, supports grieving, facilitates meaning making, restores and protects identity, and helps people connect to each other (Gucciardi *et al.* 2016; Heilferty 2018; Kelly, Cudney, and Weinert 2012; Laing *et al.* 2019; Martino and Freda 2016; Martino, Freda, and Camera 2013; Roos and Neimeyer 2007; Ryan 2006).

People naturally want to protect existing narratives, even if they're life-limiting (e.g., Distelberg *et al.* 2014). Storytelling can help people construct life-affirming stories to support life with chronic illness (Moschella 2011; Neuger 2001; White and Epston 1990), but it can be a challenging process:

> Meaning-making—something which had always seemed more or less effortless, even playful at times—felt like hard physical labor involving my whole body in the struggle against the black hole of meaninglessness. Even though I succeeded in constructing a narrative which I felt worked for me in this situation, I was constantly aware of, and affected by, alternative discourses, some of which positioned me in ways which quickly removed my hard earned serenity, my fragile sense of being "at peace." (Willig 2009, p.183)

Research suggests that writing about emotions may benefit people who are encouraged to express themselves verbally, but it doesn't help people encultured to make meaning through non-verbal methods (e.g., in meditation or through art) or people who are more comfortable writing about facts than feelings (Knowles, Wearing, and Campos 2011; Lu *et al.* 2019). In general, research shows that when people write about troubling experiences, negative emotions are short-lived and give way to enhanced well-being (Kelley, Lumley, and Leisen 1997; Kleinman 1988; Pennebaker 1997b).

Spiritual direction

In many spiritual traditions, people share stories and make meaning in ongoing relationships with spiritual directors, guides, or companions[4] (e.g., Christian: Barry and Connolly 1982; Jewish: Eilberg 2005; Buddhist: Taylor 2007; diverse traditions: Vest 2003). In one-on-one and small group spiritual direction, people focus on spirituality to enhance spiritual well-being and connection to the sacred (Dougherty 1995; Guenther 1992). Although "direction" suggests an authoritative dynamic, spiritual direction is a collaborative process in which directors respect people as the experts on their SOSs and illness experiences (Arora 2013). Because spiritual direction relationships are typically long-term (relationships may last years), they're an ideal context for ongoing conversations about loss and meaning making with chronic illness (Arora 2013; Bidwell 2004).[5] A woman living with systemic lupus erythematosus, Parkinson's disease, and depression had this to say:

> Therapy could not touch the pain I was in—it was spiritual. I was spinning helplessly—in increasingly tight circles—desperate for relief from relentless questions: WHERE WAS GOD? WHAT HAD I DONE TO DESERVE THIS?! HOW COULD I LIVE WITH THIS MEDICAL NIGHTMARE? ... Spiritual direction has done nothing short of quieting me down, helping me to grow up and into my new reality, creating a container for my fears and extreme panic, and bringing me home to myself and my God. (Karp 2010; emphasis in original)

Spiritual community

The health benefits of participating in a spiritual community are often cited in news media because this practice is associated

---

4   I use the most common terms: *spiritual director* and *spiritual direction*.

5   People can connect with spiritual directors of varied backgrounds around the world at www.sdiworld.org.

with a longer life span, particularly for women (Chida, Steptoe, and Powell 2009; Kim and VanderWeele 2019; McCullough *et al.* 2009). Hundreds of studies documented in the *Handbook of Religion and Health* affirm that spiritual support/community is associated with greater well-being for patients and their families (Koenig and McCullough 2012, first published 2001). Spiritual community relieves isolation associated with chronic illness (Helgeson *et al.* 2018; Noorani and Montagnini 2007; Penman, Oliver, and Harrington 2013), as this patient affirms: "[Spiritual community] encourages you, cos you talk about God, and then you got the company as well, you see. When I don't have any company I feel terrible" (Koffman *et al.* 2008, p.785).

Spiritual communities provide a place for lament and distraction from suffering (Anderson and Asnani 2013; Hogue 2003). They also enhance the power of other spiritual practices, including gratitude, discernment, and meaning making (Barry and Connolly 1982; Berry 2009; Maggio 2007; Moskowitz 2010; Pesek 2002). Opportunities to both receive and give care also enhance quality of life (Pagano, Post, and Johnson 2010; Pargament 1997), as described by this patient:

> At some stages in your chronic illness you'll need to vent, and you'll need to have people sympathize. When you hit a wall or want to give up, you'll need people who will pull you back up and get in your face about moving forward. You'll need people to help you keep track of progress and remind you just how far you've really come. You'll also feel the need to help others during these same experiences. Helping others to overcome their challenges keeps your skills fresh, helps you to acknowledge your accomplishments and gives your struggle a sense of purpose. (Jacqueline 2018, p.84)

Spiritual communities don't need to be formal or institutionally supported to provide benefit (e.g., Chan, Beaulieu, and Pickering 2018). This patient describes an informal spiritual community that meets in her home:

Seven members of my church come to pray with me every few weeks. They let me cry, and they join me in laughter and listening for the Spirit. They created a home altar for me and decorated my walls with inspiring words and images. (Harley 2013, p.23)

Other spiritual coping strategies

Many people connect with the sacred and experience relief from suffering through music, art, nature, and spending time with pets/animals (Baldacchino *et al.* 2012; Chen *et al.* 2018; Hunt, Nikopoulou-Smyrni, and Reynolds 2014; Pargament 2007; Pargament *et al.* 2017; Penman *et al.* 2013; Reynolds and Prior 2003a; Unantenne *et al.* 2013). These quotations from patients describe their experiences:

When I am really absorbed playing with [watercolors], I forget everything else around me and I don't feel much pain. (Kelly *et al.* 2012, p.51)

When I listen to music that makes me calm and brings me a feeling of happiness, my cells react in a positive way... I am sure something makes that cancer cells die if stress in our body and mind disappear. (Ahmadi 2013, p.157)

When we go to the countryside, my mind becomes completely at rest. I stay there and relax. (Baldacchino *et al.* 2012, p.837)

I have two dogs, I talk to them, they walk with me, we sleep together and when I wake up, they know it's time to get up. They give me strength. (Baldacchino *et al.* 2012, p.834)

[A view of nature] makes me happier. Also, it gives me a little push allowing me to think that I can cope with this situation and well, when you are close to nature you are able to cope with a lot of other things in a better way. (Timmerman, Uhrenfeldt, and Birkelund 2015, p.430)

Spiritual coping resources like these reinforce positive feelings about the self, support emotional expression, provide a sense of accomplishment, and create opportunities for social connection (Baldacchino *et al.* 2012; Bradt and Dileo 2010; Hunt *et al.* 2014; Kelly *et al.* 2012; Nakau *et al.* 2013; Reynolds and Prior 2003b).

Energy healing

Energy healing relieves physical, emotional, and spiritual suffering by addressing blockages, stagnation, and imbalances in universal life force energy (also known as *chi/qi*, *ki*, and *prana*). Reiki, healing touch, and therapeutic touch are common energy healing practices that may be offered in some healthcare settings (Burden *et al.* 2005; Demir, Can, and Celek 2013; DiNucci 2005; Jain and Mills 2010). There are many other lesser-known approaches to energy healing that support **energy body** understandings of illness (Levin 2011; Linn and Wells 2018; McFadden, Hernández, and Ito 2010).

Patients report reduced pain, depression, anxiety, and fatigue, as well as improved quality of life and spiritual well-being (Demir *et al.* 2013; Dŏgan 2018; Fleisher *et al.* 2014; Jain and Mills 2010; McManus 2017; Rao *et al.* 2016). Most people find energy healing a pleasurable experience, illustrated by these patients with cancer: "[Reiki] provided a general sense of peace and muscle relaxation over my entire body that I otherwise have not experience[d] in a few years" and "Each time I come to the clinic my progress, health wise, keeps improving. I believe these reiki sessions have a direct healing effect on my body" (Fleisher *et al.* 2014, p.66).

Core shamanism

Shamanic healing is an ancient practice in which shamans facilitate healing through direct engagement with the spirit world (Eliade 1987, first published 1957; Horrigan 2008; Hutch 2013;

Ingerman 2012; Krippner 2012; Levin 2008; Roberts and Levy 2008). Shamanic practices are experiencing a renaissance today due to greater acceptance of complementary and alternative healing practices and the efforts of contemporary practitioners to bring ancient healing techniques into the modern era (Brunton 2003; Gadit 2003; Helsel, Mochel, and Bauer 2004; Hendrickson 2015; Horrigan 2008; Kirmayer 2004; Penkala-Gawęcka 2013; Sajja and Puchalski 2017; Tick 2007).

Core shamanism encompasses "universal or near-universal shamanic methods" that are not rooted in specific religious or indigenous traditions, but belong to all of humanity (Brunton 2003, p.3; see also Hendrickson 2015). Core shamanic healing happens via a **shamanic journey**, a trance-like state of consciousness in which shamans' spirits travel to an alternate reality to engage with various helping spirits (Boring 2015; Brunton 2003; Hendrickson 2015; Penkala-Gawęcka 2013). Healing occurs while the shaman is in the spirit world, or the shaman may return to share information from the spirit world to facilitate healing in what we know as "ordinary reality" (Harner 2013).

It's not uncommon for people living with chronic illness to seek connection and support from angels, helping spirits, and loved ones who have died. For example: "My husband died… he's with God but for me he's still alive and I feel his help" (Baldacchino *et al.* 2012, p.834; see also Chase 2015; Koffman *et al.* 2008; Trimble 2010). People also pursue healing by exploring past lives (Adams 2018a):

> I really think cancer and some of these other diseases are just a manifestation of other things… Whatever it is that we've dealt with in our lives, this life or our past life, it manifests itself in some sort of tangible form. And I think in order to really fix that, we have to take responsibility. (Tatsumura *et al.* 2003, p.69)

Even though they are profound experiences, most people hide healing stories that involve connection with the spirit world for fear they'll be judged or even pathologized (Alexander 2015;

Lomax, Kripal, and Pargament 2011; Meyersbyrg and McNally 2011; Miller and C'de Baca 2001; Moody 2013; Trimble 2010; Yaden *et al.* 2016). Researchers also don't explicitly invite people to share stories of illness or healing that involve spirits (Laird *et al.* 2017). I also feel vulnerable sharing my experiences. Although intensely profound and life-changing, my story of shamanic healing has been challenging enough to integrate into my own SOS, without trying to explain it to people who may respond with skepticism or derision. I invite you to practice SNAP skills and stay curious as you enter my spiritual world.

Kelly copes

Immediately after my diagnosis with RA, my family (husband and two toddlers) continued to function much as it had before. When my husband was away on business, I had no help at home. My greatest source of practical support came from local friends who occasionally watched my children and one day of church-provided childcare each week. I had a few sessions with a faith-based counselor who helped me give myself permission to limit activities that taxed my energy.

Our family was actively involved with our local church in Kansas. Community prayer, Bible study, and healing services were helpful resources for us as a family and reinforced our understandings of the illness experience. Spiritual community also supported my personal practices of prayer, spiritual reading, and spiritual study. Years prior to diagnosis, I had learned Tai Chi. This slow, contemplative martial art form became a helpful moving meditative practice that I continue today. These spiritual coping strategies were life-affirming for me and our family for many years, even as we moved to Tulsa and later to Memphis. In Memphis, I began seeing a spiritual director every month. This relationship continued for over a decade and was critical in helping me develop a well-integrated spirituality that supported my experiences of ongoing loss and meaning making.

After our family moved to Denver in 2005, I found that spiritual community didn't help me cope with illness as it had done in the past. Other spiritual coping strategies that had served me well for many years also seemed to lack something at this stage of my life. Supported by my spiritual director in Memphis via monthly phone calls, I began to explore new practices. I particularly benefited from twice-weekly yoga classes that helped me integrate body, mind, and spirit.

When I began a PhD program in Denver, my studies broadened my thinking about suffering and challenged me to consider new ways of understanding illness. I began teaching courses about spirituality and health, and I personally explored diverse spiritual coping practices (e.g., healing touch) to enrich my teaching. Then I found a practice that would change my life. I began working with Sarah, a shaman who combines reiki with shamanic healing at a distance[6] (Roberts and Levy 2008).

After entering a deep trance state, Sarah's spirit travels to the spirit world[7] where she meets with her client's spirit, power animals, and spirit guides who support Sarah's healing work, power animals and spirit guides who support the client, angels and archangels, and the spirits of people deceased and living who also offer support. This group of spirit helpers is collectively called **Spirit**. Sarah narrates her experiences in the spirit world as they happen and later provides clients with a digital recording of this narration for their interpretation and reflection.

I have now had dozens of shamanic healing sessions with Sarah. Shamanic healing represents the epitome of **collaborative spiritual coping** as Spirit and I actively work together to heal my body, mind, and spirit (Hutch 2013). When Sarah is in the

---

6   Learn more at www.shamanicsoulguide.com.
7   Shamanic practitioners often describe journeys to an alternate spirit reality made up of Upper, Middle, and Lower Worlds where teaching and healing take place. Shamans often return to familiar locales in these worlds. Harner (2013) has collected thousands of accounts of shamanic journeys that describe the landscape of these worlds and what happens on these journeys.

spirit world, she uses reiki and various shamanic techniques to facilitate healing (e.g., retrieving energy lost during traumatic experiences) (Ingerman 2012; Krippner 2012). That said, healing is primarily the result of my willingness to act on what we learn from Spirit. I am also free to ignore what I learn, although Spirit will repeat messages that are clearly a priority for my health and well-being.

Spirit often illuminates the need for changes in life-limiting beliefs and behaviors that cause me and the people I love to suffer. Spirit has occasionally suggested specific remedies, including vitamins, diet changes, salt-water floats, aromatherapy, craniosacral therapy, and massage. I have followed through on these suggestions with beneficial results.

Most dramatically, in 2017 Spirit recommended I stop taking a powerful combination of long-term medications for RA because they had become toxic to my body. It was risky to stop taking these drugs. They were still helping me to some degree, and, once stopped, I couldn't restart the primary medication because the body often responds with an allergic reaction in that situation. I shared Spirit's message with family members, who were understandably concerned about fixing what didn't appear to be irreparably broke. But I trusted that I needed to follow through. To my surprise, my physician was amenable to the change (without knowing what prompted it), primarily because I'd taken these potent medications for years, and I was experiencing some unpleasant side effects. We agreed on a new treatment plan, and I stopped all current medications. After the insurance company approved the new plan (weeks later), I started taking one new drug in lieu of three I had been using. To everyone's delight, the new drug provides greater relief from symptoms without problematic side effects. I would not have considered such a risky change without Spirit's guidance.

While working with Sarah, I became aware of my own ability to use shamanic journeying and now regularly use this practice to heal myself. I also offer shamanic healing services to other people.[8] My personal experience of the spirit world is that it is an amazing, dreamlike place, with many parallels to the Land of Oz. Let's return now to Oz and consider how Dorothy and her companions learn to cope with their chronic health conditions.

Dorothy and her companions cope

Dorothy's companions have been living with illness on their own for some time when she meets them on the Yellow Brick Road. I use italics to highlight the diverse coping strategies identified in this section.

The Scarecrow continues to restuff himself with hay as it falls out. This coping strategy echoes a Japanese proverb I also live by: "Nana korobi ya oki," which translates to "seven falls, eight getting up." Years ago, I adopted a version of this proverb as my mantra for resilience: "*fall down, get up*, fall down, get up." The Tin Man also perseveres, continuously holding up his axe. The Lion also exhibits a *fighting spirit*, but in a more literal sense. He threatens to fight the rest of the group to demonstrate the courage he is missing. Unfortunately, this coping strategy is life-limiting for the Lion, whose verbal barbs drive people away when he really desires their support.

As a group, Dorothy and her companions use many life-affirming coping strategies. First, they *bear witness to illness narratives*. Dorothy affirms the Scarecrow's symptoms and suffering, she invites the Tin Man to share his story, and she addresses stigma by assuring the Cowardly Lion they won't be ashamed to be seen with him. The group bonds around a common goal that gives their lives purpose: find the Wizard of Oz who will cure them all. They *reinforce their shared purpose* each time they sing their missional song "We're off to see the Wizard!"

---

8   Learn more about my spiritual direction and shamanic healing practice at www.TalksWithSpirit.com.

Group members also provide *practical help and advocate for each other.* Dorothy oils/medicates the Tin Man when he rusts/ stiffens up. The Tin Man and Lion strengthen the Scarecrow (restuff him with hay) when disease flares up (monkeys attack) and knocks him off his feet. The companions support Dorothy in the poppy field when she is felled by illness-related fatigue/ medication side effects (results of the Witch's toxic curse). When the Lion is too afraid to approach the Wizard, the group says they'll represent his interests. Later, the Lion overcomes his cowardice to rescue Dorothy from the Witch's castle. In addition to receiving the support they need, these scenes remind us that even when people are ill, patients also want to offer support to loved ones.

The group also *acknowledges the reality of illness.* The Scarecrow recognizes that they face a haunted forest of emotional and physical upheaval before their illnesses improve. The Tin Man uses a narrative coping strategy to *externalize* the unpredictable attacks of illness as "lions and tigers and bears." Externalizing helps people remember that they are not their problems and prevents overidentification with illness (White and Epston 1990). Perhaps most importantly, these friends *keep hope alive* for each other. As they approach the Emerald City, they sing about a future in which they will exchange dark *illness-in-the-foreground* (IITF) experiences for the brighter world of *wellness-in-the-foreground* (WITF). When turned away at the gates of the Emerald City, the Scarecrow and Dorothy are despondent about the failed mission. The Tin Man reassures them their goals are still possible. When Dorothy is overcome by illness and locked away in the Witch's castle, the companions literally keep hope alive on Dorothy's behalf as they save Toto/hope from the Witch and return the dog unharmed to Dorothy.

The group initially uses the *self-directing coping style* these individuals used before coming together. Eventually, they shift to a *collaborative coping style* when they call on Glinda/SOS for support. This occurs when they panic in the poppy field about

Dorothy's and the Lion's life-threatening reaction to the Witch's curse/toxic medication. The Tin Man cries out for spiritual help (i.e., *prays*). Even the seemingly atheist Scarecrow (who tells the Tin Man that no one will hear his pleas) joins in the petitionary prayer for his friends' recovery. In response, Glinda appears as a luminous spirit that fills the sky. She waves her magic wand and provides a healing miracle: snow that awakens Dorothy and the Lion. This event reveals the double-headed coin of spiritual coping: what works for one person may not work for someone else. Dorothy and the Lion quickly recover, but the snow rusts the Tin Man, who requires a biomedical treatment/oil to carry on. Eventually, Dorothy's three companions find healing when the Wizard helps them *reframe* the way they understand their illnesses. We'll look at their meaning-making process in Chapter 6.

We learn much more about Dorothy's coping in this narrative because she is the primary patient. During illness onset, Dorothy's aunt and uncle reject reports of threats from Miss Gulch/illness symptoms. Dorothy tries to *avoid* the reality of the oncoming illness, singing about her desire to live "somewhere over the rainbow." Later, when Toto/hope is directly threatened by Miss Gulch/illness symptoms, Dorothy literally avoids her stressors by running away from home.

Dorothy also *consults an alternative healer*, Professor Marvel. He represents faith healers, psychologists/counselors, and other non-biomedical providers. When the Professor suggests that Dorothy's aunt may be suffering because of her disappearance, Dorothy realizes her avoidance coping strategy is life-limiting. She decides to return home, putting family before her own need for healing. Later, when she is held captive in the Witch's castle, Dorothy copes by using a crystal ball to consult with the spirit world (*shamanic practice*).

In Oz, Glinda warns Dorothy that getting stuck in an IITF experience will not support healing, and she encourages Dorothy to leave Oz/IITF as soon as she can. Glinda also affirms the importance of maintaining a *will to live* by warning Dorothy to always hold on to the ruby slippers/life force energy. When the Witch later convinces Dorothy to relinquish the ruby slippers in exchange for Toto/hope, the slippers won't come off. The Witch and Dorothy realize that Dorothy can hold on to her will to live despite threatening illness experiences.

Dorothy affirms the importance of *spiritual community*. She yearns to return home to family, which is **sacred** to her. She shares her longings at the gates of the Emerald City (crying for Aunt Em) and when she calls out for her beloved aunt while trapped in the Witch's castle. Dorothy also *reflects on her life* and regrets past actions that have placed distance between her and family. Dorothy also remains loyal to and expresses *gratitude* for her companions—her new family—on this healing journey.

Dorothy stumbles on an effective new spiritual practice when she impulsively douses the Witch with water and watches the Witch/illness disappear. Water is symbolic of the psyche (i.e., *deep inner work/healing*), baptism, and being spiritually reborn. The Witch even expresses surprise that Dorothy had the inner strength/depth to melt away the source of pain. When the Witch dies, Dorothy acquires her broom, giving her the psychological "lift" needed to re-engage with biomedical healing/the Wizard in a new, empowered way.

After presenting the Witch's broom to the Wizard, Dorothy witnesses her companions benefit from *meaning making* with the Wizard, who *reframes* their illnesses. However, Dorothy doesn't believe this coping strategy can help her. The Wizard offers her an opportunity to participate in a risky *experimental treatment*: return to Kansas by hot-air balloon. The balloon may suggest that many experimental treatments are nothing more than "hot air," but they offer hope to desperate patients. The Wizard appeals to Dorothy's flagging *hope for healing* when he tells the gathered crowd (in Latin) that *through hardship great heights are reached*.

Unfortunately, Dorothy does lose hope (Toto jumps out of the balloon). Dorothy chases after her dog, and the balloon leaves without her. She finally realizes that she has an incurable health condition. In her despair, Dorothy again *calls on a higher power*. Glinda appears, and Dorothy engages in a spiritual coping strategy that finally shifts her from an illness-in-the-foreground to a wellness-in-the-foreground perspective. *Co-creating a new understanding of her illness experience* with Glinda empowers Dorothy to heal herself. The Scarecrow asks why Glinda kept this information from Dorothy, and the Good Witch affirms that active and reflective meaning making is a spiritual coping strategy best used in later stages of the chronic illness experience, after patients learn for themselves the limits of their embedded meanings. Dorothy then engages a spiritual coping practice that aligns with her new worldview: the *meditative practice* of mantra repetition. Her mantra "There's no place like home" shifts her consciousness (in the film, we see Dorothy spinning) and suggests that a *mystic experience* transports Dorothy back to Kansas/wellness-in-the-foreground.

Dorothy and her companions clearly illustrate diversity in their use of spiritual coping strategies, and they affirm that people may need different coping strategies at different times in the illness journey. In the next chapter, we'll look at components of a healing relationship in Dorothy's interactions with Professor Marvel and the Wizard of Oz.

5

The Wizard of Oz

HEALERS AND HOPE

Dorothy and her friends embark on a pilgrimage to the Emerald City, the mecca of health care in the Land of Oz. They travel with the shared hope that the highly recommended Wizard of Oz will cure their suffering. Alas, when they arrive, they discover that the Wizard is human and fallible. Although his true nature is revealed, the Wizard is able to help Dorothy's companions. Why does the revelation of the man behind the curtain enhance the Wizard's ability to facilitate healing with these patients? How does the Wizard's relationship with the group compare with the relationship that his doppelganger, Professor Marvel, establishes with Dorothy in Kansas? In this chapter we explore characteristics of healing relationships and offer guidance on how you can be a healing presence for people living with chronic illness.

Healing relationships

In Chapter 1, I defined **healing** as a dynamic, ongoing process of seeking, restoring, and experiencing well-being through the integration of a person's physical, psychological, spiritual, and social dimensions. People *can* heal on their own, but research shows us that healing is facilitated—even enhanced—within relationships (Capps 2008; Horvath 2001; Kirmayer 2004; Levin 2011; Lomax *et al.* 2011; Luckenbaugh 2019; Mehl-Madrona 1999; Penman *et al.* 2013; Rosa 2016; Scott *et al.* 2017). Studies also tell us that the stronger the relationship between the patient and the healer, the greater the expectation of healing from this alliance (Alling 2015; Finniss *et al.* 2010; McDonough-Means, Kreitzer, and Bell 2004). What, then, are characteristics of the most effective healing relationships? This patient describes her vision of the ideal healer:

> I look to my healers to guide me, to bring comfort, to bring knowledge, to bring compassion. To be there beside me, to listen to my story. Healers, peel away the layer covering your eyes so that you may see the obvious and the not so obvious. Healers, peel away the layer covering your ears so that you might listen more carefully and attentively, even during the silences that are between us. Healers, peel away the layer covering your hearts so that you might be more compassionate in your actions and sensitive to the unspoken word. Healers, peel away the layer covering your lips so that you might be better able to utter words of encouragement and optimism even when I falter. (Luckenbaugh 2019)

This patient's plea affirms what literature on healing reveals: the most effective healing relationships include safety/trust, presence, compassion, and hope.

Safety/trust

Safety and trust are paramount in healing relationships (Adams 2018b). In a relational context, **safety** is the feeling that we can be authentic and vulnerable without fear of judgment or punishment on any level (physical, emotional, intellectual, spiritual). **Trust** describes the belief that when we share authentically of ourselves, the other person will respond with our best interests at heart. When people feel safe in a relationship, they're more likely to trust the other person to respect their sacred values, beliefs, meanings, and practices.

Research confirms that patients quickly assess a healthcare provider's comfort level with spirituality and the likelihood that this person will be compassionate or trustworthy (e.g., Ellis and Campbell 2004; Holmberg, Jensen, and Ulland 2017; Paddock 2011). As I've described in previous chapters, I created a healthcare *team* for body–mind–spirit care because, with few exceptions, I didn't trust healthcare providers with my **spiritual orienting system** (SOS). As a spiritual caregiver, you can fill in the spiritual care gap for people who also distrust biomedical providers with their SOSs (Determeyer and Kutac 2018; McCaffrey, Pugh, and O'Connor 2007; Masters 2018a; Wolinsky 2018).

Of course, people will also assess you for trustworthiness. People may be willing to talk about their spirituality with you, but they may be hesitant to share other aspects of their illness experience. For example, patients are unlikely to share private health information when they feel shame or guilt about their health/illness (e.g., if they have a **moral model** understanding that their illness is punishment for something they've done) (Phend 2012). An ongoing practice of **SNAP: Self-awareness** will help you live out your core values, beliefs, meanings, and practices without judging or imposing them on other people. Doing this inner work will help ensure that other people find you to be a trustworthy care provider (e.g., Kørup *et al.* 2018; Levin 2011; O'Grady and Richards 2010).

Spiritual caregivers also engender trust by being appropriately vulnerable about their spirituality. The risk is that we share too much, or shift focus from the other person's well-being to meet our own needs, like decreasing our own distress (Halifax 2011; Penman *et al.* 2013). Recall that **SNAP: Self-awareness** is always part of the caregiving encounter as we monitor our responses to the other person and maintain **life-affirming** power dynamics (Adams 2018b; Doehring 2015, first published 2006; Halifax 2011). Spiritual caregivers also reinforce trustworthiness when we demonstrate genuine curiosity and show respect for the other person's story and spiritual orienting system (**SNAP: A**sk questions and Let the other **P**erson guide the conversation).

Integration: Safety/trust

You can foster safety in spiritual care relationships physically, psychologically, intellectually, and spiritually by engaging in the following practices (Arora and McCulliss 2015):

- Notice if the physical location for this conversation is private, quiet, and free of distractions. If not, can you change location or alter the environment temporarily to enhance the sense of safety for the other person? Some public places offer a false sense of privacy because we assume anonymity (e.g., a coffee shop). However, the world is small, and people who know people may hear something you or your care receiver don't want them to hear. I've often used code names with conversation partners to disguise other people, places, or situations that we wanted to keep private.

- Position yourself physically to reinforce equality and collaboration. You should be able to easily look each other in the eye. Standing over or looking down on someone puts you in an awkward position of physical power over that person. This is especially important for patients who are in bed. You should also be close enough to hear each other clearly and avoid the frustration of repeating what is said.

- Reduce noise distractions where possible from televisions, computers, and phones. Demonstrate your genuine interest in the other person by silencing your cellphone.

- Notice signs of physical pain or psychological distress that suggest the other person needs assistance from family or another helping professional. Acknowledge the discomfort and determine if support is required immediately (i.e., the situation is an emergency). If the patient is too distracted by their distress to have the conversation, reassure them you can continue at another time.

- Assure the other person that your conversation is confidential, unless you learn something that requires you to respond as a mandatory reporter.[1] Even though you are providing care to someone living with a chronic illness, you need to respect the privacy of that person's health information. In the United States, the Health Information Portability and Accountability Act (HIPAA) protects health information. The person living with the chronic health condition should be the one to disclose any private health information. As a caregiver, you can ask general health-related questions (e.g., *How are you feeling today?*), and follow the other person's lead regarding the level of health information they wish to disclose.

- Determine how you can manage time in an unobtrusive way. For example, when I'm sitting in conversation, I place my (silenced) phone on my lap. I can easily *glance* down at the always-on time display in a natural way as I listen to the other person. If you don't have time for an in-depth conversation, it's helpful to set expectations at the beginning: *Hi Bill, I only have until 1 o'clock, but I really wanted to know how you're doing today. Is this a good time to talk or should we schedule a longer visit tomorrow?* When we stop people in the middle of sharing vulnerable information, it can raise questions about our genuine interest, and they may hesitate to share with us in the future.

---

1 Be aware of mandated reporting requirements in your location (e.g., suspected child abuse or elder abuse).

- Manage emotional power dynamics appropriately, so your own psycho-spiritual needs don't take precedence over the other person's needs. Develop self-care practices to maintain your health and well-being before, during, and after spiritual care conversations. Enter spiritual care conversations fully present to the other person (**SNAP**: Stay in the Now).

Presence

There is more to presence than being in the same space with another person. Spiritual caregivers can offer a **healing presence** when they move beyond "being with" the person physically and emotionally to forge spiritual connections, which may lead to "sacred moments" (McDonough-Means *et al.* 2004; Pargament *et al.* 2014). Care providers describe sacred moments as:

(a) feeling part of something bigger than themselves or [the care receiver]; (b) feeling that grace is present; (c) feeling that God is present; (d) feeling the presence of healing energies or spiritual beings; (e) feeling that something special and sacred has happened between the [caregiver], [care receiver], and God; and (f) feeling inspired to go beyond their natural abilities. (O'Grady and Richards 2010, p.64)

Being a healing presence is a dynamic practice we must cultivate in every spiritual care encounter. Our brains are wired to focus *either* on analytic tasks *or* empathic connection (Jack *et al.* 2013). So, when we're focused on tasks—even tasks associated with the caregiving relationship—we can't give our full psycho-spiritual attention to the other person. On the other hand, when we focus on the present moment, we might experience what this social worker describes: "I find that if I am settled and balanced spiritually, and if my connection with God is strong, my work is effortless and I am truly 'with' the person who has come to me for assistance" (O'Grady and Richards 2010, p.61). It takes ongoing practice to learn how to focus our attention with genuine interest on the other person as we remain aware of our own responses to this experience and the relational dynamics that we are accountable to manage (**SNAP: Self-awareness**). Like a muscle that becomes stronger with use, sustained, focused attention becomes easier with practice.

Practices of intention and attention also help us avoid "awkward silences" that often reflect our own discomfort or our current lack of focus. We can move beyond silences offered as invitations for the other person to respond. Sacred moments of spontaneous, deep connection are most likely in "compassionate silences" that arise when we are fully present to the care receiver *with* an attitude of compassion (Back *et al.* 2009, pp.1114–1115; see also O'Grady and Richards 2010). This patient describes the afterglow of a sacred moment:

> I have just returned from therapy and am struck by my change in mood as a result. Before I went, I was feeling very low and very aware of this great heavy burden that I have been dragging around with me over the last three weeks... [I]t seemed that once experience is shared and made meaningful, it becomes enlivened and energizing rather than draining. (Willig 2009, pp.186–187)

Integration: Presence

- Set your intention at the beginning of each caregiving encounter to embody the characteristics of a healing relationship: safety/trust, presence, compassion, and hope (Back *et al.* 2009; Burden *et al.* 2005; Levin 2011).

- Shift your focus from tasks to being fully present with the other person (**SNAP: Stay in the Now**). When I prepare for a spiritual care conversation, I breathe deeply and exhale my attachment to anything I bring with me to that conversation that will not serve this person. I explicitly invite Spirit (my name for the sacred) to guide the conversation and communicate through me. Another care provider describes a similar intention that guides his healing work:

> "Let me do what I'm called to do with impeccability." The outcome is between them and their Higher Power. Aligning with God first. Myself second. I'm responsible for technical knowledge/skill. I'm responsible to be a compassionate human being (but compassion for myself and my life as well—no false martyrdom or trying to earn "brownie points"). An attitude of reverence toward creation and higher power allows more of a relationship. (O'Grady and Richards 2010, p.63)

- Be aware of your body language. When I'm in a spiritual care conversation, I call on a yoga practice to lead with my heart. Is my heart open, or have I crossed my arms to protect it? Do I lean in to this person's story, physically and/or emotionally? These subtle adjustments will become automatic with practice. Take care not to overuse nodding or affirming comments like "I see" to indicate you're paying attention. These well-meaning habits can be distracting to the other person. Early in my practice as a spiritual director, I wanted the other person to know I was enthusiastically listening to what he said. Thankfully, he paused to comment on how much I nodded, helping me realize that I was actually focused on my own response instead of what he was saying.

- During spiritual care conversations, pause occasionally for a deep breath. A pause allows you both time to absorb what has been said. A pause can help you notice the person's word choice, tone of voice, emotional state, or body language. It is often in these "compassionate silences" that we experience sacred moments (Back *et al.* 2009; McDonough-Means *et al.* 2004; Patsiopoulos and Buchanan 2011).

- Cultivate your ability to focus on another person through mindful practices (Halifax 2011). In Chapter 4, I described types of meditation and mindfulness exercises. An internet search will reveal many other options. It's important to discover a practice that suits you, so that you'll maintain your practice and benefit from it. There are also many cellphone apps available that prompt you to perform mindfulness practice, time your practice, and/or guide you in a practice.

- Let the other **Person** guide the conversation (**SNAP**) as you maintain a stance of not-knowing and ask questions with genuine curiosity. When we show respect for people as the experts on their pain, their experiences, and their spiritual orienting systems, we reinforce both trust and presence (Calhoun and Tedeschi 2001). As we explore without judgment, we also demonstrate compassion, our next topic.

Compassion

Descriptions of healing relationships stress the importance of genuine compassion for the other person (Egnew 2018; Levin 2011; Penman *et al.* 2013; Scott *et al.* 2017; Sinclair *et al.* 2017; Spandler and Stickley 2011). **Compassion** is feeling with someone who is suffering without being overwhelmed by their suffering, so that we act to help alleviate the source of suffering (McDonough-Means *et al.* 2004; Wigglesworth 2013). Compassion for others may be a driving force behind your desire to serve others as a spiritual caregiver, and this aspect of your personhood may be highly developed. What is often neglected, however, is self-compassion, a practice that caregivers must embrace to be at our best (Barnard and Curry 2011; Doehring 2015; Patsiopoulos and Buchanan 2011).

Self-compassion includes three key components: (1) common humanity: we're all fallible humans; (2) self-kindness: we can acknowledge our personal fallibility without judgment; and (3) mindfulness: we don't need to attach to "negative thoughts and feelings" about ourselves (Germer and Neff 2013; see also Patsiopoulos and Buchanan 2011). Halifax (2011) illuminates the third component of non-attachment:

> In Buddhism, there are so-called near and far enemies of compassion. The far enemy is cruelty. This enemy is easy to detect. But the near enemies of compassion are often difficult to recognize. They include fear, grief, pity, anxiety, and righteous anger, all expressions of personal distress. The so-called "near enemies" can drain or destroy us. (p.151)

Integration: Compassion

- Practice regular self-care so you aren't overwhelmed by other people's emotions, experiences, or needs. This will free you to move naturally from empathy to compassionate care (Patsiopoulos and Buchanan 2011). Practice **SNAP**: Self-awareness and reflect on when you experience "peacefulness, beauty, calm, and love." Intentionally connect with these life-affirming spiritual experiences on a daily basis (Doehring 2015, pp.642, 644).

- Reflect on how you feel emotions such as anger, sorrow, overwhelm, and shame in your body (e.g., do you feel muscle tension, pain, light-headedness, or nausea?). Identify these physical sensations when they arise and acknowledge the emotions underlying them without judgment. You might find it helpful to use a "soften–allow–soothe" practice:

- Soften or relax the part of your body where you become aware of this emotion.

- Allow or acknowledge what you're feeling, physically and emotionally.

- Soothe yourself "with loving-kindness" (Germer and Neff 2013, p.864).

• Offer yourself the compassionate wisdom you would give to other people experiencing stress. Examples of my compassionate self-talk include:

- *Life is a series of problems to be solved, and I can solve this problem as I've solved others.*

- *My goal is progress, not perfection.*

- *Fall down, get up.*

• Practice meditation to enhance self-compassion (Halifax 2011). Some meditations are specifically designed for compassion, such as "loving-kindness meditation" (e.g., Schairer 2018). You can find videos and other information on the internet.

• Practice "not-knowing" (**SNAP**: Let the other **P**erson guide the conversation) as a compassionate reminder that you don't need to know everything. Respect other people as the experts on their illness experiences and spiritual orienting systems and relieve yourself of the pressure to have all the answers (Arora 2011).

Hope

Healing relationships also inspire and help sustain a person's sense of hope (Coulehan 2011; Egnew 2018; Kristiansen *et al.* 2014; Loffer 2000; Scott *et al.* 2017; Stone and Lester 2001; Underwood 2006). It's important for people to have an expansive or "deep" hope for the future (e.g., *I hope to live peacefully with my illness*, or *I hope researchers find a cure in my lifetime*) (Coulehan 2011). It's also important that people have a set of dynamic, specific, realistic, and near-term hopes (e.g., *I hope to have the energy to attend my grandson's recital next week*, or *I hope to complete a walk next month to support research for a cure*). These diverse and attainable hopes help prevent all-or-nothing thinking about the future. They also contribute to the patient's/family's well-being without reinforcing "false hope" in unrealistic outcomes (Coulehan 2011; Fischer, Cripe, and Rand 2018; Gijsberts *et al.* 2019a; Sharif *et al.* 2018).

This physician diagnosed with non-Hodgkin lymphoma describes how she determines if a hope is life-affirming or **life-limiting** for her. Her reflective process illustrates the importance of helping people with chronic illness consider the helpfulness of their hopes:

> I could ask whether [a hope] was helping me think and act in healthy ways. "Is this hope helping me take proper action or, if there's no more I can do, is it helping me wait?" Whenever the answer was "no," I let go of that hope and invested in other, more healing hopes. For example, patients undergoing evaluation naturally hope for good news. Unfortunately, that hope only exacerbated my anxiety. If the results were what I'd feared, I felt somewhat responsible, as if I hadn't hoped right. I found a more healing hope. Now while undergoing an evaluation, I repeatedly tell everyone, "I'm hoping for accurate news." That hope motivates me to hold still in the scanner to help get clear pictures. It helps me wait for results because I want my doctors to take their time scrutinizing the findings. It lessens the shock of upsetting news. It prevents despair by framing upsetting results as "useful" news. And it quiets a voice that might try to blame me. (Harpham 2018)

Healing relationships also nurture the hope that the caregiving relationship will lead to healing. We do this by subtly encouraging the **placebo effect**: the person's belief that this relationship—a harmless, nonmedical "treatment"—can enhance their quality of life and well-being (Coulehan 2011; Grassie 2011; Krippner 2012; Levin 2011; McDonough-Means *et al.* 2004). **Placebo** is Latin for "I shall please," an apt description of a patient's desire to please a caregiver by responding positively to the treatment offered. Biomedical providers have long used placebos—inactive medications or procedures—with patients who don't have clearly diagnosable physical ailments.

A placebo can be a symbol that stimulates self-healing (e.g., the sight of a healthcare provider's white coat), or a tangible means of comfort until healing happens naturally (e.g., a soothing balm) (Glynn 2013; Harrington 2008; Masters 2018b; Miller and Colloca 2009). This patient describes the symbolic and tangible aspects of the placebo effect that catalyzed her healing process:

> I was prone to coughs; I loved watching my primary care physician write prescriptions, knowing that in forty-eight hours I'd feel better. *Always*. It offered a kind of ritual satisfaction. As he recited the instructions with which I was so familiar, I'd take the first easy breath. In an important sense, it seemed to me, the cough actually ended when he handed me the prescription, as if the prescription were a telegram announcing that the enemy was retreating; the fighting might drag on for a few days, but the war was effectively over. (Thernstrom 2010, p.40; emphasis in original)

The placebo effect essentially names the "power of belief"—faith—in the healing process (Alling 2015, p.274; Grassie 2011; Levin 2009). In the narrative-based approach to spiritual care I describe in this book, conversation is the primary intervention used to promote healing. Hope-filled and compassionate conversations are so powerful (e.g., Fuentes *et al.* 2014) that one well-known physician identified conversation as a placebo in the *New York Times* (Ofri 2017). As powerful as narrative can be, people may also find non-verbal means of expression helpful to address suffering or other difficult-to-articulate aspects of their illness experiences (Fischer 1988; Graham *et al.* 2005; Plach *et al.* 2004a).

Rituals facilitate meaning making through **poesis**, storytelling that relies on metaphor, symbols, and symbolic action.

Rituals are transformative, embodied practices that create a shift from ordinary time and space to sacred time and space (Kinsley 1996; Smith 1980). In the case of people living with chronic illness, rituals can help people realize their hopes for healing through integration of belief and action (Bell 1987). There are many existing *religious* healing rituals that may be helpful for people who live with incurable health conditions (e.g., laying on hands, anointing with oil, prayer circles). You can help people connect to/participate in these rituals. You can also help people create meaningful rituals that speak to their illness experience and hopes for healing. Ritual making and enactment can also provide a measure of control when life with chronic illness feels uncertain or overwhelming (Smith 1980).

Integration: Hope

- Encourage people to engage in life-affirming spiritual practices that foster hope, particularly connection to the sacred, connection to other people, and affirming their sense of meaning or purpose in life (Coulehan 2011; Gijsberts *et al.* 2019a; Kudla *et al.* 2015; Yodchai *et al.* 2017).

- Invite people to imagine their future: *What would a good month look like? What does healthy look/feel like for you in the year ahead?* Encourage them to create a detailed description that brings these hopes to life. Support their deep hopes as you invite them to identify realistic, attainable hopes: *I also want you to be pain-free. While your healthcare team is working on that, how can I help you experience greater peace today/this week?* (Gijsberts *et al.* 2019a; Harpham 2018; Stone and Lester 2001).

- Notice when patients or family members over-emphasize the need to maintain a positive outlook under the guise of maintaining hope. The emphasis on positivity can put unnecessary pressure on people to live with illness in a particular way, and it can disenfranchise the diversity of emotions related to life with a chronic health condition (Kristiansen *et al.* 2014).

- Invite people to participate in meaningful rituals, either drawn from religious traditions or created together. Often the simplest rituals are the most effective (Hogue 1999; Mitchell and Anderson 1983). Ritual creation should consider:

  - who will participate or observe (rituals may be private or include other people as witnesses)

  - when the ritual will take place (in-the-moment or at a later time) and specific start/stop points

  - where the ritual will take place and how the space will be prepared

  - how participants will carry out the ritual (e.g., share stories; lament; use/create symbols or symbolic acts; respond to each other; read poetry or prose; sing, chant, or engage in silence; perform specific actions)

  - what meaningful objects, readings, dress, or other elements will enhance the experience

  - how participants will reflect on and integrate the ritual afterwards (e.g., silent reflection, guided integration).

  (Berry 2009; Hammerschlag and Silverman 1997; Hogue 2003; Kollar 1989; Reeves 2007)

- Consider using simple opening and/or closing rituals for your spiritual care conversations. These rituals may help people with chronic illness shift into a safe and sacred space for reflection on their illness experience (opening ritual), and then shift from a focus on illness to a hoped-for focus on wellness-in-the-foreground experiences (closing ritual).

Professor Marvel and the Wizard of Oz

When Dorothy runs away from home, she encounters her first healer: Professor Marvel. He represents complementary and alternative healers, including spiritual caregivers. The Professor has mixed results in developing a healing relationship with Dorothy. He tries to gain her trust by claiming he knows all. He uses a crystal ball, a ritual object symbolic of mystical spiritual knowledge and healing prowess, to invoke the placebo effect. Although he attempts to be a healing presence for Dorothy and her emerging narrative, he violates her privacy by rifling through her things to learn more about her. The Professor also makes broad assumptions about Dorothy's illness experience based on contextual clues (a photo of Aunt Em). He expresses compassion in gestures (lightly touching Dorothy's shoulder) and demeanor, and he expresses their shared hope that Dorothy will return to a wellness-in-the-foreground experience with her family. Their encounter is cut short by Dorothy and never fully develops its potential as a healing relationship.

Once her illness is fully manifest in the Land of Oz, Dorothy seeks a consultation with a highly regarded biomedical specialist, the Wizard of Oz. The Wizard's reputation is magnified by the challenges Dorothy and her companions face as they try to secure an appointment with him. They encounter confusing instructions when they attempt to enter the Emerald City, must provide proof that they need the Wizard's specialized expertise, cope with the disappointment of a cancelled appointment, and undergo elaborate purification rituals before they are finally allowed into the examination room.

As they approach the Wizard, the group is nearly overcome by fear and awe. Patients may experience these feelings as "white coat syndrome," raised blood pressure at the sight of a biomedical provider's ritual garment (Pope 2007). A long dark passageway and flames shooting up around the holographic image of a bellowing Wizard create an atmosphere of fear instead of safety. Members of the group tremble, kneel, faint, and respond submissively when the Wizard addresses them.

The Wizard further ignores these unbalanced power dynamics and the need to build trust as he asserts his omnipotence and omniscience, disregarding Dorothy and her friends as experts on their illness narratives. He yells at these patients and repeatedly interrupts them. Unfortunately, the latter is common behavior. On average, physicians interrupt patients within 11 seconds of beginning to describe their concerns (Ospina *et al.* 2018). The Wizard also lacks compassion, dehumanizing his patients as he refers to them by their diagnoses and shaming them as unworthy of his curative expertise. Finally, the Wizard makes a seemingly insurmountable bar for healing. They must return to him with the Witch's broom, in essence telling them they must heal themselves. The Lion is devastated by this encounter and responds to his hopelessness by jumping through a window. This healer clearly did *not* try to establish a healing relationship in this initial encounter.

Later, the group returns with the Witch's broom in hand. The Wizard is surprised, but he admires their alternate healing methods. When the group challenges him on yet another delay, the Wizard again exerts his power as biomedical expert and dismisses them. Dorothy's hope for healing is strong enough to stand up to the Wizard's bravado: Toto/hope pulls back the curtain to expose the human behind the façade of the Great and Powerful Oz. Like the Wizard, all healers can experience "imposter syndrome" and wear a symbolic "mask" to hide insecurities and help control emotional attachments and responses to care receivers. Spiritual caregivers must seek balance between being authentically vulnerable to create a trust relationship and monitoring the power dynamics in that relationship. In his vulnerable state, the Wizard is finally authentic and fully present with his patients. The group is angry at this revelation, but the Wizard builds trust by humbling himself, making a healing relationship possible.

The Wizard uses placebos for immediate healing results with the Scarecrow (a diploma), the Lion (a medal), and the Tin Man (a testimonial). In Chapter 6, we'll unpack the spiritual healing practice the Wizard also offers alongside these symbolic means of healing. Dorothy, however, recognizes that the placebo effect won't work for her. The Wizard suggests another option for Dorothy: an experimental balloon ride to Kansas under his direct care. His healing work with her companions, and further revelations about his personal journey have finally established a healing relationship with Dorothy.

Healers and hope in Kelly's world

I've worked with many healers on my chronic illness journey. During the pre-diagnosis period, my primary care physician was often equally frustrated that we couldn't pinpoint what was happening with me. My mysterious ailment was complicated because I lack common antibodies that point to rheumatoid arthritis (RA) in blood tests (i.e., I am seronegative). My **web of life** breathed a huge sigh of relief when a blood test finally indicated the culprit was RA. Over the course of my illness, I have had relationships with a number of primary care providers, rheumatologists, and nurses. I would characterize most of our interactions as typical biomedical encounters. Providers usually expressed concern for my symptoms while efficiently checking disease progress by visual cues and clinical markers.

For nearly 20 years, my primary RA medication has been delivered by intravenous infusions that take one to three hours every four weeks. Nurses have administered these infusions at each stop on my Yellow Brick Road (Kansas, Oklahoma, Tennessee, and Colorado). As a group, they have been wonderful caregivers, and I think fondly of the healing relationships they nurtured with me during disease flare-ups and other times of stress.

Recently, I made a difficult decision to change rheumatologists. I had a functional relationship with my long-term provider, but it was clear that this provider did not share, or even respect, my core value of whole-person care. When the medical assistant working for this provider treated me without compassion and delayed my treatment, the resulting disease flare-up prompted me to make a change. I chose another physician in the practice whose caring relationships I'd observed for years. I know that the power of established insurance coverage and convenience of staying with a long-term provider make it challenging for many people to consider such a change. Because I was able to stay within the practice, I circumvented those issues. I wish I'd made the change sooner. A true healing relationship with someone who respects my value of care for body–mind–spirit is a source of comfort on my Yellow Brick Road.

I have also been blessed with both professional and informal spiritual caregivers who have supported my healing for over two decades. For many years I had a healing relationship with a spiritual director. She always nurtured a safe, compassionate presence to reflect on my illness experience, co-create meaning, engage life-affirming spiritual coping practices, and re-envision hopes. Today I experience this support in a healing relationship with a shaman, my companion for the next phase of this deeply spiritual illness journey. I would be remiss if I didn't offer gratitude to my husband, daughter, and son, whose healing relationships sustain my healing and well-being.

In the next chapter, we turn to **meaning making** that typically happens in later stages of the chronic illness journey. We'll also look at how people create a new life for themselves, a life that hopefully integrates chronic illness in life-affirming ways.

6

Glinda and the Return to Kansas

MEANING MAKING
AND THE NEW NORMAL

The Wizard demands proof that Dorothy and her companions are worthy of his healing powers. The group responds to his challenge by vanquishing the Wicked Witch of the West and presenting her broom to the Wizard, a symbol of their capacity to transcend illness. The Wizard artfully uses the **placebo effect** to heal the Tin Man, Scarecrow, and Lion. However, Dorothy is skeptical of this approach. Instead, she agrees to an experimental treatment that ultimately fails (hot-air balloon ride to Kansas). Out of other options, Dorothy finally looks to her **spiritual orienting system** (SOS) for healing. With Glinda's insight into the power of the ruby slippers, Dorothy returns home to Kansas, the land of **wellness-in-the-foreground**. Back on the farm, Dorothy engages in **meaning making** with loved ones in her **web of life**. Their conversation illustrates how meanings are socially constructed. Dorothy and her family will eventually co-create a new understanding of normal life that integrates what Dorothy has learned about the two worlds she now inhabits: **illness-in-the-foreground** (IITF) and **wellness-in-the-foreground** (WITF).

As I've noted in previous chapters, each phase of the chronic illness journey is associated with a set of common tasks for patients and families to address (Doka 2014, first published 2009;

Whittemore and Dixon 2008). In the terminal phase of long-term illness, patients and families turn their attention to dying and what happens after death. Because this book focuses on *living* with chronic illness, I won't address aspects of spiritual care that are specific to the end of life. Rather, our focus in this chapter is on people like me and Dorothy, people who have moved beyond the crisis of diagnosis, through one or more chronic phases of IITF, to a period of relative relief when wellness is in the foreground. We now look at **meaning making** that often occurs later in the illness journey, consider psycho-spiritual growth as a result of chronic illness, and reflect on what it means to transition to a **new normal** that integrates illness experiences into broader life narratives. I offer guidance on how spiritual caregivers can support and collaborate in these processes to help patients and families experience well-being (Ambrosio *et al.* 2015; Sorajjakool *et al.* 2006; Ziebarth 2016).

Meaning making later in the illness experience

Recall that living with chronic illness is characterized by "shifting perspectives" between WITF and IITF (Paterson 2001). Wellness-in-the-foreground does not mean that illness disappears. More often, "the illness requires attention in order not to have to pay attention to it" (Paterson 2001, p.24). When pain and other symptoms are under control, people can shift to a WITF mindset in which they are more likely to engage in deeper spiritual reflection and meaning making, both personally and within the family system (Doka 2014, first published 2009; Heilferty 2018; Kralik 2002; Paterson 2001; Sorajjakool *et al.* 2006; Whittemore and Dixon 2008). This patient describes his awareness of a shift to WITF:

> [Chronic illness] had become woven into daily conversations as a mundane part of everyday life and I was comfortable with its presence and no longer troubled by fears and thoughts of

unfairness. What's more, with it firmly embedded into my sense of finitude, I could allow it to interact productively with opportunities for transcendence. (Adams 2016, p.52)

The shifting perspectives of chronic illness trigger ongoing meaning making, particularly when stressful IITF experiences prompt further reflection on suffering (Moskowitz and Wrubel 2005; Russell *et al.* 2006; Taves *et al.* 2018; Voltzenlogel *et al.* 2016). Finding meaning in life is "an ultimate concern" of the human experience (Yalom 1980, p.8; see also Frankl 2014, originally published 1946), with the desire for meaning increasing as we near the end of life (Araten-Bergman *et al.* 2016). Although we may wish to make meaning of illness once and move on, this woman with Lyme disease discovered the more typical recurring nature of meaning making with a chronic health condition, a process she engaged in as she wrote a book about her illness experience:

> I set out to write more influenced by a desire to have a happy ending, and have it read something like: You can get well, too! I wanted to write a book that would let people know that maybe it will get better. But in the process of writing it, I didn't experience that. It was humbling in that sense. It's magical thinking that you'll write about something and then you won't have to deal with it again. You'll move past it and into a new chapter. But I don't think that's how trauma works. Trauma's a big component of illness, of being diagnosed and being treated. (Williams 2018)

Over time, people may reflectively seek or discover a broader meaning to their illness experiences (George and Park 2016; Neimeyer, Klass, and Dennis 2014; Sherman *et al.* 2010). At least one study indicates that "pragmatically oriented persons, who may not feel compelled to search for meaning even in the wake of trauma, often fare better than those who are compelled to find meaning in difficult events" (Taves *et al.* 2018, p.214). This conclusion may indicate that some people sought meaning too soon after a traumatic event (such as diagnosis), or people may have sought meaning without the benefit of compassionate spiritual practices to support them in this process (Doehring 2019). A larger body of evidence concludes that finding meaning in one's life is a critical component of well-being and quality of life, and finding meaning of a major life event like chronic illness contributes to a greater sense of the broader meaning of one's life (Guerrero-Torrelles *et al.* 2017a; Kudla *et al.* 2015).

The meaning of an illness experience is constructed through stories told and retold to self and within families, social groups, and cultural contexts (Kristiansen *et al.* 2014; Metta *et al.* 2015; Neimeyer *et al.* 2014; Sakellariou *et al.* 2013; Zeligman *et al.* 2018). Socially constructed meanings affect both the patient and other people making meaning of their experience of this illness, in both private and public settings (Southwood 2018). All aspects of a person's social identity (e.g., sexual/affective orientation, gender, health, dis/ability, age, generational influences, religion/ spirituality, race, ethnicity, national origin, education, and socio-economic background), and the way these social identifiers intersect with each other, influence meaning making at individual and communal levels (Doehring 2015, first published 2006). When understandings of an illness conflict within the patient's web of life, it can complicate meaning making for the patient, as this person describes:

> As time went on and I talked to friends and relatives about my situation, I noticed that they had their own ways of making sense of cancer and these were often quite different from, or even opposed to, mine. I realized that, as I was so immediately and existentially affected by the situation and as I was myself still in the process of trying to make sense of it, other people's constructions of meaning could unsettle my fragile narrative and throw me back into a state of anxiety and confusion. (Willig 2009, p.184)

Narrative meaning-making practices, such as telling and recreating stories about illness experiences, help people feel in control of their lives, enhance their resiliency to cope with ongoing shifts between WITF and IITF, and experience healing (Kalitzkus and Matthiessen 2009; Kristiansen *et al.* 2014; Schuhmann and Damen 2018). Storytelling also supports well-being:

> I feel better when I talk about my life and living with diabetes. I have no one to talk to about my illness so I keep it all inside. It is like a flower that can't bloom. When you came and asked me to talk about it, I feel better and good about myself. The flower bloomed inside of me. (Rosa 2016, p.215)

In meaning making, some people readily integrate illness experiences into their spiritual orienting systems, preserving their understandings of self, the world, and the sacred. For example, in a study of Buddhist nuns, "there was widespread acceptance of the impermanence of life and a belief that karma would decide the course. For most nuns, chronic illness was just one manifestation of this impermanence" (Wijesinghe and Parshall 2016, p.162). Sometimes people need to transform their spiritual orienting systems to integrate illness experiences that remain incomprehensible within the context of their existing beliefs and meanings (McIntosh 1997). Spiritual caregivers can be an important source of support for people who need to recreate their SOSs. Changing core values, beliefs, and meanings can be challenging and this process puts the person at risk for negative health consequences (e.g., spiritual distress or crisis, depression) (Cummings and Pargament 2010; Kim, Schulz, and Carver 2007).

Benefit finding and post-traumatic growth

In addition to making sense of illness experiences, meaning making *may* include **benefit finding**: identifying **life-affirming** effects or outcomes from challenging experiences (Cummings and Pargament 2010; Sherman *et al.* 2010). People are best able to reflect on potential benefits later in their chronic illness experiences, with the advantage of viewing their experiences over a longer trajectory (Pakenham 2008). Not everyone experiences a positive side to chronic illness (Gall and Bilodeau 2017; Graffigna *et al.* 2017; Kim *et al.* 2007). Some people only associate illness with its negative effects on them and their web of life (Buonaccorso *et al.* 2019; Schroevers, Kraaij, and Garnefski 2011). A one-year study with 81 women found that "some women were unable to project themselves into a different and more optimistic future... They seemed caught in the web of illness" (Kralik 2002, p.150). Other people may experience illness as a combination of distinctly positive and negative outcomes (Golub, Gamarel, and Rendina 2014).

When people are unable to make sense of their illness experience over time or they remain stuck in IITF, they are at risk for spiritual crises and other poor health outcomes (Bray 2013; Pargament *et al.* 2004; Sherman *et al.* 2010). This woman illustrates how a person might continue to wrestle with meaning: "I still want to be the 'old me' desperately, and yet I know I can't. Trying to find the new me is hard...nothing is familiar, everything I knew about myself has changed" (Kralik 2002, p.149). Spiritual caregivers should support benefit finding as it occurs organically, rather than prescriptively encouraging a positive perspective on illness (i.e., looking for "the silver lining") because this approach can disenfranchise suffering and loss (Pakenham 2008; Sherman *et al.* 2010).

Many people experience the stress of chronic illness as a catalyst for spiritual transformation or **post-traumatic growth** (Harris and Winokuer 2016).[1] Common benefits associated with chronic illness include re-evaluating core values and beliefs (when this does not lead to lasting distress), discovering or re-engaging in life-affirming spiritual practices, finding

---

1   Some researchers use **benefit finding** and **post-traumatic growth** interchangeably. I differentiate between benefit finding as a process and post-traumatic growth as an outcome.

new meaning or purpose in life, renewing one's appreciation of life and/or health, growing stronger in faith, strengthening relationships, expanding one's social circle, and helping other people (Balboni and Balboni 2018; Bourland *et al.* 2011; Fong *et al.* 2006; Gall and Kafi 2014; Hannum *et al.* 2016; Kukulka *et al.* 2019; Nabolsi and Carson 2011; Radcliffe, Lowton, and Morgan 2013; Sarenmalm *et al.* 2009; Schroevers *et al.* 2011; Tedeschi and Calhoun 2004). These patients describe their post-traumatic growth:

> At the beginning I was dead. Then I was reborn. Now I am able to enjoy my life despite the disease. (Graffigna *et al.* 2017, p.2749)

> I think cancer shaped me into who I am today. I have a very different outlook on life... I try and live every day now, and enjoy every day that's given to me because every day is a gift. (Hannum *et al.* 2016, p.489)

> It's like a re-birth. All the knowledge you had about yourself, feelings, dreams, etc. go through a rather radical shake-up. You are a new person, the illness has made you stronger in some respects. (Kralik 2002, p.151)

> I wouldn't be who I am today and [I wouldn't] like who I am today, if I had not had cancer. Look at how much I have learned, and grown and changed... [I]t was a chance to evolve spiritually. (Mount *et al.* 2007, p.379)

Studies affirm that social support is an important ingredient for post-traumatic growth (Bray 2013; Cassidy 2013; Paredes and Pereira 2018). However, social support alone does not lead to post-traumatic growth. People need social support that is safe and compassionate to make meaning, the type of healing relationships we explored in Chapter 5 (Coor and Coolican 2010; Zeligman *et al.* 2018).

New normal: Mastering liminal space

Patients and family members may describe illness as a disruption of their life stories. Specifically, they may feel illness has disrupted time, where relatively certain understandings of self, the world, and the sacred before illness (WITF) are distinct and disconnected from relatively uncertain understandings after illness onset/ diagnosis (IITF) (Calhoun and Tedeschi 2006; Freda and Martino 2015; Germeni *et al.* 2018; Hannum *et al.* 2016; Martino and Freda 2016; Rebman *et al.* 2017). One patient talks about time disruption this way: "I keep wondering if true acceptance means to stop challenging myself to do things as I used to, which was exhausting even when I was 'normal,' and avoid the frustrating comparison with Before" (Ryan 2006, p.428).

People can integrate chronic health conditions into their lives, creating a **new normal** that bridges disruptions in their narratives and sense of time (Larsson and Grassman 2012; MacDonald 2017; Matini and Ogden 2016; Saunders 2017). A new normal is both a desired state and an ongoing process of adaptation to changes brought on by illness (Årestedt, Persson, and Benzein 2014; MacDonald 2017). Creating a new normal may mean embracing a new way of life that fully integrates chronic illness (Matini and Ogden 2016) or accepting illness as a "normal recurrent disruption" to life (Saunders 2017, p.726). A new normal is life-affirming when it helps people adapt to illness without losing sight of the significant impact illness has on life (Saunders 2017). This patient, whose SOS includes Taoist values and beliefs about balancing the yin and yang of life, describes his life-affirming new normal:

> I should live happily every day by using the positive to balance the negative. Don't fly too high or too low, that is neither be too complacent nor too depressed… Darkness is always followed by dawn. Rainbow will arise after rain. The good coexists closely with the bad. Sadness is within happiness… Then I just maximized the smallest pleasure and minimized the largest

sadness to maintain the balance and accept the reality. (Zhang, Shan, and Jiang 2013, p.536)

Acceptance and **surrender** (terms often used interchangeably in research literature) have been cited as important coping strategies to enhance quality of life for people living with chronic health conditions (Anderson and Asnani 2013; Beesley *et al.* 2018; Gall and Cornblat 2002; Greer *et al.* 2017; Rosequist *et al.* 2012; Sarenmalm *et al.* 2009; van Laarhoven *et al.* 2011). Surrender is not giving *up*, but rather giving *in* or letting go of resistance to the undesirable reality of living with chronic illness (Egnew 2018; Ironside *et al.* 2003). Surrender paves the way for acceptance: integrating illness into one's life to create a new normal (Ambrosio *et al.* 2015; Unantenne *et al.* 2013). People can live with chronic illness without accepting their reality, but they will lack a sense of control and balance needed to remain resilient when future shifts between WITF and IITF occur (Ambrosio *et al.* 2015). These patients illustrate how acceptance is itself an ongoing process:

> I'm accepting it much more but I realize that when I hit a wall again and I get really disappointed all over again, I realize you weren't accepting this as much as you said you were. (Rebman *et al.* 2017, p.539)

> What I'm recommending here is that we work on making peace with life's uncertainty since it's an inevitable part of the human experience. This is a daily practice, and on those days when we fall short and simply can't greet what's before us with curiosity and wisdom, we can at least take good care of ourselves by acknowledging with compassion how hard it is to live day in and day out with the uncertainty of chronic illness. (Bernhard 2014a)

Living a new normal with chronic illness is not without challenges (Graffigna *et al.* 2017). For example, one study found that mothers of chronically ill children were better able to live the family's new normal in the more certain and structured environment of home, but felt they were unable to fully live the new normal outside the home where they faced more variables (Germeni *et al.* 2018). Perhaps other people were not able to adjust to a person's/family's new normal in the public arena. Just because the person living with chronic illness has adjusted to a new way of life doesn't mean other people will adjust with them or accept their new normal. Recognizing that every person has limits of some kind can help people "reject unrealistic ideals or illusions of perfection" that add to the potential frustration of living a new normal (Creamer 2009, p.111).

Integration: Narrative meaning making

I offer practices you can cultivate to encourage meaning making in spiritual care relationships. Notice how **SNAP** skills (Self-awareness, Stay in the Now, Ask questions, and Let the other Person guide the conversation) play an important role in developing and maintaining healing relationships where people feel comfortable making meaning.

Let go of your assumptions about when and how meaning making should occur, as well as desired outcomes of the meaning-making process (Egnew 2018). Not every person who participates in a spiritual care conversation has meaning making as a goal. If we impose our meanings or the process of meaning making on people who aren't ready, they may respond defensively. Some people find attempts to reconsider their current understandings as "highly offensive, perhaps even blasphemous" (Calhoun and Tedeschi 2001, p.167). Unless a person's spiritual orienting system is **life-limiting** in some way, spiritual caregivers should focus on helping people frame illness in ways that "make the story integrative, meaningful, and coherent" within their existing worldview (Roos and Neimeyer 2007, p.103).

Meaning making usually happens organically (Hill 2017). People may need to lament losses and suffering before they can reflect on meaning (Stanley and Hurst 2011). As we develop authentic healing relationships over time, meaning making and the potential for post-traumatic growth become more likely (Guerrero-Torrelles *et al.* 2017b; Neimeyer *et al.* 2014; Rosa 2016; Willig 2009; Zeligman *et al.* 2018).

Some people prefer to write about their illness experience, rather than talk about it with another person. Writing about one's experiences by hand (rather than typing) encourages people to slow down and process their feelings (Arora and McCulliss 2015). Putting experiences on paper (or a computer screen) offers people symbolic distance from the experiences, providing a new vantage point from which "they can recover, revise, and thereby control the meaning of what has happened to them" (Stanley and Hurst 2011, p.46; see also Arora and McCulliss 2015; Willig 2009).

As people engage in meaning making, remain aware of your emotional responses. We don't want to inadvertently try to control the meaning-making process or impose our own meanings on the other person (DeAngelis 2018; Heyen, Walton, and Jonker 2016). Healers don't direct meaning making; they *accompany* people in meaning making (Egnew 2018). Continue to validate the person as the expert authority on his or her illness experiences (Rebman *et al.* 2017). Use their language as you talk about and reflect on their story.

Invite people into meaning making with open-ended questions such as *What have you learned from this experience?* and *How has this experience changed you?* (DeAngelis 2018). As people tell and retell their stories, notice when their story becomes stable and when it changes. Does a shift in either direction indicate that the person has found life-affirming meaning, or does it signal a struggle with meaning? Does this version of the story reinforce a life-affirming or life-limiting interpretation of illness? If someone seems stuck in the meaning making, you can suggest new ways to tell the story (Arora and McCulliss 2015):

- Create a dialogue with their body or a troubling symptom of illness.

- Write a poem or create a work of art to express what is challenging to articulate in prose.

- Tell the story from another person's point of view.

- Draft different endings to the story.

- Imagine the illness "is a human being and describe what it looks like, how it behaves, and what it says" (Graffigna *et al.* 2017, p.2741).

Notice and address signs of spiritual distress or crisis, as well as other life-limiting patterns of behavior. If people are receptive to change, help them (re)discover life-affirming understandings of what is sacred to them and consider how values, beliefs, coping strategies, and spiritual practices support a new normal that integrates illness in their life.

People often find meaning in "enduring values that emanate from three main sources: engaging in creative work or deeds of kindness; appreciating love, goodness, truth or beauty; and taking a courageous stance toward life's difficulties" (DeAngelis 2018, p.41). This research affirms the importance of a well-integrated spirituality that is flexible (adaptable to cope with changing circumstances), complex (able to support meaning making about suffering), liberative (supports freedom in the person's life), and grounded in benevolent views and experiences of life and the sacred (Doehring 2015, first published 2006; Pargament 1997).

When people experience illness as a disruption in time, the illness can become *the* defining moment of their life and identity (Martino and Freda 2016). Using metaphors of illness as a journey or illness as shifting perspectives (WITF/IITF) may help people reintegrate illness across time (Baldwin *et al.* 2018). Another way to help people reconnect life before and after diagnosis is to ask what they want to carry with them from life before illness into the new normal and ask them to consider what else they might need for the future (Doka 2014, first published 2009). Meaning making should support visions of the future that are realistic and align with both the person's SOS (existing or evolving) and the new normal (Schulman-Green *et al.* 2012). Just as we want to promote realistic and diverse hopes for the future, we can affirm that "everyday activities—tasks as simple as helping a person get dressed or taking a stroll together—can be as valuable as loftier or more ambitious goals" in helping people find meaning in life (DeAngelis 2018, p.44; see also Schroevers *et al.* 2011). Affirm the progress people make to motivate them to continue challenging integration of illness experiences (Kralik 2002).

Making meaning with a spiritual caregiver is helpful, but meaning making will be even more beneficial if the process is shared with and supported by the person's partner, spouse, and/ or other people in the patient's **web of life** (Årestedt *et al.* 2016; Epstein and Street 2011; Neimeyer *et al.* 2014; Radcliffe *et al.* 2013; Sakellariou *et al.* 2013). You can encourage and possibly facilitate these conversations.

Dorothy's meaning making and new normal

Dorothy and her companions deliver the Wicked Witch's broom to the Wizard with the expectation that he will cure them. As we know, the Wizard cannot provide a *cure* for any member of the group, but he wisely engages the Tin Man, the Scarecrow, and the Lion in meaning making that leads to their *healing*. These interactions illustrate the social construction of meaning as the Wizard reframes illness experiences in ways that are life-affirming for each character.

The Scarecrow's brain disease isn't eradicated, but a diploma signifies that he has significant intellectual capacity to live a full life. The Lion has allowed his illness to limit his engagement with life. Meaning making with the Wizard helps the Lion recognize that he can still do what is important to him, and he has other strengths to draw on, namely wisdom. The Wizard presents the Lion with a medal in the shape of a cross. The cross symbolizes the spiritual resource of wisdom gained from experience. This resource will help the Lion continue to meet the challenges of living with chronic illness without pushing away the support he needs. The Tin Man seeks a cure for his heart/emotional condition. The Wizard reframes the Tin Man's purpose in life by assigning greater importance to the way other people are affected by the Tin Man's love for them. This process removes the emotional limitations the Tin Man believed held him back from a life of meaning.

At last, it's Dorothy's turn for the Wizard's attention. Her companions are encouraged by their own experiences of healing and believe Dorothy will also benefit from co-creating new meanings of her illness experience with the Wizard. However, Dorothy isn't convinced that reframing will restore her to wholeness—she is not yet ready to revisit her understandings of illness. Instead, she agrees to one last experimental treatment (a hot-air balloon ride to Kansas/WITF), in part because she now trusts the Wizard and his limited success with the balloon. You will also find that people are willing to take the road less traveled with someone who has walked the path before them. Unfortunately for Dorothy, the balloon takes off without her. Now, Dorothy believes she has exhausted her resources for healing. Like many people with nowhere else to turn, Dorothy finally seeks a spiritual solution to her struggles.

Glinda/Dorothy's SOS appears. Glinda observes that Dorothy wasn't ready to make new meanings of her illness experience until she reached this point in her journey. With Glinda's support, Dorothy moves from an understanding of illness as a random event (**biomedical model**) to a mind–body–spirit wholistic **energy body understanding** in which she has the power to heal herself. The ruby slippers symbolize Dorothy's life force energy, which she uses to amplify the power of new spiritual coping strategies that result in her healing.

When Dorothy learns she can return "home" to Kansas, she also repairs the time disruption of illness she experienced at diagnosis (when the tornado dropped the farmhouse into the Land of Oz). This revelation bridges the worlds of illness-in-the-foreground and wellness-in-the-foreground, linking her past in Kansas to the present in Oz and a future that will likely include experiences in both locations. Dorothy makes the shift to WITF using two new spiritual coping strategies: positive thinking (believing in her inner capacity to heal) and mindfulness meditation (focused repetition of a meaningful mantra). Both practices are embodied in the iconic phrase Dorothy repeats as she makes the shift: "There's no place like home." Glinda notes that Dorothy has always had access to these inner spiritual resources, but Dorothy is only now learning to mobilize them for ongoing healing.

As Dorothy chants her mantra, she enters a recovery phase of illness that shifts her from IITF to WITF and shifts the film from Oz (color) to Kansas (black and white). Dorothy wakes up in her bed at the farmhouse, where she is greeted with relief and celebration by her aunt, uncle, the farmhands, and Professor Marvel (the folk/psychological healer Dorothy visited prior to diagnosis). This group begins to co-construct meaning of Dorothy's experience. However, there are clear differences between Dorothy's full-color experience of illness and the black-and-white interpretation offered by the people in her web of life.

Group members patronize Dorothy's description of illness and characterize the IITF period as a dream best forgotten, invalidating and disenfranchising Dorothy's complex and vivid experience. Dorothy will have to reconcile her reality separate from their experiences of the illness. Dorothy's family and friends may be challenged to socially construct meaning of the illness experience at this time because they're still overwhelmed by their fear that Dorothy wouldn't recover from the chronic phase of illness. Left to make meaning on her own, Dorothy characterizes her IITF experience as challenging but meaningful, a **moral model** pedagogical understanding. She acknowledges that she still has hope/Toto. Finally, she names the new normal that will help her retain her core identity: to always stay close to home where she can be her true self. For Dorothy, post-traumatic growth includes spiritual transformation, renewed appreciation for home and family, and a commitment to be her authentic self.

Kelly's meaning making and new normal

As I described in Chapter 2, I initially made meaning of my illness (rheumatoid arthritis/RA) as a natural part of human finitude, an understanding that fits within the **biomedical model** of illness. This belief aligned with embedded family beliefs about health and illness. Later, as my spirituality evolved to include Buddhist teachings, I reframed this belief slightly. My illness aptly represented the Buddhist perspective that life is suffering, and illness is one way we suffer.

Early in my illness journey, I resisted creating a new normal for our family by absorbing as much of the impact of frequent pain, chronic fatigue, and constant healthcare appointments as I could handle on my own (**self-directing spiritual coping**). My husband did the same with the burdens and losses he experienced as a result of my physical limitations. My children were too young to know me/our family without RA. The way I cared for their physical needs naturally evolved to accommodate pain and fatigue over time. About four years into RA, we hired college students to clean the house, freeing some of my energy to attend graduate school. That was a short-term adjustment. When we moved to Memphis two years later, I not only took on house cleaning, but remodeling as well, even as I continued my graduate studies.

One benefit of having an often-invisible disease (as long as inflammation was managed with medication) was being able to control who knew about my illness. I could pass for healthy unless it was advantageous for me to reveal otherwise. For many years, this ability to live stealthily with chronic illness likely squelched the need for further meaning making.

During seminary, I began seeing a spiritual director on a regular basis. My understandings of illness were certainly shaped by both the academic milieu and my personal reflective practice. As my spiritual director and I discerned God's presence in my life (**collaborative style of spiritual coping**), I ascribed the lessons illness had taught me to God (**moral model** understanding). In the context of this **healing relationship**, I could identify these lessons as gifts from the illness (**benefit finding**) without disenfranchising negative experiences of pain and suffering. This understanding of illness also aligned with personal, family, and social values and beliefs about a loving God who is present in all life experiences.

I formally and more thoroughly refined my ideas about the meaning of illness during my doctoral studies, which began about eight years after diagnosis. As I reviewed the literature on meaning making that shaped Chapter 2 of this book, I explored my ideas in assignments, publications, and my dissertation. I had the advantage of situating my private meaning making within a broader theological/spiritual framework. I could consider the meaning of my story in relation to diverse illness narratives and understandings of suffering. Academic exploration and critical theological reflection augmented personal meaning making within my web of life.

The greatest shift in meaning making came when I began working with a shaman, more than ten years after diagnosis. I wasn't explicitly looking to make meaning of my illness through shamanic healing/journeying, but this deep spiritual work continues to offer rich insights with direct bearing on my understandings of illness. My experiences bear out the truth in this description of shamanic healing:

> In the shamanic form of transpersonal care the spirits, rather than the clinician, are in charge and guide the process of treatment.

> The questions this framework asks are different as well: "What's trying to happen?" and "What's *right* with this person?" and "If this symptom had a voice, what might it be saying?" This model views health and illness as a dynamic process, a trajectory of growth for the person at all levels. (Carson 2013, p.3)

I now understand my illness to be the result of complex mind–body–spirit interactions, some of which occurred in previous lifetimes and have been reinforced through my beliefs, behaviors, and relationships in this lifetime (**energy body model**). I believe I have the power and the responsibility to collaborate with Spirit for my healing and to help others with their healing. Healthcare providers are still critical members of my support team, but they are no longer the primary healers. Do I expect a complete cure from RA? No. Nor do I particularly desire a cure. RA has been a helpful teacher for me, symbolically pointing to deeper psychological and spiritual pain that I needed (and still need) to address. I expect to continue learning from my illness-as-teacher for the rest of my life.

Integration: SNAP review and final thoughts

I wrote this book to highlight common psycho-spiritual experiences of chronic illness and equip informal and professional caregivers to ease suffering and support healing for people living with long-term health conditions. I hope you have a greater appreciation of the diversity of losses, psycho-spiritual responses to loss and uncertainty, shifting perspectives of illness-in-the-foreground and wellness-in-the-foreground, spiritual struggles, and spiritual coping strategies that you may encounter with your own health condition or when offering care to someone living with chronic illness.

Using the guidelines and tools in this book, you can help people discover and draw on life-affirming values, beliefs, meanings, and practices to develop and sustain well-integrated spiritualities that are complex and flexible enough to account for the full reality of life with an incurable disease. Always keep in mind that healing is both a process and a dynamic state of well-being that you can facilitate but can never create or sustain for another person. I find spiritual care to be most rewarding when I let go of my attachment to the outcomes of the spiritual encounter or relationship. People will change when they are ready to change,[2] just as Dorothy needed time to grow and learn before she was ready to hear and act on Glinda's wisdom (her SOS).

Although every spiritual care conversation is unique to that person at that time, SNAP skills are the foundation of ongoing healing relationships in which people experience you as a safe and compassionate presence who bears witness to their stories and offers hope for the future. As you practice **SNAP** skills, you will be rewarded with invitations to explore the amazing and magical spiritual worlds other people inhabit.

- Self-awareness: Know yourself so that you don't inadvertently impose your own values, beliefs, meanings, or practices on other people. Attend to relationship dynamics. Reflect on spiritual care conversations to note areas for growth in the way you practice spiritual care.

- Stay in the Now: Keep your attention focused in the present moment and the care receiver. Contemplative, mindful practices can help you offer compassionate, invitational silences during care conversations.

- Ask questions: Remain curious, with an attitude of "not-knowing" about the other person and the ways their experiences and SOS differ from your experiences and SOS.

---

2   Rollnick and Miller (1995) offer a helpful understanding of when and why people change.

- Let the other **Person** guide the conversation: Build trust by using the other person's preferred vocabulary to talk about spirituality and their illness experience. Don't assume you know what the other person means when they use specific words or phrases; ask for clarification. Respect other people as the experts on their experiences and SOSs.

I have previously noted the importance of meaning making for living well with chronic illness. People initially make meaning of the cause of their illness to answer the question *Why?* Many people later make meaning to reflect on *how* the illness has transformed them, perhaps offering benefits as they discover a new normal, their way of "finding a place for illness…and keeping the illness in its place" (Patterson and Garwick 1994, p.138). Ongoing spiritual care relationships may be ideal crucibles for such life-affirming meaning making.

I hope you found this retelling of Dorothy's visit to Oz a helpful and compelling metaphor for the chronic illness journey, further illuminated by my story and the stories of many other people from research studies and personal accounts of illness. *The Wizard of Oz* film also underscores how the worlds of IITF and WITF can be as starkly different as living in black and white versus living in color. Of course, people may also experience these shifts in more nuanced ways. As I've emphasized throughout the book, the millions of people worldwide who live with chronic illness (as patients and within a patient's web of life) will have unique illness experiences. What remains true for everyone is, as Dorothy says, the fact that there is "no place like home." We all want to feel at home in our bodies and in our lives. Spiritual caregivers can help people find their way home again and again, reconnecting body, mind, and spirit to find meaning and purpose in life and live as their authentic selves. I wish you well on the healing journey and will look for you on the Yellow Brick Road.

Glossary

Acceptance: Integrating illness into one's life to create a **new normal**

Anxiety: Worry, concern, or fear about what might happen in the future

Benefit finding: Identifying life-affirming effects or outcomes from challenging experiences

Biographical disruption: A change in a person's self-understanding or identity

Biomedical model: The belief that illness is caused by poor health habits, genetics, aging, germs, viruses, accidents, environmental toxins, or random acts of nature

Caregiver burden: The negative impact of illness on a family caregiver

Chi/ki/qi/prana: Layers of life force energy associated with specific vibrations, sounds, colors, pathways (meridians), and locations in the body known as chakras

Chronic illness: The subjective experience of living with an incurable health condition

Collaborative style of spiritual coping: Managing stress by partnering with God/a higher power

Compassion: Acting on empathic feelings to help alleviate another person's suffering

Compassion fatigue: Feeling indifferent to another person's suffering because one has already given so much of themselves in support

Coping: Attempts to manage stressful or threatening experiences

Core shamanism: Seeking guidance and healing through direct communications from/with the spirit realm (God, angels, spirit guides, and deceased loved ones)

Curing: Eliminating disease

Death anxiety: Worry or fear about the process of dying or ceasing to live

Deferring style of spiritual coping: Managing stress by giving control of the situation to God/a higher power

Demoralization syndrome: Feelings of helplessness, hopelessness, and loss of meaning that last longer than two weeks

Depression: Feelings of sadness and loss of interest in life that last longer than two weeks

Desire for hastened death: A wish to die sooner than one would die from the natural progression of disease

Disease: A medically defined condition in which physiological structure and/or function are impaired

Disenfranchised grief: Sadness that is not acknowledged by the person who is grieving and/or by other people

Energy body model: The belief that illness is caused by mental/spiritual imbalances or specific imbalances, blockages, or disharmony in life force energy

Family system: All people considered family by the patient

Grief: A response to loss

Grieving: Internal expression of grief, including sadness, numbness, heartache, regret, anger, and shame; often used interchangeably with **mourning**

Healing: A dynamic and ongoing process of seeking, restoring, and experiencing well-being of mind, body, and spirit

Healing presence: Experiencing a **sacred** or spiritual connection in a caregiving interaction

Helplessness: Feelings of being trapped, lacking control, and/or a sense of failure

Hero's journey: An archetypal tale in which a person is called to an adventure, faces trials and tribulations, meets guides and helpers, overcomes challenges, and returns home transformed

Hopelessness: Feeling that life will never get better

Illness/illness experience: A person's subjective experience of living with disease

Illness narrative: The story a person tells to make sense of an **illness experience**

Illness-in-the-foreground (IITF): Periods in which illness and suffering are the focus of attention; life may feel chaotic, uncertain, and/or unstable

Informal family caregivers: Unpaid family members who provide care to people who are ill

Intercultural spiritual care: A care relationship in which the caregiver practices self-awareness; respects the uniqueness of the other person; affirms the other person as the expert authority on their experiences and **spiritual orienting system**; and attends to the complex, multi-layered, and contextual nature of each person's experiences within interconnected familial, social, and cultural systems

Interspiritual dialogue: Conversation between two or more people about their unique **spiritual orienting systems**

Life-affirming: Describes various ways people respond to chronic health conditions to support or enhance positive life experiences

Life-limiting: Describes various ways chronic health conditions negatively affect a person's ability to experience life as they would like to experience it. A life-limiting illness may or may not include a shortened lifespan

Liminal: An ambiguous time or place; neither here nor there

Living human document: A metaphor used to describe people as the embodiment of their life stories

Living web: See **web of life**

Loss: The experience of something that once existed but is no longer present or available

Meaning making: The process of developing a coherent understanding of a life experience

Moral model: The belief that illness is caused by gods, demons, or other supernatural powers in relation to sin, one's thinking (positive or negative), karma, divine favor, life lessons, or opportunities for growth and transformation

Mourning: External expression of grief, including talking about feelings, crying, yelling, punching something, or writing about the loss; often used interchangeably with **grieving**

Narrative approaches to spiritual care: Care that focuses on the stories people tell to construct meaning and make sense of life experiences

Negative spiritual coping: Life-limiting ways to manage stress (e.g., spiritual struggle and doubt, belief in a punishing God/higher power, or belief that demonic forces are responsible for illness)

New normal: A way of life that integrates chronic illness or accepts chronic illness as a normal interruption to life

None/religious resistor/spiritual but not religious/unaffiliated: Terms used to describe people who do not identify with a **religion**

Pain: Negative experiences associated with actual or potential tissue damage; in practice, pain is defined by the person experiencing it

Palliative care: Specialized health care that eases physical, psychological, social, and spiritual suffering and improves quality of life for people and families living with serious and life-limiting illnesses

Placebo: A harmless treatment given to promote healing

Placebo effect: Healing through belief in a treatment assumed by the care provider to be harmless or ineffective

Poesis: Storytelling that relies on metaphor, symbols, and symbolic action

Positive spiritual coping: Life-affirming ways to manage stress (e.g., belief in a loving God/higher power, spiritual connection with other people, collaborative spiritual coping, or spiritual support)

Post-traumatic growth: Personal transformation as a result of struggle or crisis

Primary loss: The first loss that leads to other losses (e.g., health is the primary loss with chronic illness)

Reciprocal suffering: Suffering experienced within the patient's **web of life** as a result of the shared illness experience; each person is affected differently, and each person copes differently

Religion: An established set of values, beliefs, practices, meanings, and relationships shared among a group of people within public and private institutions that are themselves focused on **spirituality** (e.g., the Church of Jesus Christ of Latter-day Saints or Hinduism)

Rituals: Practices that help people realize their hopes for healing through embodied integration of belief and action

(The) Sacred: What is of ultimate importance to someone; used as a placeholder for the diverse ways people name what is transcendent, boundless, and infinite

Safety: The feeling that we can be authentic and vulnerable without fear of judgment or punishment

Secondary loss: A loss that results from a **primary loss** (e.g., with chronic illness, loss of identity may follow the primary loss of health)

Self-compassion: Kind, non-judgmental, and mindful thoughts and feelings toward oneself as a fallible human being who deserves positive life experiences

Self-directing style of spiritual coping: Managing stress without reliance on God/a higher power

Shamanic journey: A trance-like state of consciousness in which a person's spirit travels to the spirit world to engage with a variety of helping spirits for guidance and healing

Sick role: A social agreement in which people who are ill are relieved of their responsibilities at work and/or home in exchange for managing their condition without taking undue advantage of others

SNAP: An easy-to-remember mnemonic for **interspiritual dialogue**: Self-awareness, Stay in the Now, Ask questions, and Let the other Person guide the conversation

Social determinants of health: Individual, systemic, communal, and cultural factors that affect the health of individuals and communities (e.g., socio-economic status, racism, access to healthcare services)

Social model: The belief that illness is caused by systemic, communal, and cultural factors (e.g., socio-economic status, racism, access to healthcare services)

Spirit: In core shamanism, a term for the higher consciousness/universal creative energy and/or group of spirit helpers who offer guidance and healing in shamanic journeys (e.g., power animals, spirit guides, angels and archangels, and the spirits of people deceased and living)

Spiritual coping: Relying on spiritual resources to manage stress

Spiritual crisis: An overwhelming disruption in a person's **spiritual orienting system** that leads to disconnection with the sacred, the inability to make meaning of life experiences, and loss of well-being

Spiritual distress: The experience of **spiritual struggles** or challenges to a person's **spiritual orienting system**; spiritual distress can coexist with spiritual **well-being**

Spiritual orienting system (SOS): The unique set of values, beliefs, meanings, and practices that guide a person's behaviors and decision making, and help people understand who they are and their purpose in the world

Spiritual struggles: Conflicts related to some aspects of a person's **spiritual orienting system**

Spirituality: An individual's dynamic search for and expression of meaning and purpose, and their connection with self, others, nature, and **the sacred**

Spiritually fluid: People who seek and express a dynamic **spirituality** that integrates diverse life experiences (which may or may not include religious values, beliefs, meaning, or practices) to stay connected to self, others, nature, and **the sacred** and maintain a coherent understanding of life

Suffering: A person's subjective response to pain and other physical, psychological, social, and spiritual distress

Surrender: Giving in or letting go of resistance to the undesirable reality of living with chronic illness

Surrender style of spiritual coping: Managing stress by seeking the will of God/a higher power, and acquiescing to that path, even though other—even preferred—options are available

Tertiary loss: Loss experienced by someone in the patient's **web of life**

Trust: The belief that when we share authentically of ourselves, the other person will respond with our best interests at heart

Visitor test: Using the patient's likely response to the news of an upcoming visit from a loved one to assess if the patient might be experiencing **depression** or **demoralization syndrome**

Web of life/living web: The dynamic environment in which a person lives; the web includes human and non-human elements, systems, and contexts

Well-being: A subjective feeling of life satisfaction or contentment

Well-integrated spirituality: A **spiritual orienting system** that is flexible (adaptable to cope with changings circumstances), complex (able to support meaning making about suffering), grounded in benevolent views and experiences of life and the sacred, and liberative (supports freedom in the person's life)

Wellness-in-the-foreground (WITF): Periods in which illness is not the person's focus (although it may still require attention) and the person experiences a sense of control and stability

Wholeness/wholistic healing/care: Addressing and/or integrating all dimensions of a person's life

References

Abercrombie, B. (2002) *Writing Out the Storm: Reading and Writing Your Way Through Serious Illness or Injury.* New York, NY: St. Martin's Griffin.

Abu-Raiya, H., Pargament, K. I., and Exline, J. J. (2015a) "Understanding and addressing religious and spiritual struggles in health care." *Health and Social Work 40,* 4, 126–134.

Abu-Raiya, H., Pargament, K. I., Krause, N., and Ironson, G. (2015b) "Robust links between religious/spiritual struggles, psychological distress, and well-being in a national sample of American adults." *American Journal of Orthospsychiatry 85,* 6, 565–575.

Aburub, A. S., Gagnon, B., Ahmed, S., Rodríguez, A. M., and Mayo, N. E. (2018) "Impact of reconceptualization response shift on rating of quality of life over time among people with advanced cancer." *Supportive Care in Cancer 26,* 3063–3071.

Adams, H. (2018a) "Calling on past lives to solve the problems of the present." Religion News Service. Accessed on June 22, 2018 at https://religionnews.com/2018/06/22/calling-on-past-lives-to-solve-the-problems-of-the-present.

Adams, K. (2018b) "Defining and operationalizing chaplain presence: A review." *Journal of Religion and Health 58,* 4, 1–13.

Adams, P. J. (2016) "Responding to the existentials of non-life-threatening chronic conditions." *Medical Hypothesis 93,* 48–52.

Adelman, R. D., Tmanova, L. L., Delgado, D., Dion, S., and Lachs, M. S. (2014) "Caregiver burden: A clinical review." *JAMA 311,* 10, 1052–1059.

Agrimson, L. B. and Taft, L. B. (2008) "Spiritual crisis: A concept analysis." *Journal of Advanced Nursing 65,* 2, 454–461.

Ahaddour, C. and Broeckaert, B. (2018) "'For every illness there is a cure': Attitudes and beliefs of Moroccan Muslim women regarding health, illness and medicine." *Journal of Religion and Health 57,* 1285–1303.

Ahmadi, F. (2013) "Music as a method of coping with cancer: A qualitative study among cancer patients in Sweden." *Arts and Health 5,* 2, 152–165.

Ahmadmehrabi, S. (2018) "The day when the white coat can be worn with no hesitation at all." KevinMD. Accessed on December 11, 2018 at www.kevinmd.com/blog/2018/12/the-day-when-the-white-coat-can-be-worn-with-no-hesitation-at-all.html.

Alexander, E. (2015) "Near-death experiences, the mind-body debate and the nature of reality." *Missouri Medicine 112,* 1, 17-21.

Alling, F. A. (2015) "The healing effects of belief in medical practices and spirituality." *Explore 11,* 273–280.

Alradaydeh, M. and Khalil, A. A. (2018) "The association of spiritual well-being and depression among patients receiving hemodialysis." *Perspectives in Psychiatric Care* 54, 341–347.

Ambrosio, L., García, J. M. S., Fernández, M. R., Bravo, S. A., *et al.* (2015) "Living with chronic illness in adults: A concept analysis." *Journal of Clinical Nursing 24*, 2357–2367.

Anderson, H. (2001) "Spiritual care: The power of an adjective." *Journal of Pastoral Care* 55, 3, 233–237.

Anderson, M. and Asnani, M. (2013) "'You just have to deal with it': Coping with sickle cell disease in Jamaica." *Qualitative Health Research 23*, 5, 655–664.

Ankrom, S. (2019) "Proper breathing to reduce anxiety." Very Well Mind. Accessed on February 6, 2019 at www.verywellmind.com/abdominal-breathing-2584115.

Ano, G. G. and Vasconcelles, E. B. (2005) "Religious coping and psychological adjustment to stress: A meta-analysis." *Journal of Clinical Psychology 61*, 4, 461–480.

Antonio, E., Arora, K., Doehring, C., and Hernández, A. (2014) "Theological education and economic revitalization: Creating sustainable organizations through authentic engagement." *Theological Education 48*, 2, 57–67.

Anxiety Canada (2018) "How to do progressive muscle relaxation." Anxiety Canada. Accessed on February 6, 2019 at www.anxietycanada.com/sites/default/files/MuscleRelaxation.pdf.

Applebaum, A. J. and Breitbart, W. (2013) "Care for the cancer caregiver: A systematic review." *Palliative and Supportive Care 11*, 3, 231–252.

Appleby, A., Swinton, J., Bradbury, I., and Wilson, P. (2018a) "GPs and spiritual care: Signed up or souled out? A quantitative analysis of GP trainers' understanding and application of the concept of spirituality." *Education for Primary Care 29*, 6, 1–9.

Appleby, A., Wilson, P., and Swinton, J. (2018b) "Spiritual care in general practice: Rushing in or fearing to tread? An integrative review of qualitative literature." *Journal of Religion and Health 57*, 1108–1124.

Arabiat, D. H., Al Jabery, M., Abdelkader, R. H., and Mahadeen, A. (2013) "Jordanian mothers' beliefs about the causes of cancer in their children and their impact on the maternal role." *Journal of Transcultural Nursing 24*, 3, 246–253.

Araten-Bergman, T., Avieli, H., Mushkin, P., and Band-Winterstein, T. (2016) "How aging individuals with schizophrenia experience the self-etiology of their illness: A reflective lifeworld research approach." *Aging and Mental Health 20*, 11, 1147–1156.

Årestedt, L., Benzein, E., Persson, C., and Margareta, R. (2016) "The meaning of place for family well-being in families living with chronic illness." *International Journal of Qualitative Studies on Health and Well-being 11*, 1, 1–10.

Årestedt, L., Persson, C., and Benzein, E. (2014) "Living as a family in the midst of chronic illness." *Scandinavian Journal of Caring Sciences 28*, 29–37.

Arora, K. R. (2009) "Models of understanding chronic illness: Implications for pastoral theology and care." *Journal of Pastoral Theology 19*, 1, 22–37.

Arora, K. R. (2011) "Not-knowing in spiritual direction: Reflections on social identity." *Presence: An International Journal of Spiritual Direction 17*, 2, 19–26.

Arora, K. R. (2013) "Spiritual Direction as Psychospiritual Care for Women with Autoimmune Diseases." In R. Green, D. Y. Schumm, and M. J. Stoltzfus (eds) *Chronic Illness and Spirituality: Diverse Disciplinary, Religious, and Cultural Perspectives*. New York, NY: Palgrave Macmillan.

Arora, K. R. and McCulliss, D. (2015) "Illness narratives in spiritual direction: Healing through story." *Presence: An International Journal of Spiritual Direction 21*, 1, 34–40.

Association of Religion Data Archives (2012) "Portraits of American Life Study." Accessed on August 4, 2018 at www.thearda.com/pals.

Attig, T. (2001) "Relearning the World: Making and Finding Meanings." In R. A. Neimeyer (ed.) *Meaning Reconstruction and the Experience of Loss.* Washington, DC: American Psychological Association.

Avert (2018) "HIV stigma and discrimination." Accessed on November 1, 2018 at www.avert.org/professionals/hiv-social-issues/stigma-discrimination.

Back, A. L., Bauer-Wu, S. M., Rushton, C. H., and Halifax, J. (2009) "Compassionate silence in the patient-clinician encounter: A contemplative approach." *Journal of Palliative Medicine 12*, 12, 1113–1117.

Badaracco, C. H. (2007) *Prescribing Faith: Medicine, Media, and Religion in American Culture.* Waco, TX: Baylor University Press.

Baider, L. (2012) "Cultural diversity: Family path through terminal illness." *Annals of Oncology 23*, Supplement 3, iii62–iii65.

Balboni, T. A. and Balboni, M. J. (2018) "The spiritual event of serious illness." *Journal of Pain and Symptom Management 56*, 5, 816–822.

Baldacchino, D. (2003) *Spirituality in Illness and Care.* Blata L-Bajda, Malta: Preca Library.

Baldacchino, D. R., Borg, J., Muscat, C., and Sturgeon, C. (2012) "Psychology and theology meet: Illness appraisal and spiritual coping." *Western Journal of Nursing Research 34*, 6, 818–847.

Baldwin, M., Landau, M. J., and Swanson, T. J. (2018) "Metaphors can give life meaning." *Self and Identity 17*, 2, 163–193.

Barnard, L. K. and Curry, J. F. (2011) "Self-compassion: Conceptualizations, correlates, and interventions." *Review of General Psychology 15*, 4, 289–303.

Barrett, J. (1995) "Multiple sclerosis: The experience of a disease." *Women's Studies International Forum 18*, 2, 159–171.

Barry, W. A. and Connolly, W. J. (1982) *The Practice of Spiritual Direction.* San Francisco, CA: HarperSanFrancisco.

Barton, K. S., Tate, T., Lau, N., Taliesin, K. B., Waldman, E. D., and Rosenberg, A. R. (2018) "'I'm not a spiritual person.' How hope might facilitate conversations about spirituality among teens and young adults with cancer." *Journal of Pain and Symptom Management 55*, 6, 1599–1608.

Baum, L. F. (1899) *The Wonderful Wizard of Oz.* Chicago, IL: George M. Hill Company.

Beck, J. (2014) "When doctors make you feel guilty." *The Atlantic*, January 22, 2014. Accessed on July 25, 2019 at www.theatlantic.com/health/archive/2014/01/when-doctors-make-you-feel-guilty/283218.

Beck, M. (2007) "Illness, disease and sin: The connection between genetics and spirituality." *Christian Bioethics 13*, 67–89.

Beesley, V. L., Smith, D. D., Nagle, C. M., Friedlander, M., *et al.* (2018) "Coping strategies, trajectories, and their associations with patient-reported outcomes among women with ovarian cancer." *Supportive Care in Cancer 26*, 4133–4142.

Bell, C. (1987) "Discourse and dichotomies: The structure of ritual theory." *Religion 17*, 95–118.

Benson, H. and Klipper, M. Z. (1975) *The Relaxation Response.* New York, NY: HarperTorch.

Berger, A. S. (2013) "The evil eye: A cautious look." *Journal of Religion and Health 52*, 785–788.

Bernard, M., Strasser, F., Gamondi, C., Braunschweig, G., *et al.* (2017) "Relationship between spirituality, meaning in life, psychological distress, wish for hastened death, and their influence on quality of life in palliative care patients." *Journal of Pain and Symptom Management 54*, 4, 415–522.

Bernhard, T. (2010) *How to Be Sick: A Buddhist-inspired Guide for the Chronically Ill and Their Caregivers.* Boston, MA: Wisdom Publications.

Bernhard, T. (2013) "What chronic pain and illness make me miss the most." KevinMD. Accessed on May 30, 2013 at www.kevinmd.com/blog/2013/05/chronic-pain-illness. html.

Bernhard, T. (2014a) "The uncertainty that the chronically ill face." KevinMD. Accessed on June 29, 2014 at www.kevinmd.com/blog/2014/06/uncertainty-chronically-ill-face.html.

Bernhard, T. (2014b) "A not-to-do list for caregivers of the chronically ill." *Psychology Today.* Accessed on January 23, 2014 at www.psychologytoday.com/us/blog/turning-straw-gold/201401/not-do-list-caregivers-the-chronically-ill.

Berry, J. (2009) *Ritual Making Women: Shaping Rites for Changing Lives.* London: Equinox Publishing.

Betcher, S. V. (2001) "Rehabilitating religious discourse: Bringing disability studies to the theological venue." *Religious Studies Review 27,* 4, 341–348.

Bichell, R. E. (2017) "Scientists start to tease out the subtler ways racism hurts health." Shots: Health News from NPR. Accessed on November 11, 2017 at www.npr.org/sections/health-shots/2017/11/11/562623815/scientists-start-to-tease-out-the-subtler-ways-racism-hurts-health.

Bidwell, D. R. (2004) "Real/izing the sacred: Spiritual direction and social constructionism." *Journal of Pastoral Theology 14,* 1, 59–74.

Bidwell, D. R. (2018) *When One Religion Isn't Enough: The Lives of Spiritually Fluid People.* Boston, MA: Beacon Press.

Blinne, K. C. (2012) "(Re)storying illness identity: A five-element perspective." *Health Communication 27,* 314–317.

Boring, F. M. (2015) "Walking in the shaman's shoes: A transformational walk with the family soul." *Revision 32,* 2/3, 46–53.

Boston, P., Bruce, A., and Schreiber, R. (2011) "Existential suffering in the palliative care setting: An integrated literature review." *Journal of Pain and Symptom Management 41,* 3, 604–618.

Boston, P. H. and Mount, B. M. (2006) "The caregiver's perspective on existential and spiritual distress in palliative care." *Journal of Pain and Symptom Management 32,* 1, 13–26.

Bourgeault, C. (2004) *Centering Prayer and Inner Awakening.* Cambridge, MA: Cowley Publications.

Bourland, E. L. R., Neville, M. A., and Pickens, N. D. (2011) "Loss, gain, and the reframing of perspectives in long-term stroke survivors: A dynamic experience of quality of life." *Topics in Stroke Rehabilitation 18,* 5, 437–449.

Bradt, J. and Dileo, C. (2010) "Music therapy for end-of-life care (Review)." *Cochrane Database of Systematic Reviews,* 1.

Branigan, M. (2015) "Desire for hastened death: Exploring the emotions and the ethics." *Current Opinion in Supportive and Palliative Care 9,* 1, 64–71.

Bray, P. (2013) "Bereavement and transformation: A psycho-spiritual and post-traumatic growth perspective." *Journal of Religion and Health 52,* 890–903.

Bregman, L. (2004) "Defining spirituality: Multiple uses and murky meanings of an incredibly popular term." *Journal of Pastoral Care and Counseling 58,* 3, 157–167.

Breitbart, W. and Dickerman, A. L. (2018) "Assessment and management of depression in palliative care." UpToDate. Accessed on July 9, 2019 at www.uptodate.com/contents/assessment-and-management-of-depression-in-palliative-care/print.

Briggs, D. (2016) "Why believing in miracles could be hazardous to your health." *Washington Post.* Accessed on October 4, 2016 at www.washingtonpost.com/news/acts-of-faith/wp/2016/10/04/why-believing-in-miracles-could-be-hazardous-to-your-health/?utm_term=.0d38f447e8b2.

Brody, J. E. (2015) "Healthy in a falling apart sort of way." *New York Times.* Accessed on March 2, 2015 at http://well.blogs.nytimes.com/2015/03/02/healthy-in-a-falling-apart-sort-of-way/?em_pos=medium&emc=edit_hh_20150303&nl=subscription-3&nlid=65079564&ref=headline.

Brunton, B. (2003) "The reawakening of shamanism in the West." Foundation for Shamanic Studies. Accessed on October 5, 2018 at https://shamanism.org/articles/article13.html.

Buchholz, L. (2015) "Exploring the promise of mindfulness as medicine." *JAMA 314,* 13, 1327–1329.

Buonaccorso, L., Martucci, G., Miccinesi, G., Maruelli, A., and Ripamonti, C. (2019) "Construction of new personal meanings by cancer patients: A qualitative analysis in an Italian patient population." *Supportive Care in Cancer 27,* 5, 1911–1918.

Burden, B., Herron-Marx, S., and Clifford, C. (2005) "The increasing use of reiki as a complementary therapy in specialist palliative care." *International Journal of Palliative Nursing 11,* 5, 248–253.

Burke, A. (2012) "Comparing individual preferences for four meditation techniques: Zen, vipassana (mindfulness), Qigong, and mantra." *Explore 8,* 4, 237–242.

Burton, C. M. and King, L. A. (2010) "Effects of (very) brief writing on health: The two-minute miracle." *British Journal of Health Psychology 13,* 1, 9–14.

Bury, M. (1982) "Chronic illness as biographical disruption." *Sociology of Health and Illness 4,* 2, 167–182.

Byczkowski, A. (2013) "In today's society, chronic illness is viewed as a personal failing." KevinMD. Accessed on May 16, 2013 at www.kevinmd.com/blog/2013/05/todays-society-chronic-illness-viewed-personal-failing.html.

Cain, C. L., Surbone, A., Elk, R., and Kagawa-Singer, M. (2018) "Culture and palliative care: Preferences, communication, meaning, and mutual decision making." *Journal of Pain and Symptom Management 55,* 5, 1408–1419.

Calhoun, L. G. and Tedeschi, R. G. (2001) "Posttraumatic Growth: The Positive Lessons of Loss." In R. A. Neimeyer (ed.) *Meaning Reconstruction and the Experience of Loss.* Washington, DC: American Psychological Association.

Calhoun, L. G. and Tedeschi, R. G. (2006) "The Foundations of Posttraumatic Growth: An Expanded Framework." In L. G. Calhoun and R. G. Tedeschi (eds) *Handbook of Posttraumatic Growth Research and Practice.* Mahwah, NJ: Lawrence Erlbaum Associates.

Campbell, J. (2008) *The Hero with a Thousand Faces.* Novato, CA: New World Library.

Camus, J. T. W. (2009) "Metaphors of cancer in scientific popularization articles in the British press." *Discourse Studies 11,* 4, 465–495.

Capps, D. (2008) *Jesus the Village Psychiatrist.* Louisville, KY: Westminster John Knox Press.

Carney, L. M. and Park, C. L. (2018) "Cancer survivors' understanding of the cause and cure of their illness: Religious and secular appraisals." *Pscyho-Oncology 27,* 1553–1558.

Carr, E. C. J., McCaffery, G., and Ortiz, M. M. (2017) "The suffering of chronic pain patients on wait lists: Are they amenable to narrative therapy?" *Canadian Journal of Pain 1,* 1, 14–21.

Carson, C. (2013) "Mastery and Mystery: Models for Today's Healthcare." In C. Carson (ed.) *Spirited Medicine: Shamanism in Contemporary Healthcare.* Baltimore, MD: Otter Bay Books.

Caruso, R., Nanni, M. G., Riba, M., Sabato, S., *et al.* (2017) "Depressive spectrum disorders in cancer: Prevalence, risk factors and screening for depression: A critical review." *ACTA Oncologica 56,* 2, 146–155.

Cassell, D. K. and Rose, N. R. (2003) *The Encyclopedia of Autoimmune Diseases.* New York, NY: Facts on File.

Cassell, E. J. (2004, first published 1991) *The Nature of Suffering and the Goals of Medicine*. New York, NY: Oxford University Press.

Cassidy, T. (2013) "Benefit finding through caring: The cancer caregiver experience." *Psychology and Health 28*, 3, 250–266.

Centers for Disease Control and Prevention (2019) National Center for Chronic Disease and Health Promotion. Accessed on September 14, 2018 at www.cdc.gov/chronicdisease/index.htm.

Chaar, E. A., Hallit, S., Hajj, A., Aaraj, R., *et al.* (2018) "Evaluating the impact of spirituality on the quality of life, anxiety, and depression among patients with cancer: An observational transversal study." *Supportive Care in Cancer 26*, 2581–2590.

Chan, R. R., Beaulieu, J., and Pickering, C. E. Z. (2018) "Building sangha in the American healthcare setting for persons with chronic disease." *Explore 14*, 122–130.

Chan, R. R. and Larson, J. L. (2015) "Meditation interventions for chronic disease populations: A systematic review." *Journal of Holistic Nursing 33*, 3, 351–365.

Charmaz, K. (1995) "The body, identity, and self: Adapting to impairment." *Sociological Quarterly 36*, 4, 657–680.

Charon, R. (2006) *Narrative Medicine: Honoring the Stories of Illness*. New York, NY: Oxford University Press.

Chase, L. (2015) "Losing my husband—and finding him again through a medium." *Elle*. Accessed on October 5, 2015 at www.elle.com/life-love/news/a30986/losing-my-husband-and-finding-him-through-a-medium.

Chen, S.-C., Chou, C.-C., Chang, H.-J., and Lin, M.-F. (2018) "Comparison of group vs self-directed music interventions to reduce chemotherapy-related distress and cognitive appraisal: An exploratory study." *Supportive Care in Cancer 26*, 461–469.

Chen, S.-L., Tsai, J.-C., and Chou, K.-R. (2011) "Illness perceptions and adherence to therapeutic regimens among patients with hypertension: A structural modeling approach." *International Journal of Nursing Studies 48*, 235–245.

Cheng, Q., Xu, X., Liu, X., Mao, T., and Chen, Y. (2018) "Spiritual needs and their associated factors among cancer patients in China: A cross-sectional study." *Supportive Care in Cancer 26*, 3405–3412.

Chida, Y., Steptoe, A., and Powell, L. H. (2009) "Religiosity/spirituality and mortality." *Psychotherapy and Psychosomatics 78*, 2, 81–90.

Chisea, A. and Serretti, A. (2011) "Mindfulness-based interventions for chronic pain: A systematic review of the evidence." *Journal of Alternative and Complementary Medicine 17*, 1, 83–93.

Clayton, M. (2013) "Contemplative chaplaincy? A view from a children's hospice." *Practical Theology 6*, 1, 35–50.

Clegg, C. (2014) "Emerging paradigm shifts in spiritual care services in Scotland." *Health and Social Care Chaplaincy 2*, 1, 41–49.

Clow, B. (2001) "Who's afraid of Susan Sontag? Or, the myths and metaphors of cancer revisited." *Society for the Social History of Medicine 14*, 2, 293–312.

Coble, R. (2017) *The Chaplain's Presence and Medical Power: Rethinking Loss in the Hospital System*. Lanham, MD: Lexington Books.

Cohen, D. (2000) *Turning Suffering Inside Out: A Zen Approach to Living with Physical and Emotional Pain*. Boston, MA: Shambhala.

Cohen, S. (2016) "Medical students need exposure to chronic pain patients." KevinMD. Accessed on September 27, 2016 at www.kevinmd.com/blog/2016/09/medical-students-need-exposure-chronic-pain-patients.html.

Connell, S. and Beardsley, C. (2014) "'Hospitality of the heart—hospitality for the human spirit': How healthcare chaplains can discover, create and offer spaces for spiritual care in the hospital setting." *Health and Social Care Chaplaincy 2*, 1, 65–78.

Cooper, R. S., Ferguson, A., Bodurtha, J. N., and Smith, T. J. (2014) "AMEN in challenging conversations: Bridging the gaps between faith, hope, and medicine." *Journal of Oncology Practice 10*, 4, e191–e195.

Cooper-White, P. (2004) *Shared Wisdom: Use of the Self in Pastoral Care and Counseling.* Minneapolis, MN: Fortress Press.

Coor, C. A. and Coolican, M. B. (2010) "Understanding bereavement, grief, and mourning: Implications for donation and transplant professionals." *Progress in Transplantation 20*, 169–177.

Coruh, B., Ayele, H., Pugh, M., and Mulligan, T. (2005) "Does religious activity improve health outcomes? A critical review of the recent literature." *Explore (NY) 1*, 3, 186–191.

Coulehan, J. (2011) "Deep hope: A song without words." *Theoretical Medicine and Bioethics 32*, 143–160.

Cousins, N. (1979) *Anatomy of an Illness as Perceived by the Patient: Reflections on Healing and Regeneration.* New York, NY: W. W. Norton and Co.

Creamer, D. B. (2009) *Disability and Christian Theology: Embodied Limits and Constructive Possibilities.* New York, NY: Oxford University Press.

Crislip, A. T. (2005) *From Monastery to Hospital: Christian Monasticism and the Transformation of Health Care in Late Antiquity.* Ann Arbor, MI: University of Michigan Press.

Cruz, J. P., Colet, P. C., Alquwez, N., Inocian, E. P., Al-Otaibi, R. S., and Islam, S. M. S. (2017) "Influence of religiosity and spiritual coping on health-related quality of life in Saudi haemodialysis patients." *Hemodialysis International 21*, 1, 125–132.

Cubukcu, M. (2018) "Evaluation of quality of life in caregivers who are providing home care to cancer patients." *Supportive Care in Cancer 26*, 1457–1463.

Cummings, J. P. and Pargament, K. I. (2010) "Medicine for the spirit: Religious coping in individuals with medical conditions." *Religions 1*, 28–53.

Dale, O. and Smith, R. (2013, first published 2003) *Human Behavior and the Social Environment: Social Systems Theory.* Boston, MA: Pearson Education.

Daly, L., Fahey-McCarthy, E., and Timmins, F. (2019) "The experience of spirituality from the perspective of people living with dementia: A systematic review and meta-synthesis." *Dementia 18*, 2, 448–470.

Damen, A., Labuschagne, D., Fosler, L., O'Mahony, S., Levine, S., and Fitchett, G. (2018) "What do chaplains do: The views of palliative care physicians, nurses, and social workers." *American Journal of Hospice and Palliative Medicine 36*, 5, 1–6.

Davidson, R. J. and Kaszniak, A. W. (2015) "Conceptual and methodological issues in research on mindfulness and meditation." *American Psychologist 70*, 7, 581–592.

DeAngelis, T. (2018) "In search of meaning." *Monitor on Psychology 49*, 9, 38–44.

Defenbaugh, N. L. (2013) "Revealing and concealing ill identity: A performance narrative of IBD disclosure." *Health Communication 28*, 2, 159–169.

Delbyck, C. (2018) "Sarah Hyland reveals she was 'contemplating suicide' before second kidney transplant." HuffPost. Accessed on July 9, 2019 at www.huffingtonpost.co.uk/entry/sarah-hyland-reveals-she-contemplated-suicide-before-second-kidney-transplant_n_5c0e9912e4b08bcb27eb0aa8.

Delgado-Guay, M. O., Parsons, H. A., Hui, D., De la Cruz, M. G., Thorney, S., and Bruera, E. (2012) "Spirituality, religiosity, and spiritual pain among caregivers of patients with advanced cancer." *American Journal of Hospice and Palliative Medicine 30*, 5, 455–461.

Demir, M., Can, G., and Celek, E. (2013) "Effect of reiki on symptom management in oncology." *Asian Pacific Journal of Cancer Prevention 14*, 8, 4931–4933.

Deshpande, A. (2018) "Yoga for palliative care." *Integrative Medicine Research 7*, 211–213.

Desy, P. L. (2019) "Five layers of the human energy field." Learn Religions. Accessed on April 2, 2019 at www.thoughtco.com/layers-of-human-energy-field-1729677.

Determeyer, P. L. and Kutac, J. E. (2018) "Touching the spirit: Re-enchanting the person in the body." *Journal of Religion and Health 57*, 1679–1689.

Di Benedetto, M., Lindner, H., Aucote, H., Churcher, J., *et al.* (2014) "Co-morbid depression and chronic illness related to coping and physical and mental health status." *Psychology, Health and Medicine 19*, 3, 253–262.

DiNucci, E. M. (2005) "Energy healing: A complementary treatment for othopaedic and other conditions." *Orthopaedic Nursing 24*, 4, 259–269.

Distelberg, B., Williams-Reade, J., Tapanes, D., Montgomery, S., and Pandit, M. (2014) "Evaluation of a family systems intervention for managing pediatric chronic illness: Mastering Each New Direction (MEND)." *Family Process 53*, 2, 194–213.

Djivre, S. E., Levin, E., Schinke, R. J., and Porter, E. (2012) "Five residents speak: The meaning of living with dying in a long-term care home." *Death Studies 36*, 487–518.

Doehring, C. (2010) "Pastoral Care and Counseling in a Postmodern Context." In G. H. Asquith (ed.) *The Concise Dictionary of Pastoral Care and Counseling.* Nashville, TN: Abingdon Press.

Doehring, C. (2011) "Meditation as a Spiritually Integrative Practice for Coping with Stress." In C. Morgenthaler, I. Noth, and K. Greider (eds) *Pastoral Psychology and Psychology of Religion in Dialogue: Implications for Pastoral Care.* Stuttgart: Theologische Fakultät Kohlhammer Verlag.

Doehring, C. (2013) "The Practice of Relational-Ethical Pastoral Care." In M. Riemslagh, R. Burggraeve, C. Jozef, and A. Liégeois (eds) *After You: The Ethics of the Pastoral Counselling Process.* Leuven, Belgium: Uitgeverij Peeters.

Doehring, C. (2015) "Resilience as the relational ability to spiritually integrate moral stress." *Pastoral Psychology 64*, 635–649.

Doehring, C. (2015, first published 2006) *The Practice of Pastoral Care: A Postmodern Approach.* Louisville, KY: Westminster John Knox Press.

Doehring, C. (2019) "Searching for wholeness amidst traumatic grief: The role of spiritual practices that reveal compassion in embodied, relational, and transcendent ways." *Pastoral Psychology 68*, 3, 241–259.

Dŏgan, M. D. (2018) "The effect of reiki on pain: A meta-analysis." *Complementary Therapies in Clinical Practice 31*, 384–387.

Doka, K. J. (2014, first published 2009) *Counseling Individuals with Life-Threatening Illness.* New York, NY: Springer.

Doka, K. J. (2016) *Grief Is a Journey: Finding Your Path Through Loss.* New York, NY: Atria Books.

Doka, K. J. and Aber, R. A. (2002) "Psychosocial Loss and Grief." In K. J. Doka (ed.) *Disenfranchised Grief: New Directions, Challenges and Strategies for Practice.* Champaign, IL: Research Press.

Doka, K. J. and Martin, T. L. (2002) "How We Grieve: Culture, Class, and Gender." In K. J. Doka (ed.) *Disenfranchised Grief: New Directions, Challenges and Strategies for Practice.* Champaign, IL: Research Press.

Dose, A. M. and Rhudy, L. M. (2018) "Perspectives of newly diagnosed advanced cancer patients receiving dignity therapy during cancer treatment." *Supportive Care in Cancer 26*, 187–195.

Dossey, L. (1996) *Prayer Is Good Medicine: How to Reap the Healing Benefits of Prayer.* San Francisco, CA: HarperSanFrancisco.

Dossey, L. (1997) *Be Careful What You Pray For…You Might Just Get It.* San Francisco, CA: HarperSanFrancisco.

Dougherty, R. M. (1995) *Group Spiritual Direction: Community for Discernment.* New York, NY: Paulist Press.

Douglas, C., Windsor, C., and Wollin, J. (2008) "Understanding chronic pain complicating disability: Finding meaning through focus group methodology." *Journal of Neuroscience Nursing 40*, 3, 158–168.

Dumit, N. Y., Magilvy, J. K., and Afifi, R. (2016) "The cultural meaning of cardiac illness and self-care among Lebanese patients with coronary artery disease." *Journal of Transcultural Nursing 27*, 4, 385–391.

Duval, M. L. (1984) "Psychosocial metaphors of physical distress among MS patients." *Social Science and Medicine 19*, 6, 635–638.

Dyer, A. R. (2011) "The need for a new 'New Medical Model': A bio-psychosocial-spiritual model." *Southern Medical Journal 104*, 4, 297–298.

Edwards, R. C. (2018) "Butterfly symbolism and meaning." Gardens with Wings. Accessed on November 9, 2018 at www.gardenswithwings.com/butterfly-stories/butterfly-symbolism.html.

Egnew, T. R. (2018) "A narrative approach to healing chronic illness." *Annals of Family Medicine 16*, 160–165.

Eiesland, N. L. (1994) *The Disabled God: Toward a Liberatory Theology of Disability.* Nashville, TN: Abingdon.

Eilberg, A. (2005) "Jewish theologies of spiritual direction." *Presence: An International Journal of Spiritual Direction 11*, 3, 28–32.

Eliade, M. (1987, first published 1957) *The Sacred and the Profane: The Nature of Religion.* San Diego, CA: Harcourt.

Ellis, M. R. and Campbell, J. D. (2004) "Patients' views about discussing spiritual issues with primary care physicians." *Southern Medical Journal 97*, 12, 1158–1164.

Ellis, M. R., Thomlinson, P., Gemmill, C., and Harris, W. (2013) "The spiritual needs and resources of hospitalized primary care patients." *Journal of Religion and Health 52*, 1306–1318.

Epstein, R. M. and Street, R. L. (2011) "Shared mind: Communication, decision making, and autonomy in serious illness." *Annals of Family Medicine 9*, 5, 454–461.

Eriksson, M. and Svedlund, M. (2005) "'The intruder': Spouses' narratives about life with a chronically ill partner." *Journal of Clinical Nursing 15*, 324–333.

Esmaeili, R., Hesamzadeh, A., Bagheri-Nesami, M., and Berger, V. L. (2015) "Exploring the religious and spiritual coping experiences of cases via cancer: A qualitative research." *Journal of Medicine and Life 8*, Special Issue 3, 222–228.

Fadiman, A. (1997) *The Spirit Catches You and You Fall Down: A Hmong Child, Her American Doctors, and the Collision of Two Cultures.* New York, NY: Farrar, Straus and Giroux.

Faith & Leadership (2018) "Kate Bowler: Not all pain has to be explained." Accessed on February 6, 2018 at www.faithandleadership.com/kate-bowler-not-all-pain-has-be-explained?utm_source=FL_newsletter&utm_medium=content&utm_campaign=FL_topstory.

Faraj, C. A. (2019) "Remove your blindfold to your patient's pain." KevinMD. Accessed on March 8, 2019 at www.kevinmd.com/blog/2019/03/remove-your-blindfold-to-your-patients-pain.html.

Ferrell, B., Wittenberg, E., Battista, V., and Walker, G. (2016) "Nurses' experiences of spiritual communication with seriously ill children." *Journal of Palliative Medicine 19*, 11, 1166–1170.

Fetters, M. D. (2006) "The Wizard of Osler: A brief educational intervention combining film and medical readers' theater to teach about power in medicine." *Family Medicine 38*, 5, 323–325.

Finniss, D. G., Kaptchuk, T. J., Miller, F., and Benedetti, F. (2010) "Biological, clinical, and ethical advances of placebo effects." *Lancet 375*, 9715, 686–695.

Fischer, I. C., Cripe, L. D., and Rand, K. L. (2018) "Predicting symptoms of anxiety and depression in patients living with advanced cancer: The differential roles of hope and optimism." *Supportive Care in Cancer 26*, 3471–3477.

Fischer, K. (1988) *Women at the Well: Feminist Perspectives on Spiritual Direction.* New York, NY: Paulist Press.

Fitchett, G., Murphy, P. E., Kim, J., Gibbons, J. L., Cameron, J. R., and Davis, J. A. (2004) "Religious struggle: Prevalence, correlates and mental health risks in diabetic, congestive heart failure, and oncology patients." *International Journal of Psychiatry in Medicine 34*, 2, 179–196.

Fitchett, G., Nieuwsma, J. A., Bates, M. J., Rhodes, J. E., and Meador, K. G. (2014) "Evidence-based chaplaincy care: Attitudes and practices in diverse healthcare chaplain samples." *Journal of Health Care Chaplaincy 20*, 144–160.

Fleisher, K. A., Mackenzie, E. R., Frankel, E. S., Seluzicki, C., Casarett, D., and Mao, J. J. (2014) "Integrative reiki for cancer patients: A program evaluation." *Integrative Cancer Therapies 13*, 1, 62–67.

Fleming, V. and Vidor, K. (1939) *The Wizard of Oz*. United States, Metro-Goldwyn-Mayer (101 minutes).

Folk, K. (2013) "The difference between concentration and insight meditation." Accessed on March 14, 2019 at www.youtube.com/watch?v=xKun84Bs6BM.

Fong, T., Finlayson, M., and Peacock, N. (2006) "The social experience of aging with a chronic illness: Perspectives of older adults with multiple sclerosis." *Disability and Rehabilitation 28*, 11, 695–705.

Fortney, L. and Taylor, M. (2010) "Meditation in medical practice: A review of the evidence and practice." *Primary Care 37*, 1, 81–90.

Frank, A. W. (2013, first published 1995) *The Wounded Storyteller: Body, Illness, and Ethics*. Chicago, IL: University of Chicago Press.

Frank, A. W. (2016) "From sick role to narrative subject: An analytic memoir." *Health 20*, 1, 9–21.

Frank, A. W. (2017) "An illness of one's own: Memoir as art form and research as witness." *Cogent Arts and Humanities 4*, 1, 1343654.

Frankl, V. E. (2014, first published 1946) *Man's Search for Meaning*. Boston, MA: Beacon Press.

Franzen, A. B. (2018) "Influence of physicians' beliefs on propensity to include religion/spirituality in patient interactions." *Journal of Religion and Health 57*, 1581–1597.

Frazier, L. D., Cotrell, V., and Hooker, K. (2003) "Possible selves and illness: A comparison of individuals with Parkinson's disease, early-stage Alzheimer's disease, and healthy older adults." *International Journal of Behavioral Development 27*, 1, 1–11.

Freda, M. F. and Martino, M. L. (2015) "Health and writing: Meaning-making processes in the narratives of parents of children with leukemia." *Qualitative Health Research 25*, 3, 348–359.

Freeman, A. (1998) "Spirituality, well-being, and ministry." *Journal of Pastoral Care 52*, 1, 7–17.

Frosch, D. L. and Elwyn, G. (2010) "I believe, therefore I do." *Journal of General Internal Medicine 26*, 1, 2–4.

Fuentes, J., Armijo-Olivo, S., Funabashi, M., Miciak, M., *et al.* (2014) "Enhanced therapeutic alliance modulates pain intensity and muscle pain sensitivity in patients with chronic low back pain: An experimental controlled study." *Physical Therapy 94*, 4, 477–489.

Furnham, A. (1994) "Explaining health and illness lay perceptions on current and future health, the cause of illness, and the nature of recovery." *Social Science Medicine 39*, 5, 715–725.

Gadit, A. A. (2003) "Health services delivery by shamans: A local experience in Pakistan." *International Journal of Mental Health 32*, 2, 63–83.

Gall, T. L. (2003) "The role of religious resources for older adults coping with illness." *Journal of Pastoral Care and Counseling 57*, 2, 211–224.

Gall, T. L. and Bilodeau, C. (2017) "'Why me?'—Women's use of spiritual causal attirubtions in making sense of breast cancer." *Psychology and Health 32*, 6, 709–727.

Gall, T. L. and Cornblat, M. W. (2002) "Breast cancer survivors give voice: A qualitative analysis of spiritual factors in long-term adjustment." *Psycho-Oncology 11*, 524–535.

Gall, T. L. and Grant, K. (2005) "Spiritual disposition and understanding illness." *Pastoral Psychology 53*, 6, 515–533.

Gall, T. L. and Kafi, S. (2014) "The impact of breast cancer on the mother–daughter relationship: Implications of relationship with God on attachment." *Journal of Spirituality in Mental Health 16*, 111–132.

Gallagher, N. (2013) *Moonlight Sonata at the Mayo Clinic*. New York, NY: Knopf.

Gao, J., Fan, J., Wu, B. W., Halkias, G. T., *et al.* (2017) "Repetitive religious chanting modulates the late-stage brain response to fear- and stress-provoking pictures." *Frontiers in Psychology 7*, 1–12.

Garssen, B., Uwland-Sikkema, N. F., and Visser, A. (2014) "How spirituality helps cancer patients with the adjustment to their disease." *Journal of Religion and Health 54*, 1249–1265.

Gaudette, H. and Jankowski, K. R. B. (2013) "Spiritual coping and anxiety in palliative care patients: A pilot study." *Journal of Health Care Chaplaincy 19*, 131–139.

Gecewicz, C. (2018) "'New Age' beliefs common among both religious and nonreligious Americans." Pew Research Center. Accessed on October 2, 2018 at www.pewresearch. org/fact-tank/2018/10/01/new-age-beliefs-common-among-both-religious-and-nonreligious-americans.

Geertz, C. (1973) *The Interpretation of Cultures: Selected Essays*. New York, NY: Basic Books.

George, L. S. and Park, C. L. (2016) "Meaning in life as comprehension, purpose, and mattering: Toward integration and new research questions." *Review of General Psychology 20*, 3, 205–220.

Gerkin, C. V. (1984) *The Living Human Document: Re-Visioning Pastoral Counseling in a Hermeneutical Mode*. Nashville, TN: Abingdon.

Germeni, E., Vallini, I., Bianchetti, M. G., and Schulz, P. J. (2018) "Reconstructing normality following the diagnosis of a childhood chronic disease: Does 'rare' make a difference?" *European Journal of Pediatrics 177*, 489–495.

Germer, C. K. and Neff, K. D. (2013) "Self-compassion in clinical practice." *Journal of Clinical Psychology 69*, 8, 856–867.

Giffords, E. D. (2003) "Understanding and managing systemic lupus erythematosus (SLE)." *Journal of Social Work in Health Care 37*, 4, 57–72.

Gijsberts, M.-J., Liefbroer, A. I., Otten, R., and Olsman, E. (2019a) "Spiritual care in palliative care: A systematic review of the recent European literature." *Medical Sciences 7*, 25, 1–21.

Gijsberts, M.-J. H. E., van der Steen, J. T., Hertogh, C. M. P., and Deliens, L. (2019b) "Spiritual care provided by nursing home physicians: A nationwide survey." *BMJ Supportive Palliative Care*. doi: 10.1136/bmjspcare-2018-001756.

Glucklich, A. (2001) *Sacred Pain: Hurting the Body for the Sake of the Soul*. New York, NY: Oxford University Press.

Glynn, S. (2013) "97% of doctors prescribe placebos, UK." Medical News Today. Accessed on August 21, 2019 at www.medicalnewstoday.com/articles/258048.php.

Goldberg, P. (2010) *American Veda: From Emerson and the Beatles to Yoga and Meditation—How Indian Spirituality Changed the West*. New York, NY: Three Rivers Press.

Goldstein, L. H., Atkins, L., Landau, S., Brown, R., and Leigh, P. N. (2006) "Predictors of psychological distress in carers of people with amyotrophic lateral sclerosis: A longitudinal study." *Psychological Medicine 36*, 865–875.

Golub, S. A., Gamarel, K. E., and Rendina, J. (2014) "Loss and growth: Identity processes with distinct and complementary impacts on well-being among those living with chronic illness." *Psychology, Health and Medicine 19*, 5, 572–579.

Goodman, D., Morrissey, S., Graham, D., and Bossingham, D. (2005) "Illness representations of systemic lupus erythematosus." *Qualitative Health Research 15*, 5, 606–619.

Gordon, P. A., Feldman, D., Crose, R., Schoen, E., Griffing, G., and Shankar, J. (2002) "The role of religious beliefs in coping with chronic illness." *Counseling and Values 46*, 162–174.

Graffigna, G., Cecchini, I., Breccia, M., Capochiani, E., *et al.* (2017) "Recovering from chronic myeloid leukemia: The patients' perspective seen through the lens of narrative medicine." *Quality of Life Research 26*, 2739–2754.

Graham, E., Walton, H., and Ward, F. (2005) *Theological Reflection: Methods*. London: SCM Press.

Grant, D., Sallaz, J., and Cain, C. (2016) "Bridging science and religion: How health-care workers as storytellers construct spiritual meanings." *Journal for the Scientific Study of Religion 55*, 3, 465–484.

Grant, T. (2016) "I was my husband's caregiver as he was dying of cancer. It was the best seven months of my life." *Washington Post*. Accessed on December 12, 2018 at www.washingtonpost.com/news/inspired-life/wp/2016/08/30/i-was-my-husbands-caregiver-as-he-was-dying-of-cancer-it-was-the-best-seven-months-of-my-life/?noredirect=on&utm_term=.4e91e271ad82.

Grassi, L. and Nanni, M. G. (2016) "Demoralization syndrome: New insights in psychosocial cancer care." *Cancer 122*, 14, 2030–2133.

Grassie, W. (2011) "What's the problem with a good placebo? Or, the deep semiotics of health." Religion Dispatches. Accessed on January 28, 2011 at www.religiondispatches.org/archive/culture/3806/what%E2%80%99s_the_problem_with_a_good_placebo.

Graves, H., Scott, D. L., Lempp, H., and Weinman, J. (2009) "Illness beliefs predict disability in rheumatoid arthritis." *Journal of Psychosomatic Research 67*, 417–423.

Gray, E. (2018) "Christine Blasey Ford didn't have the luxury of being angry." HuffPost. Accessed on September 28, 2018 at www.huffingtonpost.co.uk/entry/christine-blasey-ford-brett-kavanaugh-courtesy-rage_n_5bad53f5e4b09d41eb9fe35a.

Greer, J. A., Jacobs, J. M., El-Jawahri, A., Nipp, R. D., *et al.* (2017) "Role of patient coping strategies in understanding the effects of early palliative care on quality of life and mood." *Journal of Clinical Oncology 36*, 53–60.

Greider, K. J. (2018) "Caring from a Distance: Intersectional Pastoral Theology amid Plurality Regarding Spirituality and Religion." In N. J. Ramsay (ed.) *Pastoral Theology and Care: Critical Trajectories in Theory and Practice*. Oxford: Wiley Blackwell.

Griffiths, J. (2016) "Photos of how life changes when your 20-year-old girlfriend gets cancer." VICE. Accessed on June 25, 2016 at www.vice.com/read/its-cancer-photos-johnny-griffiths-yasmin-jeffery.

Grubbs, J. B., Exline, J. J., Campbell, W. K., Twenge, J. M., and Pargament, K. I. (2018) "God owes me: The role of divine entitlement in predicting struggles with a deity." *Psychology of Religion and Spirituality 10*, 4, 356–367.

Grue, J. (2016) "The social meaning of disability: A reflection on categorisation, stigma and identity." *Sociology of Health and Illness 38*, 6, 957–964.

Grytten, N. and Mäseide, P. (2005) "'What is expressed is not always what is felt': Coping with stigma and the embodiment of perceived illegitimacy of multiple sclerosis." *Chronic Illness 1*, 3, 231–243.

Gubar, S. (2014) "Living with cancer: Practicing loss." *New York Times*. Accessed on April 24, 2014 at http://well.blogs.nytimes.com/2014/04/24/living-with-cancer-practicing-loss/?emc=edit_tnt_20140425&nlid=65079564&tntemail0=y.

Gucciardi, E., Jean-Pierre, N., Karam, G., and Sidani, S. (2016) "Designing and delivering facilitated storytelling interventions for chronic disease self-management: A scoping review." *BMC Health Services Research 16*, 249, 1–13.

Guenther, M. (1992) *Holy Listening: The Art of Spiritual Direction.* Boston, MA: Cowley Publications.

Guerrero-Torrelles, M., Monforte-Royo, C., Rodríquez-Prat, A., Porta-Sales, J., and Balaguer, A. (2017a) "Understanding meaning in life interventions in patients with advanced diseases: A systematic review and realist synthesis." *Palliative Medicine 31*, 9, 798–813.

Guerrero-Torrelles, M., Monforte-Royo, C., Tomás-Sábado, J., Marimon, F., Porta-Sales, J., and Balaguer, A. (2017b) "Meaning in life as a mediator between physical impairment and the wish to hasten death in patients with advanced cancer." *Journal of Pain and Symptom Management 54*, 6, 826–834.

Hafiz, Y. (2013) "Atheist study reveals that non-believers are just as varied as people of faith." HuffPost. Accessed on July 13, 2013 at www.huffingtonpost.com/2013/07/13/atheist-study_n_3587748.html.

Hale-Smith, A., Park, C. L., and Edmondson, D. (2012) "Measuring beliefs about suffering: Development of the Views of Suffering Scale." *Psychological Assessment 24*, 4, 855–866.

Halifax, J. (2011) "The precious necessity of compassion." *Journal of Pain and Symptom Management 41*, 1, 146–153.

Hall, E. H., Meador, K. G., and Koenig, H. G. (2008) "Measuring religiousness in health research: Review and critique." *Journal of Religion and Health 47*, 134–163.

Hamilton, J. B., Moore, A. D., Johnson, K. A., and Koenig, H. G. (2013) "Reading the Bible for guidance, comfort, and strength during stressful life events." *Nursing Research 62*, 3, 178–184.

Hammerschlag, C. A. and Silverman, H. D. (1997) *Healing Ceremonies: Creating Personal Rituals for Spiritual, Emotional, Physical and Mental Health.* New York, NY: Berkeley Publishing Group.

Hanh, T. N. and Anh-Huong, N. (2006) *Walking Meditation.* Louisville, CO: Sounds True.

Hannum, S. M., Smith, K. C., Coa, K., and Klassen, A. C. (2016) "Identity reconstruction among older cancer survivors: Age and meaning in the context of life-altering illness." *Journal of Psychosocial Oncology 34*, 6, 477–492.

Hanson, L. C., Dobbs, D., Usher, B. M., Williams, S., Rawlings, J., and Daaleman, T. P. (2008) "Providers and types of spiritual care during serious illness." *Journal of Palliative Medicine 11*, 6, 906–914.

Hanson, M. J. (1999) "Bioethics and the Challenge of Theodicy." In M. E. Mohrmann and M. J. Hanson (eds) *Pain Seeking Understanding.* Cleveland, OH: The Pilgrim Press.

Haozous, E. A. and Knobf, M. T. (2013) "'All my tears were gone': Suffering and cancer pain in Southwest American Indians." *Journal of Pain and Symptom Management 45*, 6, 1050–1059.

Harley, J. R. (2013) "My life with ALS." *Christian Century 130*, 23–25.

Harner, M. (2013) *Cave and Cosmos: Shamanic Encounters with Another Reality.* Berkeley, CA: North Atlantic Books.

Harnett, S. (2017) "The painful side of positive health care marketing." Shots: Health News from NPR. Accessed on December 4, 2017 at www.npr.org/sections/health-shots/2017/10/08/555370189/the-painful-side-of-positive-health-care-marketing.

Harpham, W. S. (2018) "What cancer taught this physician about hope." KevinMD. Accessed on December 13, 2018 at www.kevinmd.com/blog/2018/12/what-cancer-taught-this-physician-about-hope.html.

Harrington, A. (2008) *The Cure Within: A History of Mind-Body Medicine.* New York, NY: W. W. Norton & Company.

Harris, D. L. and Winokuer, H. R. (2016) *Principles and Practice of Grief Counseling.* New York, NY: Springer Publishing.

Harris, J. I., Usset, T., Krause, L., Schill, D., *et al.* (2018) "Spiritual/religious distress is associated with pain catastrophizing and interference in veterans with chronic pain." *Pain Medicine 19*, 4, 757–763.

Harrison, M. O., Koenig, H. G., Hays, J. C., Eme-Akwari, A. G., and Pargament, K. I. (2001) "The epidemiology of religious coping: A review of recent literature." *International Review of Psychiatry 13*, 86–93.

Harvey, I. S. (2009) "Spiritual self-management: A look at older adults with chronic illness." *Journal of Religion, Spirituality and Aging 21*, 3, 200–218.

Harvey, I. S. and Silverman, M. (2007) "The role of spirituality in the self-management of chronic illness among older African and Whites." *Journal of Cross-Cultural Gerontology 22*, 2, 205–220.

Hashemi, M., Irajpour, A., and Taleghani, F. (2018) "Caregivers needing care: The unmet needs of family caregivers of end-of-life cancer patients." *Supportive Care in Cancer 26*, 759–766.

Haug, S. H. K., DeMarinis, V., Danbolt, L. J., and Kvigne, K. (2016) "The illness reframing process in an ethnic-majority population of older people with incurable cancer: Variations of cultural- and existential meaning-making adjustments." *Mental Health, Religion and Culture 19*, 2, 150–163.

Hay, L. (2004, first published 1984) *You Can Heal Your Life.* Carlsbad, CA: Hay House Publishing.

HealthCare Chaplaincy Network (2018) "Making spiritual care a priority." Accessed on September 25, 2018 at https://spiritualcareassociation.org.

Heilferty, C. M. (2018) "'Hopefully this will all make sense at some point': Meaning and performance in illness blogs." *Journal of Pediatric Oncology Nursing 35*, 4, 287–295.

Helgeson, V. S., Jakubiak, B., Van Vleet, M., and Zajdel, M. (2018) "Communal coping and adjustment to chronic illness: Theory update and evidence." *Personality and Social Psychology Review 22*, 2, 170–195.

Helsel, D. G., Mochel, M., and Bauer, R. (2004) "Shamans in a Hmong American community." *Journal of Alternative and Complementary Medicine 10*, 6, 933–938.

Hendrickson, B. (2015) "Neo-shamans, curanderismo and scholars: Metaphysical blending in contemporary Mexican American folk healing." *Nova Religio: The Journal of Alternative and Emergent Religions 19*, 1, 25–44.

Heyen, H., Walton, M. N., and Jonker, E. (2016) "Spiritual care and logotherapy." *Health and Social Care Chaplaincy 4*, 1, 35–50.

Hilbert, R. A. (1984) "The acultural dimensions of chronic pain: Flawed reality construction and the problem of meaning." *Social Problems 31*, 4, 365–378.

Hill, C. E. (2017) "Therapists' perspectives about working with meaning in life in psychotherapy: A survey." *Counselling Psychology Quarterly 30*, 4, 373–391.

Hirsch, M. L. (2018) *Invisible: How Young Women with Serious Health Issues Navigate Work, Relationships, and the Pressure to Seem Just Fine.* Boston, MA: Beacon Press.

Hogue, D. A. (1999) "Shelters and pathways: Ritual and pastoral counseling." *Journal of Supervision and Training in Ministry 19*, 57–67.

Hogue, D. A. (2003) *Remembering the Future, Imagining the Past: Story, Ritual, and the Human Brain.* Cleveland, OH: Pilgrim Press.

Holmberg, A., Jensen, P., and Ulland, D. (2017) "To make room or not to make room: Clients' narratives about exclusion and inclusion of spirituality in family therapy practice." *Australian and New Zealand Journal of Family Therapy 38*, 1, 15–26.

Holmes, L. (2017a) "What not to say to someone with cancer, in one comic: Attention all friends and family." HuffPost. Accessed on March 4, 2019 at www.huffpost.com/entry/what-not-to-say-to-someone-who-is-a-cancer-patient-in-one-comic_n_594975f6e4b0e84975505144.

Holmes, L. (2017b) "Cancer doesn't choose who survives based on how hard someone fights." Accessed on July 9, 2019 at www.huffingtonpost.co.uk/entry/cancer-john-mccain-fighter_n_5970ae8de4b0aa14ea77f55b.

Horrigan, B. (2008) "Alberto Villodo, PhD: Healing and the four levels of existence." *Explore 4*, 2, 140–147.

Horvath, A. O. (2001) "The therapeutic alliance: Concepts, research and training." *Australian Psychologist 36*, 2, 170–176.

Houston, J. (2012) *The Wizard of Us: Transformational Lessons from Oz.* New York, NY: Atria Books.

Huber, M., Knottnerus, A. J., Green, L., van der Horst, H., *et al.* (2011) "How should we define health?" *British Medical Journal 343*, d4163, 1–3.

Hunt, L., Nikopoulou-Smyrni, P., and Reynolds, F. (2014) "'It gave me something big in my life to wonder and think about which took over the space…and not MS': Managing well-being in multiple sclerosis through art-making." *Disability and Rehabilitation 36*, 14, 1139–1147.

Hunt, L. M., Jordan, B., and Irwin, S. (1989) "Views of what's wrong: Diagnosis and patients' concepts of illness." *Social Science and Medicine 28*, 9, 945–956.

Hutch, R. A. (2013) "Health and healing: Spiritual, pharmaceutical, and mechanical medicine." *Journal of Religion and Health 52*, 955–965.

Ingerman, S. (2012) "The power of shamanism to heal emotional and physical illness." Accessed on July 14, 2018 at www.sandraingerman.com/sandrasarticles/abstractonshamanism.html.

International Association for the Study of Pain (2018) "IASP terminology." Accessed on September 29, 2018 at www.iasp-pain.org/Education/Content.aspx?ItemNumber=1698.

Ironside, P. M., Scheckel, M., Wessels, C., Bailey, M. E., Powers, S., and Seeley, D. K. (2003) "Experiencing chronic illness: Cocreating new understandings." *Qualitative Health Research 13*, 2, 171–183.

Irvine, H., Davidson, C., Hoy, K., and Lowe-Strong, A. (2009) "Psychosocial adjustment to multiple sclerosis: Exploration of identity redefinition." *Disability and Rehabilitation 31*, 8, 599–606.

Jack, A. I., Dawson, A. J., Begany, K. L., Leckie, R. L., *et al.* (2013) "fMRI reveals reciprocal inhibition between social and physical cognitive domains." *NeuroImage 66*, 385–401.

Jacob, J. A. (2016) "As opioid prescribing guidelines tighten, mindfulness meditation holds promise for pain relief." JAMA Network. Accessed on October 10, 2019 at http://jamanetwork.com/journals/jama/article-abstract/2524308.

Jacqueline, I. (2018) *Surviving and Thriving with an Invisible Chronic Illness.* Oakland, CA: New Harbinger Publications.

Jain, S. and Mills, P. J. (2010) "Biofield therapies: Helpful or full of hype? A best-evidence synthesis." *International Journal of Behavioral Medicine 17*, 1–16.

Jakoby, N. R. (2012) "Grief as a social emotion: Theoretical perspectives." *Death Studies 36*, 8, 679–711.

James, W. (2002, first published 1994) *The Varieties of Religious Experience: A Study in Human Nature.* New York, NY: Modern Library.

Jampolsky, G. (1993) *The Tao of Healing: Meditations for Body and Spirit.* Novato, CA: New World Library.

Jaquad, S. (2015) "Life, interrupted: The 100 day project." *New York Times.* Accessed on October 15, 2015 at https://well.blogs.nytimes.com/author/suleika-jaouad.

Jette, A. M. and Keysor, J. J. (2003) "Disability models: Implications for arthritis exercise and physical activity interventions." *Arthritis and Rheumatism (Arthritis Care and Research) 49*, 1, 114–120.

Johnsdotter, S., Ingvarsdotter, K., Ostman, M., and Carlbom, A. (2011) "Koran reading and negotiation with jinn: Strategies to deal with mental ill health among Swedish Somalis." *Mental Health, Religion and Culture 14*, 8, 741–755.

Jors, K., Büssing, A., Hvidt, N. C., and Baumann, K. (2015) "Personal prayer in patients dealing with chronic illness: A review of the research literature." *Evidence-based Complementary and Alternative Medicine 2015*, 1–12.

Jou, J. and Johnson, P. J. (2016) "Nondisclosure of complementary and alternative medicine to primary care physicians: Findings from the 2012 National Health Interview Survey." *JAMA 176*, 4, 545–546.

Jurecic, A. (2012) *Illness as Narrative*. Pittsburgh, PA: University of Pittsburgh Press.

Jyotsna, V. P., Joshi, A., Ambekar, S., Kumar, N., Dhawan, A., and Sreenivas, V. (2012) "Comprehensive yogic breathing program improves quality of life in patients with diabetes." *Indian Journal of Endocrinology and Metabolism 16*, 3, 423–428.

Kabat-Zinn, J. (1990) *Full Catastrophe Living: Using the Wisdom of Your Body and Mind to Face Stress, Pain, and Illness*. New York, NY: Bantam Dell.

Kagawa-Singer, M., Dressler, W., and George, S. (2016) "Culture: The missing link in health research." *Social Science and Medicine 170*, 237–246.

Kahn, Z. H. and Watson, P. J. (2006) "Construction of the Pakistani Religious Coping Practices Scale: Correlations with religious coping, religious orientation, and reactions to stress among Muslim university students." *International Journal for the Psychology of Religion 16*, 2, 101–112.

Kalitzkus, V. and Matthiessen, P. F. (2009) "Narrative-based medicine: Potential, pitfalls, and practice." *Permanente Journal 13*, 1, 80–86.

Karp, M. (2010) "What has spiritual direction opened for you?" SDI. Accessed on July 2, 2010 at http://info.sdiworld.org/post/what-has-spiritual-direction-opened-for-you.

Kaufman, P. (2018) "Writing and teaching with a terminal illness." *The Chronicle of Higher Education*. Accessed on July 9, 2019 at www.chronicle.com/article/WritingTeaching-With-a/245183.

Kayser, K. and Sormanti, M. (2002) "Identity and the illness experience: Issues faced by mothers with cancer." *Illness, Crisis and Loss 10*, 1, 10–26.

Keefe, F. J., Affleck, G., Lefebvre, J., Underwood, L., *et al.* (2001) "Living with rheumatoid arthritis: The role of daily spirituality and daily religious and spiritual coping." *Journal of Pain 2*, 2, 101–110.

Keefe, F. J., Smith, S., Buffington, A. L. H., Gibson, J., Studts, J. L., and Caldwell, D. S. (2002) "Recent advances and future directions in the biopsychosocial assessment and treatment of arthritis." *Journal of Consulting and Clinical Psychology 70*, 3, 640–655.

Kelley, J. E., Lumley, M. A., and Leisen, J. C. C. (1997) "Health effects of emotional disclosure in rheumatoid arthritis patients." *Health Psychology 16*, 4, 331–340.

Kelly, C. G., Cudney, S., and Weinert, C. (2012) "Use of creative arts as a complementary therapy by rural women coping with chronic illness." *Journal of Holistic Nursing 30*, 1, 48–54.

Kelly, J. A., May, C. S., and Maurer, S. H. (2016) "Assessment of the spiritual needs of primary caregivers of children with life-limiting illnesses is valuable yet inconsistently performed in the hospital." *Journal of Palliative Medicine 19*, 7, 763–766.

Keshet, Y. and Liberman, I. (2014) "Coping with illness and threat: Why non-religious Jews choose to consult rabbis on healthcare issues." *Journal of Religion and Health 53*, 4, 1146–1160.

Kim, E. S. and VanderWeele, T. J. (2019) "Mediators of the association between religious service attendance and mortality." *American Journal of Epidemiology 188*, 1, 96–101.

Kim, H., Lee, S., Cheon, J., Hong, S., and Chang, M. (2018) "A comparative study to identify factors of caregiver burden between baby boomers and post baby boomers: A secondary analysis of a US online caregiver survey." *BMC Public Health 18*, 579, 1–9.

Kim, Y., Carver, C. S., Shaffer, K. M., Gansler, T., and Cannady, R. S. (2015) "Cancer caregiving predicts physical impairments: Roles of earlier caregiving stress and being a spousal caregiver." *Cancer 121*, 1302–1310.

Kim, Y., Schulz, R., and Carver, C. S. (2007) "Benefit finding in the cancer caregiving experience." *Psychosomatic Medicine 69*, 283–291.

King, S. D. W., Fitchett, G., Murphy, P. E., Pargament, K. I., Harrison, D. A., and Loggers, E. T. (2017a) "Determining the best methods to screen for religious/spiritual distress." *Supportive Care in Cancer 25*, 471–479.

King, S. D. W., Fitchett, G., Murphy, P. E., Pargament, K. I., *et al.* (2017b) "Spiritual or religious struggle in hematopoietic cell transplant survivors." *Pscyho-Oncology 26*, 270–277.

Kinsley, D. (1996) *Health, Healing, and Religion: A Cross-Cultural Perspective.* Upper Saddle River, NJ: Prentice Hall.

Kirmayer, L. J. (2004) "The cultural diversity of healing: Meaning, metaphor and mechanism." *British Medical Bulletin 69*, 33–48.

Kirmayer, L. J. and Sartorius, N. (2007) "Cultural models and somatic syndromes." *Psychosomatic Medicine 69*, 832–840.

Kistner, U. (1998) "Illness as metaphor? The role of linguistic categories in the history of medicine." *Studies in 20th Century Literature 22*, 1, article 3.

Klass, P. (2014) "Illness not as metaphor." *New England Journal of Medicine 371*, 22, 2057–2059.

Kleinman, A. (1988) *The Illness Narratives: Suffering, Healing, and the Human Condition.* New York, NY: Basic Books.

Knitter, P. F. (2009) *Without Buddha I Could Not Be a Christian.* London: Oneworld Publications.

Knowles, E. D., Wearing, J. R., and Campos, B. (2011) "Culture and health benefits of expressive writing." *Social Psychological and Personality Science 2*, 4, 408–415.

Koenig, H. G. (2000) "Religion and medicine I: Historical background and reasons for separation." *International Journal of Psychiatry in Medicine 30*, 4, 385–398.

Koenig, H. G. and McCullough, M. E. (2012, first published 2001) *Handbook of Religion and Health.* New York, NY: Oxford University Press.

Koffman, J., Morgan, M., Edmonds, P., Speck, P., and Higginson, I. J. (2008) "'I know he controls cancer': The meanings of religion among Black Caribbean and White British patients with advanced cancer." *Social Science and Medicine 67*, 780–789.

Kollar, N. R. (1989) "Rituals and the Disenfranchised Griever." In K. J. Doka (ed.) *Disenfranchised Grief: Recognizing Hidden Sorrow.* Lexington, MA: Lexington Books.

Kørup, A. K., Søndergaard, J., Christensen, R. D., Nielsen, C. T., *et al.* (2018) "Religious values in clinical practice are here to stay." *Journal of Religion and Health.* doi: 10.1007/s10943-018-0715-y.

Kralik, D. (2002) "The quest for ordinariness: Transition experienced by midlife women living with chronic illness." *Journal of Advanced Nursing 39*, 2, 146–154.

Kralik, D., Brown, M., and Koch, T. (2001) "Women's experiences of 'being diagnosed' with a long-term illness." *Journal of Advanced Nursing 33*, 5, 594–602.

Krause, N. and Pargament, K. I. (2018) "Reading the Bible, stressful life events, and hope: Assessing an overlooked coping resource." *Journal of Religion and Health 57*, 1428–1439.

Krippner, S. (2012) "Shamans as healers, counselors, and psychotherapists." *International Journal of Transpersonal Studies 31*, 2, 72–79.

Kristiansen, M., Irshad, T., Worth, A., Bhopal, R., Lawton, J., and Sheikh, A. (2014) "The practice of hope: A longitudinal, multi-perspective qualitative study among South Asian Sikhs and Muslims with life-limiting illness in Scotland." *Ethnicity and Health 19*, 1, 1–19.

Kristofferzon, M.-L., Engström, M., and Nilsson, A. (2018) "Coping mediates the relationship between sense of coherence and mental quality of life in patients with chronic illness: A cross-sectional study." *Quality of Life Research 27*, 1855–1863.

Kroenke, K., Spitzer, R. L., Williams, J. B. W., and Löwe, B. (2010) "The Patient Health Questionnaire Somatic, Anxiety and Depressive Symptom Scales: A systematic review." *General Hospital Psychiatry 32*, 345–359.

Kruizinga, R., Scherer-Rath, M., Schilderman, H. J. B. A. M., Puchalski, C. M., and van Laarhoven, H. H. W. M. (2018) "Toward a fully fledged integration of spiritual care and medical care." *Journal of Pain and Symptom Management 55*, 3, 1035–1039.

Kübler-Ross, E. (1969) On *Death and Dying*. New York, NY: Scribner.

Kudla, D., Kujur, J., Tigga, S., Tirkey, P., Rai, P., and Fegg, M. J. (2015) "Meaning in life experiences at the end of life: Validation of the Hindi version of the schedule for meaning in life evaluation and a cross-cultural comparison between Indian and German palliative care patients." *Journal of Pain and Symptom Management 49*, 1, 79–88.

Kukulka, K., Washington, K. T., Govindarajan, R., and Mehr, D. R. (2019) "Stakeholder perspectives on the biopsychosocial and spiritual realities of living with ALS: Implications for palliative care teams." *American Journal of Hospice and Palliative Medicine*. doi: 10.1177/1049909119834493.

Kuluski, K., Bensimon, C. M., Alvaro, C., Lyons, R. F., Schaink, A. K., and Tobias, R. (2014) "Life interrupted: The impact of complex chronic disease from the perspective of hospitalized patients." *Illness, Crisis and Loss 22*, 2, 127–144.

Kurapati, R. (2018) "Do doctors see patients as machines?" KevinMD. Accessed on March 7, 2018 at www.kevinmd.com/blog/2018/03/doctors-see-patients-machines.html.

Kutz, I. (2000) "Job and his 'doctors': Bedside wisdom in the Book of Job." *British Medical Journal 321*, 7276, 1613–1615.

Laing, C. M., Moules, N. J., Sinclair, S., and Estefan, A. (2019) "Digital storytelling as a psychosocial tool for adult cancer survivors." *Oncology Nursing Forum 46*, 2, 147–154.

Laird, L. D., Curtis, C. E., and Morgan, J. R. (2017) "Finding spirits in spirituality: What are we measuring in spirituality and health research?" *Journal of Religion and Health 56*, 1–20.

Larsen, P. D. (2016) "Chronicity." Nurse Key. Accessed on October 17, 2018 at https://nursekey.com/chronicity.

Larsson, A. T. and Grassman, E. J. (2012) "Bodily changes among people living with physical impairments and chronic illnesses: Biographical disruption or normal illness?" *Sociology of Health and Illness 34*, 8, 1156–1169.

Lartey, E. Y. (2003) In *Living Color: An Intercultural Approach to Pastoral Care and Counseling*. London: Jessica Kingsley Publishers.

Leavey, G., Loewenthal, K., and King, M. (2016) "Locating the social origins of mental illness: The explanatory models of mental illness among clergy from different ethnic and faith backgrounds." *Journal of Religion and Health 55*, 1607–1622.

Lempp, H., Scott, D., and Kingsley, G. (2006) "The personal impact of rheumatoid arthritis on patients' identity: A qualitative study." *Chronic Illness 2*, 109–120.

Leng, S. (2013) "The medical model versus the nursing model: A difference in philosophy." KevinMD. Accessed on May 13, 2013 at www.kevinmd.com/blog/2013/05/medical-model-nursing-model-difference-philosophy.html.

Leonardi-Warren, K., Wenger, B., and Fink, R. (2016) "Sexual health: Exploring patient needs and healthcare provider comfort and knowledge." *Clinical Journal of Oncology Nursing 20*, 6, E1–E6.

Levin, J. (2008) "Esoteric healing traditions: A conceptual overview." *Explore 4*, 2, 101–112.

Levin, J. (2009) "How faith heals: A theoretical model." *Explore 5*, 2, 77–96.

Levin, J. (2011) "Energy healers: Who they are and what they do." *Explore 7*, 1, 13–26.

Levin, J. (2016) "Prevalence and religious predictors of healing prayer use in the USA: Findings from the Baylor Religion Survey." *Journal of Religion and Health 55*, 4, 1136–1158.

Library of Congress (2018) "The Wizard of Oz: An American Fairy Tale." Accessed on September 12, 2018 at www.loc.gov/exhibits/oz/ozsect2.html.

Liebhold, P. (2016) "Populism and the World of Oz." National Museum of American History. Accessed on September 12, 2018 at http://americanhistory.si.edu/blog/populism-oz.

Linn, D. and Wells, S. J. (2018) *Searching… A Peek into the Invisible World of Energy and Healing*. Bloomington, IN: Balboa Press.

Lipka, M. (2013) "Five facts about atheists." Pew Research Center. Accessed on October 23, 2013 at www.pewresearch.org/fact-tank/2013/10/23/5-facts-about-atheists.

Livneh, H. (2001) "Psychosocial adaptation to chronic illness and disability: A conceptual framework." *Rehabilitation Counseling Bulletin 44*, 3, 151–160.

Loffer, S. L. (2000) "Returning to ourselves: Women thriving with chronic illness." Doctoral dissertation, Institute of Transpersonal Psychology.

Lomax, J. W., Kripal, J. J., and Pargament, K. I. (2011) "Perspectives on 'sacred moments' in psychotherapy." *American Journal of Psychiatry 168*, 1, 12–18.

Lopez, G., Milbury, K., Chen, M., Li, Y., Bruera, E., and Cohen, L. (2019) "Couples' symptom burden in oncology care: Perception of self and the other." *Supportive Care in Cancer 27*, 139–145.

Lu, Q., Dong, L., Wu, I. H. C., You, J., Huang, J., and Hu, Y. (2019) "The impact of an expressive writing intervention on quality of life among Chinese breast cancer patients undergoing chemotherapy." *Supportive Care in Cancer 27*, 165–173.

Lucette, A., Ironson, G., Pargament, K. I., and Krause, N. (2016) "Spirituality and religiousness are associated with fewer depressive symptoms in individuals with medical conditions." *Psychosomatics 57*, 505–513.

Luckenbaugh, M. (2019) "Healers: Peel away the layers." KevinMD. Accessed on February 20, 2019 at www.kevinmd.com/blog/2019/02/healers-peel-away-the-layers.html.

Lyketsos, C. G. and Chisolm, M. S. (2009) "The trap of meaning: A public health tragedy." *JAMA 302*, 4, 432–433.

Lyons, R. F. and Sullivan, M. J. L. (1998) "Curbing Loss in Illness and Disability: A Relationship Perspective." In J. H. Harvey (ed.) *Perspectives on Loss: A Sourcebook*. Philadelphia, PA: Brunner/Mazel.

McCaffrey, A. M., Pugh, G. F., and O'Connor, B. B. (2007) "Understanding patient preference for integrative medical care: Results from patient focus groups." *Journal of General Internal Medicine 22*, 11, 1500–1505.

McCaffrey, N., Bradley, S., Ratcliffe, J., and Currow, D. C. (2016) "What aspects of quality of life are important from palliative care patients' perspectives? A systematic review of qualitative research." *Journal of Pain and Symptom Management 52*, 2, 318–328. e315.

McConnell, K. M. and Pargament, K. I. (2006) "Examining the links between spiritual struggles and symptoms of psychopathology in a national sample." *Journal of Clinical Psychology 62*, 12, 1469–1484.

McCullough, M. E., Friedman, H. S., Enders, C. K., and Martin, L. R. (2009) "Does devoutness delay death? Psychological investment in religion and its association with longevity in the Terman sample." *Journal of Personality and Social Psychology 97*, 5, 866–882.

MacDonald, K. (2017) "Using poetry to explore normalcy as a coping mechanism for young people with cystic fibrosis." *Journal of Research in Nursing 22*, 6–7, 479–491.

McDonough-Means, S. I., Kreitzer, M. J., and Bell, I. R. (2004) "Fostering a healing presence and investigating its mediators." *Journal of Alternative and Complementary Medicine 10*, Supplement 1, S25–S41.

McFadden, K. L., Hernández, T. D., and Ito, T. A. (2010) "Attitudes toward complementary and alternative medicine influence its use." *Explore 6*, 6, 380–388.

McGlensey, M. (2015) "31 secrets of people who live with anxiety." The Mighty. Accessed on May 19, 2015 at https://Themighty.com/2015/05/what-anxiety-feels-like.

McIntosh, D. N. (1997) "Religion-as-Schema, with Implications for the Relation between Religion and Coping." In B. Spilka and D. N. McIntosh (eds) *The Psychology of Religion: Theoretical Approaches*. Boulder, CO: Westview Press.

MacLean, C. D., Susi, B., Phifer, N., Schultz, L., *et al.* (2003) "Patient preference for physician discussion and practice of spirituality." *Journal of General Internal Medicine 18*, 38–43.

MacLeod, R. D., Wilson, D. M., and Phillipa, M. (2012) "Assisted or hastened death: The healthcare practitioner's dilemma." *Global Journal of Health Science 4*, 6, 87–98.

McManus, D. E. (2017) "Reiki is better than placebo and has broad potential as a complementary health therapy." *Journal of Evidence-Based Complementary and Alternative Medicine 22*, 4, 1051–1057.

Maggio, L. M. (2007) "Externalizing lupus: A therapist's/patient's challenge." *Professional Psychology: Research and Practice 38*, 6, 576–581.

Mahdavi, B., Fallahi-Khoshknab, M., Mohammadi, F., Hossenini, M. A., and Haghi, M. (2017) "Effects of spiritual group therapy on caregiver strain in home caregivers of the elderly with Alzheimer's disease." *Archives of Psychiatric Nursing 31*, 3, 269–273.

Mahon, G., O'Brien, B., and O'Conor, L. (2014) "The experience of chronic illness among a group of Irish patients: A qualitative study." *Journal of Research in Nursing 19*, 4, 330–342.

Maiko, S., Johns, S. A., Helft, P. R., Slaven, J. E., Cottingham, A. H., and Torke, A. M. (2019) "Spiritual experiences of adults with advanced cancer in outpatient clinical settings." *Journal of Pain and Symptom Management 57*, 3, 576–586.e1.

Mann, S. B. (1982) *Being Ill: Personal and Social Meaning*. New York, NY: Irvington Publishers.

Martino, M. L. and Freda, M. F. (2016) "Meaning-making process related to temporality during breast cancer traumatic experience: The clinical use of narrative to promote a new continuity of life." *Europe's Journal of Psychology 12*, 4, 622–634.

Martino, M. L., Freda, M. F., and Camera, F. (2013) "Effects of guided written disclosure protocol on mood states and psychological symptoms among parents of off-therapy acute lymphoblastic leukemia children." *Journal of Health Psychology 18*, 727–736.

Masters, P. (2018a) "Are physicians losing the healing touch?" KevinMD. Accessed on July 9, 2019 at www.kevinmd.com/blog/2018/01/physicians-losing-healing-touch.html.

Masters, P. (2018b) "The power of the tincture of time." KevinMD. Accessed on December 6, 2018 at www.kevinmd.com/blog/2018/12/the-power-of-the-tincture-of-time.html.

Matini, L. and Ogden, J. (2016) "A qualitative study of patients' experience of living with inflammatory bowel disease: A preliminary focus on the notion of adaptation." *Journal of Health Psychology 21*, 11, 2493–2505.

Matzo, M. (2015) "Sexuality." In B. R. Ferrell, N. Coyle, and J. A. Paice (eds) *Oxford Textbook of Palliative Nursing*. Oxford: Oxford University Press.

Mehl-Madrona, L. E. (1999) "Native American medicine in the treatment of chronic illness: Developing an integrated program and evaluating its effectiveness." *Alternative Therapies in Health and Medicine 5*, 1, 36–44.

Mehta, A. and Cohen, S. R. (2009) "Palliative care: A need for a family systems approach." *Palliative and Supportive Care 7*, 235–243.

Melnick, M. (2017) "Meditation health benefits: What the practice does to your body." HuffPost. Accessed on October 10, 2019 at www.huffpost.com/entry/meditation-health-benefits_n_3178731.

Mercadante, L. (2012) "The seeker next door: What drives the 'spiritual but not religious'?" *Christian Century 129*, 11, 30–33.

Merritt, J. (2018) "It's getting harder to talk about God." *New York Times*. Accessed on October 16, 2018 at www.nytimes.com/2018/10/13/opinion/sunday/talk-god-sprituality-christian.html.

Metta, E., Bailey, A., Kessy, F., Geubbels, E., Hutter, I., and Haisma, H. (2015) "'In a situation of rescuing life': Meanings given to diabetes symptoms and care-seeking practices among adults in Southeastern Tanzania: A qualitative inquiry." *BMC Public Health 15*, 224, 1–12.

Meyersbyrg, C. A. and McNally, R. J. (2011) "Reduced death distress and greater meaning in life among individuals reporting past life memory." *Personality and Individual Differences 50*, 1218–1221.

Michigan Medicine (2018) "Guided imagery podcasts." Rogel Cancer Center. Accessed on February 6, 2019 at www.rogelcancercenter.org/podcasts/guided-imagery-podcasts.

Michlig, G. J., Westergaard, R. P., Lam, Y., Ahmadi, A., *et al.* (2018) "Avoidance, meaning and grief: Psychosocial factors influencing engagement in HIV care." *AIDS Care 30*, 4, 511–517.

Middleton-Green, L. and Chatterjee, J. (2017) *End of Life Care for People with Dementia*. London: Jessica Kingsley Publishers.

Miles, A. (2009) "Of butterflies and wolves: Enacting lupus transformations on the Internet." *Anthropology and Medicine 16*, 1, 1–12.

Miller, E. (2014) "How I feel after chemotherapy." KevinMD. Accessed on July 9, 2018 at www.kevinmd.com/blog/2014/02/feel-chemotherapy.html.

Miller, F. G. and Colloca, L. (2009) "The legitimacy of placebo treatments in clinical practice: Evidence and ethics." *American Journal of Bioethics 9*, 12, 39–47.

Miller, G. (2010) "Beyond DSM: Seeking a brain-based classification of mental illness." *Science 327*, 5972, 1437.

Miller, W. R. and C'de Baca, J. (2001) *Quantum Change: When Epiphanies and Sudden Insights Transform Ordinary Lives*. New York, NY: Guilford Press.

Miller-McLemore, B. J. (1988) "Doing wrong, getting sick, and dying." *Christian Century 105*, 6, 186–190.

Miller-McLemore, B. J. (2008) "Revisiting the living human web: Theological education and the role of clinical pastoral education." *Journal of Pastoral Care and Counseling 62*, 1–2, 3–18.

Mitchell, K. R. and Anderson, H. (1983) *All Our Losses, All Our Griefs: Resources for Pastoral Care*. Louisville, KY: Westminster John Knox Press.

Möllerberg, M.-L., Sandgren, A., Swahnberg, K., and Benzein, E. (2017) "Familial interaction patterns during the palliative phase of a family member living with cancer." *Journal of Hospice and Palliative Nursing 19*, 1, 68–74.

Molzahn, A., Sheilds, L., Bruce, A., Stajduhar, K., *et al.* (2012) "People living with serious illness: Stories of spirituality." *Journal of Clinical Nursing 21*, 2347–2356.

Monaghan, L. F. and Gabe, J. (2015) "Chronic illness as biographical contingency? Young people's experiences of asthma." *Sociology of Health and Illness 37*, 8, 1236–1253.

Moody, R. A. (2013) "Near-death experiences: An essay in medicine and philosophy." *Missouri Medicine 110*, 5, 368–371.

Morone, N. E., Lynch, C. S., Greco, C. M., Tindle, H. A., and Weiner, D. K. (2008) "'I felt like a new person.' The effects of mindfulness meditation on older adults with chronic pain: Qualitative narrative analysis of diary entries." *Journal of Pain 9*, 9, 841–848.

Moschella, M. C. (2011) "Spiritual autobiography and older adults." *Pastoral Psychology* 60, 95–98.

Moschella, M. C. (2018) "Practice Matters: New Directions in Ethnography and Qualitative Research." In N. J. Ramsay (ed.) *Pastoral Theology and Care: Critical Trajectories in Theory and Practice.* Oxford: John Wiley and Sons.

Moskowitz, J. T. (2010) "Positive Affect at the Onset of Chronic Illness: Planting the Seeds of Resilience." In J. W. Reich, A. J. Zautra, and J. S. Hall (eds) *Handbook of Adult Resilience.* New York, NY: Guilford Press.

Moskowitz, J. T. and Wrubel, J. (2005) "Coping with HIV as a chronic illness: A longitudinal analysis of illness appraisals." *Psychology and Health 20,* 4, 509–531.

Mount, B. M., Boston, P. H., and Cohen, S. R. (2007) "Healing connections: On moving from suffering to a sense of well-being." *Journal of Pain and Symptom Management* 33, 4, 372–388.

Munck, B., Fridlund, B., and Mårtensson, J. (2008) "Next-of-kin caregivers in palliative home care—from control to loss of control." *Journal of Advanced Nursing 64,* 6, 578–586.

Murray, S. A., Kendall, M., Boyd, K., Worth, A., and Benton, T. F. (2004) "Exploring the spiritual needs of people dying of lung cancer or heart failure: A prospective qualitative interview study of patients and their carers." *Palliative Medicine 18,* 39–45.

Nabolsi, M. M. and Carson, A. M. (2011) "Spirituality, illness and personal responsibility: The experience of Jordanian Muslim men with coronary artery disease." *Scandinavian Journal of Caring Sciences 25,* 716–724.

Nakau, M., Imanishi, J., Imanishi, J., Watanabe, S., *et al.* (2013) "Spiritual care of cancer patients by integrated medicine in urban green space: A pilot study." *Explore 9,* 2, 87–90.

National Consensus Project for Quality Palliative Care (2018) *Clinical Practice Guidelines for Quality Palliative Care.* Pittsburgh, PA: National Consensus Project for Quality Palliative Care.

Neimeyer, R. A., Klass, D., and Dennis, M. R. (2014) "A social constructionist account of grief: Loss and the narration of meaning." *Death Studies 38,* 485–498.

Nelson, S. (2003) "Facing evil: Evil's many faces. Five paradigms for understanding evil." *Interpretation 57,* 4, 398–413.

Neuger, C. C. (2001) *Counseling Women: A Narrative, Pastoral Approach.* Minneapolis, MN: Fortress Press.

Ngyuyen, H. T., Yamada, A. M., and Dinh, T. Q. (2012) "Religious leaders' assessment and attribution of the causes of mental illness: An in-depth exploration of Vietnamese American Buddhist leaders." *Mental Health, Religion and Culture 15,* 5, 511–527.

Nichols, L. M. and Hunt, B. (2011) "The significance of spirituality for individuals with chronic illness: Implications for mental health counseling." *Journal of Mental Health Counseling 33,* 1, 51–66.

Nissen, K. G., Trevino, K. M., Lange, T., and Prigerson, H. G. (2016) "Family relationships and psychosocial dysfunction among family caregivers of patients with advanced cancer." *Journal of Pain and Symptom Management 52,* 6, 841–849.

Nissim, R., Gagliese, L., and Rodin, G. (2009) "The desire for hastened death in individuals with advanced cancer: A longitudinal qualitative study." *Social Science and Medicine 69,* 2, 165–171.

Noorani, N. H. and Montagnini, M. (2007) "Recognizing depression in palliative care patients." *Journal of Palliative Medicine 10,* 2, 458–464.

Nyatanga, B. (2016) "Death anxiety and palliative nursing." *British Journal of Community Nursing 21,* 12, 636.

O'Grady, K. A. and Richards, P. S. (2010) "The role of inspiration in the helping professions." *Psychology of Religion and Spirituality 2,* 1, 57–66.

O'Neill, E. S. and Morrow, L. L. (2001) "The symptom experience of women with chronic illness." *Journal of Advanced Nursing 33*, 2, 257–268.

Ofri, D. (2017) "The conversation placebo." *New York Times*. Accessed on January 19, 2017 at www.nytimes.com/2017/01/19/opinion/sunday/the-conversation-placebo.html?_r=0.

Orsi, R. A. (2005) *Between Heaven and Earth: The Religious Worlds People Make and the Scholars Who Study Them*. Princeton, NJ: Princeton University Press.

Ospina, N. S., Phillips, K. A., Rodriguez-Gutierrez, R., Castaneda-Guarderas, A., *et al*. (2018) "Eliciting the patient's agenda: Secondary analysis of recorded clinical encounters." *Journal of General Internal Medicine 34*, 1, 36–40.

Paddock, C. (2011) "Body language of empathy is genetically wired say scientists." Medical News Today. Accessed on November 16, 2011 at www.medicalnewstoday.com/articles/237743.php.

Paden, W. E. (1994) *Religious Worlds: The Comparative Study of Religion*. Boston, MA: Beacon Press.

Pagano, M. E., Post, S. G., and Johnson, S. M. (2010) "Alcoholics anonymous-related helping and the helper therapy principle." *Alcohol Treatment Quarterly 29*, 1, 23–34.

Pakenham, K. I. (2008) "Making sense of illness or disability: The nature of sense making in multiple sclerosis (MS)." *Journal of Health Psychology 13*, 1, 93–105.

Paredes, A. C. and Pereira, M. G. (2018) "Spirituality, distress and posttraumatic growth in breast cancer patients." *Journal of Religion and Health 57*, 1606–1617.

Pargament, K. I. (1997) *The Psychology of Religion and Coping: Theory, Research, Practice*. New York, NY: Guilford Press.

Pargament, K. I. (2007) *Spiritually Integrated Psychotherapy: Understanding and Addressing the Sacred*. New York, NY: Guilford Press.

Pargament, K. I., Ano, G. G., and Wachholtz, A. B. (2005a) "The Religious Dimension of Coping: Advances in Theory, Research, and Practice." In R. F. Paloutzian and C. L. Park (eds) *Handbook of the Psychology of Religion and Spirituality*. New York, NY: Guilford Press.

Pargament, K. I., Kennell, J., Hathaway, W., Grevengoed, N., Newman, J., and Jones, W. (1988) "Religion and the problem-solving process: Three styles of coping." *Journal for the Scientific Study of Religion 27*, 1, 90–104.

Pargament, K. I., Koenig, H. G., and Perez, L. M. (2000) "The many methods of religious coping: Development and initial validation of the RCOPE." *Journal of Clinical Psychology 56*, 4, 519–543.

Pargament, K. I., Koenig, H. G., Tarakeshwar, N., and Hahn, J. (2004) "Religious coping methods as predictors of psychological, physical and spiritual outcomes among medically ill elderly patients: A two-year longitudinal study." *Journal of Health Psychology 9*, 6, 713–730.

Pargament, K. I., Lomax, J. W., McGee, J. S., and Fang, Q. (2014) "Sacred moments in psychotherapy from the perspectives of mental health providers and clients: Prevalence, predictors, and consequences." *Spirituality in Clinical Practice 1*, 4, 248–262.

Pargament, K. I., Murray-Swank, N. A., Magyar, G. M., and Ano, G. G. (2005b) "Spiritual struggle: A phenomenon of interest to psychology and religion." In W. R. Miller and H. D. Delaney (eds) *Judeo-Christian Perspectives on Psychology*. Washington, DC: American Psychological Association.

Pargament, K. I., Oman, D., Pomerleau, J., and Mahoney, A. (2017) "Some contributions of a psychological approach to the study of the sacred." *Religion 47*, 4, 718–744.

Pargament, K. I., Smith, B. W., Koenig, H. G., and Perez, L. M. (1998) "Patterns of positive and negative religious coping with major life stressors." *Journal for the Scientific Study of Religion 37*, 4, 710–724.

Park, C. L. (2007) "Religiousness/spirituality and health: A meaning systems perspective." *Journal of Behavioral Medicine 30*, 319–328.

Park, H.-K. H. (2014) "Toward a pastoral theological phenomenology: Constructing a reflexive and relational phenomenological method from a postcolonial perspective." *Journal of Pastoral Theology 24*, 1, 3.1–3.21.

Patel, N. R., Kennedy, A., Blickem, C., Rogers, A., Reeves, D., and Chew-Graham, C. (2014) "Having diabetes and having to fast: A qualitative study of British Muslims with diabetes." *Health Expectations 18*, 5, 1698–1708.

Paterson, B. L. (2001) "The shifting perspectives model of chronic illness." *Journal of Nursing Scholarship 33*, 1, 21–26.

Patsiopoulos, A. T. and Buchanan, M. J. (2011) "The practice of self-compassion in counseling: A narrative inquiry." *Professional Psychology: Research and Practice 42*, 4, 301–307.

Patterson, J. M. and Garwick, A. (1994) "The impact of chronic illness on families: A family systems perspective." *Annals of Behavioral Medicine 16*, 2, 131–142.

Pattison, S. (1989) *Alive and Kicking: Towards a Practical Theology of Illness and Healing.* London: SCM Press.

Peale, N. V. (2003, first published 1952) *The Power of Positive Thinking.* New York, NY: Fireside.

Penkala-Gawęcka (2013) "Mentally ill or chosen by spirits? 'Shamanic illness' and the revival of Kazakh traditional medicine in post-Soviet Kazaakhstan." *Central Asian Survey 32*, 1, 37–51.

Penman, J., Oliver, M., and Harrington, A. (2013) "The relational model of spiritual engagement depicted by palliative care clients and caregivers." *International Journal of Nursing Practice 19*, 39–46.

Pennebaker, J. W. (1997a) "Writing about emotional experiences as a therapeutic process." *Psychological Science 8*, 3, 162–166.

Pennebaker, J. W. (1997b) *Opening Up: The Healing Power of Expressing Emotions.* New York, NY: Guilford Press.

Pérez, J. E. and Smith, A. R. (2015) "Intrinsic religiousness and well-being among cancer patients: The mediating role of control-related religious coping and self-efficacy for coping with cancer." *Journal of Behavioral Medicine 38*, 183–193.

Perry, B. L. (2011) "The labeling paradox: Stigma, the sick role, and social networks in mental illness." *Journal of Health and Social Behavior 52*, 4, 460–477.

Pesek, E. M. (2002) "The Role of Support Groups in Disenfranchised Grief." In K. J. Doka (ed.) *Disenfranchised Grief: New Directions, Challenges, and Strategies for Practice.* Champaign, IL: Research Press.

Petrie, K. J. and Weinman, J. (2012) "Patients' perceptions of their illness: The dynamo of volition in health care." *Current Directions in Psychological Science 21*, 1, 60–65.

Pew Research Center (2012) "Religion and the unaffiliated: 'Nones' on the rise." Accessed on October 9, 2012 at www.pewforum.org/2012/10/09/nones-on-the-rise-religion/#belief-in-god.

Pew Research Center (2018) "The religious typology: A new way to categorize Americans by religion." Accessed on July 9, 2019 at www.pewforum.org/2018/08/29/the-religious-typology.

Phend, C. (2012) "Millions of smokers don't tell docs that they light up." MedPage Today. Accessed on July 9, 2019 at www.medpagetoday.com/primarycare/smoking/30607.

Phillips, R. E., Cheng, C. M., Oemig, C., Hietbrink, L., and Vonnegut, E. (2012) "Validation of a Buddhist coping measure among primarily non-Asian Buddhists in the United States." *Journal for the Scientific Study of Religion 51*, 1, 156–172.

Piburn, G. (1999) *Beyond Chaos: One Man's Journey Alongside His Chronically Ill Wife.* Atlanta, GA: Arthritis Foundation.

Piderman, K. M., Marek, D. M., Jenkins, S. M., Johnson, M. E., Buryska, J. F., and Mueller, P. S. (2008) "Patients' expectations of hospital chaplains." *Mayo Clinic Proceedings 83*, 1, 58–65.

Pirschel, C. (2018) "Remembering Margo McCaffery's contributions to pain management." ONS Voice. Accessed on July 22, 2019 at https://voice.ons.org/news-and-views/remembering-margo-mccafferys-contributions-to-pain-management.

Plach, S. K., Stevens, P. E., and Moss, V. A. (2004a) "Corporeality: Women's experiences of a body with rheumatoid arthritis." *Clinical Nursing Research 13*, 2, 137–155.

Plach, S. K., Stevens, P. E., and Moss, V. A. (2004b) "Social role experiences of women living with rheumatoid arthritis." *Journal of Family Nursing 10*, 33–49.

Polusny, M. A., Erbes, C. R., Thuras, P., Moran, A., *et al.* (2015) "Mindfulness-based stress reduction for posttraumatic stress disorder among veterans: A randomized clinical trial." *JAMA 314*, 5, 456–465.

Pope, R. A. (2007) "White Coat Syndrome." In S. DasGupta and M. Hurst (eds) *Stories of Illness and Healing: Women Write Their Bodies*. Kent, OH: Kent State University Press.

Puchalski, C. M. (2006) *A Time for Listening and Caring: Spirituality and the Care of the Chronically Ill and Dying*. New York, NY: Oxford University Press.

Puchalski, C. M., Vtillo, R., Hull, S. K., and Reller, N. (2014) "Improving the spiritual dimension of whole person care: Reaching national and international consensus." *Journal of Palliative Medicine 17*, 6, 642–656.

Pumariega, A. (2018) "6 questions you can ask a loved one to help screen for suicide risk." *The Conversation*. Accessed on December 9, 2018 at http://theconversation.com/6-questions-you-can-ask-a-loved-one-to-help-screen-for-suicide-risk-102026.

Quill, T. R., Arnold, R., and Back, A. L. (2009) "Discussing treatment preferences with patients who want 'everything.'" *Annals of Internal Medicine 151*, 5, 345–349.

Quinn, H. (2018) "29 things people said that were actually code for 'I'm anxious.'" HuffPost. Accessed on July 9, 2019 at www.huffingtonpost.co.uk/the-mighty/29-things-people-said-that-were-actually-code-for-im-anxious_a_23381187.

Radcliffe, E., Lowton, K., and Morgan, M. (2013) "Co-construction of chronic illness narratives by older stroke survivors and their spouses." *Sociology of Health and Illness 35*, 7, 993–1007.

Rafferty, K. A., Billig, A. K., and Mosack, K. E. (2015) "Spirituality, religion, and health: The role of communication, appraisals, and coping for individuals living with chronic illness." *Journal of Religion and Health 54*, 1870–1885.

Ramsay, N. J. (2004) *Pastoral Care and Counseling: Redefining the Paradigms*. Nashville, TN: Abingdon.

Rao, A., Hickman, L. D., Sibbritt, D., Newton, P. J., and Phillips, J. L. (2016) "Is energy healing an effective non-pharmacological therapy for improving symptom management of chronic illnesses? A systematic review." *Complementary Therapies in Clinical Practice 25*, 26–41.

Ratanakul, P. (2008) "Health, disease, and healing: The Buddhist contribution." *Dharma World Magazine*. Accessed on August 20, 2017 at https://rk-world.org/dharmaworld/dw_2008odhealth.aspx.

Rebman, A. W., Aucott, J. N., Weinstein, E. R., Bechtold, K. T., Smith, K. C., and Leonard, L. (2017) "Living in limbo: Contested narratives of patients with chronic symptoms following Lyme disease." *Qualitative Health Research 27*, 4, 534–546.

Redelman, M. J. (2008) "Is there a place for sexuality in the holistic care of patients in the palliative care phase of life?" *American Journal of Hospice and Palliative Medicine 25*, 5, 366–371.

Reeves, N. (2007) "Grief and spirituality." *Presence: An International Journal of Spiritual Direction 13*, 4, 34–40.

Reyes-Ortiz, C. A., Rodriguez, M., and Markides, K. S. (2009) "The role of spirituality healing with perceptions of the medical encounter among Latinos." *Journal of General Internal Medicine 24*, S3, 542–547.

Reynolds, F. and Prior, S. (2003a) "'A lifestyle coat-hanger': A phenomenological study of the meanings of artwork for women coping with chronic illness and disability." *Disability and Rehabilitation 25*, 14, 785–794.

Reynolds, F. and Prior, S. (2003b) "'Sticking jewels in your life': Exploring women's strategies for negotiating an acceptable quality of life with multiple sclerosis." *Qualitative Health Research 13*, 9, 1225–1251.

Reynolds, N., Mrug, S., Britton, L., Guion, K., Wolfe, K., and Gutierrez, H. (2014) "Spiritual coping predicts 5-year health outcomes in adolescents with cystic fibrosis." *Journal of Cystic Fibrosis 13*, 5, 593–600.

Reynolds, N., Mrug, S., and Guion, K. (2013) "Spiritual coping and psychosocial adjustment of adolescents with chronic illness: The role of cognitive attributions, age and disease group." *Journal of Adolescent Health 52*, 559–565.

Reynolds, N., Mrug, S., Wolfe, K., Schwebel, D., and Wallander, J. (2016) "Spiritual coping, psychosocial adjustment, and physical health in youth with chronic illness: A meta-analytic review." *Health Psychology Review 10*, 2, 226–243.

Risk, J. L. (2013) "Building a new life: A chaplain's theory based case study of chronic illness." *Journal of Health Care Chaplaincy 19*, 3, 81–98.

Roberts, L. and Levy, R. (2008) *Shamanic Reiki: Expanded Ways of Working with Universal Life Force Energy*. Winchester, UK: O Books.

Robinson, J. A. and Crawford, G. B. (2005) "Identifying palliative care patients with symptoms of depression: An algorithm." *Palliative Medicine 19*, 278–287.

Robinson, P. (2016) *My Journey Through Chronic Pain*. Maitland, FL: Xulon Press.

Robinson, S., Kissane, D. W., Brooker, J., and Burney, S. (2016) "A review of the construct of demoralization: History, definitions, and future directions for palliative care." *American Journal of Hospice and Palliative Medicine 33*, 1, 93–101.

Rodin, G., Lo, C., Mikulincer, M., Donner, A., Gagliese, L., and Zimmermann, C. (2009) "Pathways to distress: The multiple determinants of depression, hopelessness, and the desire for hastened death in metastatic cancer patients." *Social Science and Medicine 68*, 3, 562–569.

Rolland, J. S. (1994) "In sickness and in health: The impact of illness on couples' relationships." *Journal of Marital and Family Therapy 20*, 4, 327–348.

Rollnick, S. and Miller, W. R. (1995) "Motivational interviewing: What is MI?" *Behavioural and Cognitive Psychotherapy 23*, 325–334.

Romm, C. (2014) "Understanding how grief weakens the body." Accessed on December 7, 2018 at www.theatlantic.com/health/archive/2014/09/understanding-how-grief-weakens-the-body/380006.

Roos, S. and Neimeyer, R. A. (2007) "Reauthoring the Self: Chronic Sorrow and Posttraumatic Stress Following the Onset of CID." In E. Martz and H. Livneh (eds) *Coping with Chronic Illness and Disability: Theoretical, Empirical, and Clinical Aspects*. New York, NY: Springer Science+Business Media.

Rosa, K. C. (2016) "Integrative review on the use of Newman Praxis Relationship in chronic illness." *Nursing Science Quarterly 29*, 3, 211–218.

Rosequist, L., Wall, K., Corwin, D., Achterberg, J., and Koopman, C. (2012) "Surrender as a form of active acceptance among breast cancer survivors receiving psycho-spiritual integrative therapy." *Supportive Care in Cancer 20*, 2821–2827.

Roth, D. L., Fredman, L., and Haley, W. E. (2015) "Informal caregiving and its impact on health: A reappraisal from population-based studies." *The Gerontologist 55*, 2, 309–319.

Rowe, M. M. and Allen, R. G. (2004) "Spirituality as a means of coping with chronic illness." *American Journal of Health Studies 19*, 1, 62–67.

Roze des Ordons, A., Sinuff, T., Stelfox, H. T., Kondejewski, J., and Sinclair, S. (2018) "Spiritual distress within inpatient settings: A scoping review of patients' and families' experiences." *Journal of Pain and Symptom Management 56*, 1, 122–145.

Russell, C. S., White, M. B., and White, C. P. (2006) "Why me? Why now? Why multiple sclerosis? Making meaning and perceived quality of life in a Midwestern sample of patients with multiple sclerosis." *Families, Systems, and Health 24*, 1, 65–81.

Ryan, E. B. (2006) "Finding a new voice: Writing through health adversity." *Journal of Language and Social Psychology 25*, 4, 423–436.

Sajja, A. and Puchalski, C. (2017) "Healing in modern medicine." *Annals of Palliative Medicine 6*, 3, 206–210.

Sakellariou, D., Boniface, G., and Brown, P. (2013) "Using joint interviews in a narrative-based study on illness experiences." *Qualitative Health Research 23*, 11, 1563–1570.

Salwitz, J. C. (2013) "Why don't doctors talk about death with their patients?" KevinMD. Accessed on February 21, 2013 at www.kevinmd.com/blog/2013/02/doctors-talk-death-patients.html.

Saniotis, A. (2018) "Understanding mind/body medicine from Muslim religious practices of salat and dhikr." *Journal of Religion and Health 57*, 849–857.

Sapey, B. (2004) "Impairment, disability, and loss: Reassessing the rejection of loss." *Illness, Crisis and Loss 12*, 1, 90–101.

Sarenmalm, E. K., Thorén-Jönsson, A.-L., Gaston-Johansson, F., and Öhlén, J. (2009) "Making sense of living under the shadow of death: Adjusting to a recurrent breast cancer illness." *Qualitative Health Research 19*, 8, 1116–1130.

Saunders, B. (2017) "'It seems like you're going around in circles': Recurrent biographical disruption constructed through the past, present and anticipated future in the narratives of young adults with inflammatory bowel disease." *Sociology of Health and Illness 39*, 5, 726–740.

Schairer, S. (2018) "3 meditations that cultivate compassion." The Chopra Center. Accessed on February 22, 2019 at https://chopra.com/articles/3-meditations-that-cultivate-compassion.

Schellinger, S. E., Anderson, E. W., Frazer, M. S., and Cain, C. L. (2018) "Patient self-defined goals: Essentials of person-centered care for serious illness." *American Journal of Hospice and Palliative Medicine 35*, 1, 159–165.

Schmohl, C. (2017) "'You've done very well' ('Das haban Sie sehr schon gemacht'): On courage and presence of mind in spiritual issues." *Health and Social Care Chaplaincy 5*, 2, 174–193.

Schneiders, S. M. (2005) "A Hermeneutical Approach to the Study of Christian Spirituality." In E. A. Dreyer and M. S. Burrows (eds) *Minding the Spirit: The Study of Christian Spirituality.* Baltimore, MD: Johns Hopkins University Press.

Scholl, T. (2014) *Walking the Labyrinth: A Place to Pray and Seek God.* Downers Grove, IL: IVP Books.

Schroevers, M. J., Kraaij, V., and Garnefski, N. (2011) "Cancer patients' experience of positive and negative changes due to the illness: Relationships with psychological well-being, coping, and goal reengagement." *Psycho-Oncology 20*, 165–172.

Schuhmann, C. and Damen, A. (2018) "Representing the good: Pastoral care in a secular age." *Pastoral Psychology 67*, 405–417.

Schulman-Green, D., Jaser, S., Martin, F., Alonzo, A., *et al.* (2012) "Processes of self-management in chronic illness." *Journal of Nursing Scholarship 44*, 2, 136–144.

Schultz, M., Meged-Book, T., Mashiach, T., and Bar-Sela, G. (2017) "Distinguishing between spiritual distress, general distress, spiritual well-being, and spiritual pain among cancer patients during oncology treatment." *Journal of Pain and Symptom Management 54*, 1, 66–72.

Scott, J. G., Warber, S. L., Dieppe, P., Jones, D., and Strange, K. C. (2017) "Healing journey: A qualitative analysis of the healing experiences of Americans suffering from trauma and illness." *British Medical Journal Open 7*, e016771.

Seawell, A. H. and Danoff-Burg, S. (2005) "Body image and sexuality in women with and without systemic lupus erythematosus." *Sex Roles 53*, 11/12, 865–876.

Seligman, M. E. P. and Csikszentmihalyi, M. (2000) "Positive psychology: An introduction." *American Psychologist 55*, 1, 5–14.

Selman, L., Harding, R., Gysels, M., Speck, P., and Higginson, I. J. (2011) "The measurement of spirituality in palliative care and the content of tools validated cross-culturally: A systematic review." *Journal of Pain and Symptom Management 41*, 4, 728–753.

Seo, M., Kang, H. S., Lee, Y. J., and Chae, S. M. (2015) "Narrative therapy with an emotional approach for people with depression: Improved symptom and cognitive-emotional outcomes." *Journal of Psychiatric and Mental Health Nursing 22*, 379–389.

Sethi, S. (2016) "How spirituality can help motivate patients." KevinMD. Accessed on July 9, 2016 at www.kevinmd.com/blog/2016/07/spirituality-can-help-motivate-patients.html.

Sharabi, A. (2014) "Deep healing: Ritual healing in the teshuvah movement." *Anthropology and Medicine 21*, 3, 277–289.

Sharif, S. P., Lehto, R. H., Nia, H. S., Goudarzian, A. H., *et al.* (2018) "Religious coping and death depression in Iranian patients with cancer: Relationships to disease stage." *Supportive Care in Cancer 26*, 2571–2579.

Sherman, A. C. and Simonton, S. (2012) "Effects of personal meaning among patients in primary and specialized care: Associations with psychosocial and physical outcomes." *Psychology and Health 27*, 4, 475–490.

Sherman, A. C., Simonton, S., Latif, U., and Bracy, L. (2010) "Effects of global meaning and illness-specific meaning on health outcomes among breast cancer patients." *Journal of Behavioral Medicine 33*, 364–377.

Shinall, M. C., Stahl, D., and Bibler, T. M. (2018) "Addressing a patient's hope for a miracle." *Journal of Pain and Symptom Management 55*, 2, 535–539.

Shoard, C. (2010) "The Wizard of Oz: 71 facts for the film's 71st birthday." *The Guardian.* Accessed on September 25, 2018 at www.theguardian.com/film/2010/aug/12/the-wizard-of-oz-google-doodle.

Shukla, R., Thakur, E., Bradford, A., and Hou, J. K. (2018) "Caregiver burden in adults with inflammatory bowel disease." *Clinical Gastroenterology and Hepatology 16*, 7–15.

Siegel, B. S. (1998, first published 1986) *Love, Medicine, and Miracles: Lessons Learned about Self-Healing from a Surgeon's Experience with Exceptional Patients.* New York, NY: HarperPerennial.

Silk, S. and Goldman, B. (2013) "How not to say the wrong thing." *Los Angeles Times,* April 7, 2013. Accessed on July 25, 2019 at http://articles.latimes.com/2013/apr/07/opinion/la-oe-0407-silk-ring-theory-20130407.

Sinclair, S., Beamer, K., Hack, T. F., McClement, S., *et al.* (2017) "Sympathy, empathy, and compassion: A grounded theory study of palliative care patients' understandings, experiences, and preferences." *Palliative Medicine 31*, 5, 437–447.

Sinclair, S., Jaggi, P., Hack, T. F., McClement, S. E., Raffin-Bouchal, S., and Singh, P. (2018) "Assessing the credibility and transferability of the patient compassion model in non-cancer palliative populations." *BMC Palliative Care 17*, 108, 1–10.

Sirois, F. M., Molnar, D. S., and Hirsch, J. K. (2015) "Self-compassion, stress, and coping in the context of chronic illness." *Self and Identity 14*, 3, 334–347.

Skinner, M. and Mitchell, D. (2016) "'What? So what? Now what?' Applying Borton and Rolfe's models of reflexive practice in healthcare contexts." *Health and Social Care Chaplaincy 4*, 1, 10–19.

Sloan, R. P. (2011) "A fighting spirit won't save your life." *New York Times*. Accessed on July 9, 2019 at www.nytimes.com/2011/01/25/opinion/25sloan.html.

Smart, J. F. and Smart, D. W. (2006) "Models of disability: Implications for the counseling profession." *Journal of Counseling and Development 84*, 29–40.

Smith, B. W., Dalen, J., Wiggins, K. T., Christopher, P. J., Bernard, J. F., and Shelley, B. M. (2008) "Who is willing to use complementary and alternative medicine?" *Explore 4*, 6, 359–367.

Smith, J. Z. (1980) "The bare facts of ritual." *History of Religions 19*, 4, 112–127.

Sontag, S. (2001, first published 1978) *Illness as Metaphor and AIDS and Its Metaphors*. London: Picador.

Sorajjakool, S., Aveling, L., Thompson, K. M., and Earl, A. (2006) "Chronic pain, meaning, and spirituality: A qualitative study of the healing process in relation to the role of meaning and spirituality." *Journal of Pastoral Care and Counseling 60*, 4, 369–378.

Southwood, K. (2018) "'You are all quacks; if only you would shut up' (Job 13.4b–5a): Sin and illness in the sacred and the secular, the ancient and the modern." *Theology 12*, 2, 84–91.

Spandler, H. and Stickley, T. (2011) "No hope without compassion: The importance of compassion in recovery-focused mental health services." *Journal of Mental Health 20*, 6, 555–566.

St. John of the Cross (2003, first translated 1959) *Dark Night of the Soul*. New York, NY: Image Books.

Stanley, P. B. and Hurst, M. (2011) "Narrative palliative care: A method for building empathy." *Journal of Social Work in End-of-Life and Palliative Care 7*, 1, 39–55.

Steinhauser, K. E., Christakis, N. A., Clipp, E. C., McNeilly, M., McIntyre, L., and Tulsky, J. A. (2000) "Factors considered important at the end of life by patients, family, physicians, and other care providers." *JAMA 284*, 19, 2476–2482.

Sterba, K. R., DeVellis, R. F., Lewis, M. A., DeVellis, B. M., Jordan, J. M., and Baucom, D. H. (2008) "Effect of couple illness perception congruence on psychological adjustment in women with rheumatoid arthritis." *Health Psychology 27*, 2, 221–229.

Stoklosa, J., Patterson, K., Rosielle, D., and Arnold, R. M. (2011) "Anxiety in palliative care: Causes and diagnosis #186." *Journal of Palliative Medicine 14*, 10, 1173–1174.

Stone, H. and Lester, A. (2001) "Hope and possibility: Envisioning the future in pastoral conversation." *Journal of Pastoral Care 55*, 3, 259–269.

Strada, E. A. (2016) *Management of Depression and Anxiety in Advanced Illness*. New York, NY: MJHS Institute for Innovation in Palliative Care.

Street, R. L. and Haidet, P. (2010) "How well do doctors know their patients? Factors affecting physician understanding of patients' health beliefs." *Journal of General Internal Medicine 26*, 1, 21–27.

Sun, J., Buys, N., and Jayasinghe, R. (2014) "Effects of community-based meditative Tai Chi programme on improving quality of life, physical and mental health in chronic heart-failure participants." *Aging and Mental Health 18*, 3, 289–295.

Swain, J. and French, S. (2000) "Towards an affirmation model of disability." *Disability and Society 15*, 4, 569–582.

Swinton, J. (2007) *Raging with Compassion: Pastoral Responses to the Problem of Evil*. Grand Rapids, MI: William B. Eerdmans Publishing.

Taïeb, O., Bricou, O., Baubet, T., Gaboulaud, V., *et al.* (2010) "Patients' beliefs about the causes of systemic lupus erythematosus." *Rheumatology 49*, 3, 592–599.

Tan, H., Wutthilert, C., and O'Connor, M. (2011) "Spirituality and quality of life in older people with chronic illness in Thailand." *Progress in Palliative Care 19*, 4, 177–184.

Tang, S. Y. S. and Anderson, J. M. (1999) "Human agency and the process of healing: Lessons learned from women living with a chronic illness—'rewriting the expert.'" *Nursing Inquiry 6*, 83–93.

Tarakeshwar, N., Pargament, K. I., and Mahoney, A. (2003) "Initial development of a measure of religious coping among Hindus." *Journal of Community Psychology 31*, 6, 607–628.

Tarlow, B. J., Wisniewski, S. R., Belle, S. H., Rubert, M., Ory, M. G., and Gallagher-Thompson, D. (2004) "Positive aspects of caregiving: Contributions of the REACH Project to the development of new measures for Alzheimer's care." *Research on Aging 26*, 4, 429–453.

Tatsumura, Y., Maskarinec, G., Kakai, H., and Shumay, D. M. (2003) "Religious and spiritual resources, CAM, and conventional treatment in the lives of cancer patients." *Alternative Therapies in Health and Medicine 9*, 3, 64–71.

Taves, A., Asprem, E., and Ihm, E. (2018) "Psychology, meaning making, and the study of worldviews: Beyond religion and non-religion." *Psychology of Religion and Spirituality 10*, 3, 201–217.

Taylor, B. B. (2010) "Pain by number." *Christian Century 127*, 19, 35.

Taylor, E. J., Gober-Park, C., Schoonover-Shoffner, K., Mamier, I., Somaiya, C. K., and Bahjri, K. (2018) "Nurse opinions about initiating spiritual conversation and prayer in patient care." *Journal of Advanced Nursing 74*, 2381–2392.

Taylor, S. (2007) "What to expect in Buddhist spiritual direction." *Presence: An International Journal of Spiritual Direction 13*, 3, 46–52.

Tedeschi, R. G. and Calhoun, L. G. (2004) "Posttraumatic growth: Conceptual foundations and empirical evidence." *Psychological Inquiry 15*, 1–18.

Thagard, P. (2018) "Science and philosophy offer more for grief than religion: Bereavement is horrible, but religion is false comfort." *Psychology Today*. Accessed on July 16, 2018 at www.psychologytoday.com/us/blog/hot-thought/201807/science-and-philosophy-offer-more-grief-religion.

Thauvoye, E., Vanhooren, S., Vandenhoeck, A., and Dezutter, J. (2018) "Spirituality and well-being in old age: Exploring the dimensions of spirituality in relation to late-life functioning." *Journal of Religion and Health 57*, 2167–2181.

Thernstrom, M. (2010) *The Pain Chronicles: Cures, Myths, Mysteries, Prayers, Diaries, Brain Scans, Healing, and the Science of Suffering*. New York, NY: Farrar, Straus, and Giroux.

Thomas, C. (2004) "How is disability understood? An examination of sociological approaches." *Disability and Society 19*, 6, 569–583.

Thomas, H., Mitchell, G., Rich, J., and Best, M. (2018) "Definition of whole person care in general practice in the English language literature: A systematic review." *BMJ Open 8*, e023758, 1–12.

Thomas Jefferson University (2012) "Meditation combined with art therapy can change your brain and lower anxiety." Jefferson Health. Accessed on December 4, 2012 at https://hospitals.jefferson.edu/news/2012/12/meditation-combined-with-art-therapy-can-change-your-brain-and-lower-anxiety.

Thomsen, T. G., Hansen, S. R., and Wagner, L. (2011) "How to be a patient in a palliative life experience? A qualitative study to enhance knowledge about coping abilities in advanced cancer patients." *Journal of Psychosocial Oncology 29*, 3, 254–273.

Thorne, S., McCormick, J., and Carty, E. (1997) "Deconstructing the gender neutrality of chronic illness and disability." *Health Care for Women International 18*, 1, 1–16.

Tick, E. (2007) "Healing mysteries in a Vietnamese village." *Explore 3*, 2, 149–152.

Timmerman, C., Uhrenfeldt, L., and Birkelund, R. (2015) "Room for caring: Patients' experiences of well-being, relief and hope during serious illness." *Scandinavian Journal of Caring Sciences 29*, 426–434.

Timmins, F., Caldeira, S., Murphy, M., Pujol, N., *et al.* (2018) "The role of the healthcare chaplain: A literature review." *Journal of Health Care Chaplaincy 24*, 87–106.

Traeger, L., Greer, J. A., Fernandez-Robles, C., Temel, J. S., and Pirl, W. F. (2012) "Evidence-based treatment of anxiety in patients with cancer." *Journal of Clinical Oncology 30*, 11, 1197–1205.

Trevino, K. M., Prigerson, H. G., and Maciejewski, P. K. (2017) "Advanced cancer caregiving as a risk for major depressive episodes and generalized anxiety disorder." *Psycho-Oncology 27*, 243–249.

Trimble, J. E. (2010) "Bear spends time in our dreams now: Magical thinking and cultural empathy in multicultural counselling theory and practice." *Counselling Psychology Quarterly 23*, 3, 241–253.

Tsoulis-Reay, A. (2016) "What it's like to have severe Lyme disease." The Cut. Accessed on June 15, 2015 at http://nymag.com/scienceofus/2015/06/what-its-like-to-have-severe-lyme-disease.html?ncid=newsltushpmg00000003.

Unantenne, N., Warren, N., Canaway, R., and Manderson, L. (2013) "The strength to cope: Spirituality and faith in chronic disease." *Journal of Religion and Health 52*, 1147–1161.

Underwood, R. L. (2006) "Enlarging hope for wholeness: Ministry with persons in pain." *Journal of Pastoral Care and Counseling 60*, 1–2, 3–12.

Van Gorp, B. and Vercruysse, T. (2012) "Frames and counter-frames giving meaning to dementia: A framing analysis of media content." *Social Science and Medicine 74*, 1274–1281.

Van Laarhoven, H. W. M., Schilderman, J., Bleijenberg, G., Donders, R., *et al.* (2011) "Coping, quality of life, depression and hopelessness in cancer patients in a curative and palliative end of life care setting." *Cancer Nursing 34*, 4, 302–313.

Van Laarhoven, H. W. M., Schilderman, J., Vissers, K. C., Verhagen, C. A., and Prins, J. B. (2010) "Images of God in relation to coping strategies of palliative care patients." *Journal of Pain and Symptom Management 40*, 4, 495–501.

Vander Zee, J. (2002) "The Chronically Ill Patient." In R. B. Gilbert (ed.) *Health Care and Spirituality: Listening, Assessing, Caring.* Amityville, NY: Baywood Publishing.

VanderWeele, T. J., Balboni, T. A., and Koh, H. K. (2017) "Health and spirituality." *JAMA 318*, 6, 519–520.

Vassilev, I., Rogers, A., Sanders, C., Cheraghi-Sohi, S., *et al.* (2014) "Social status and living with a chronic illness: An exploration of assessment and meaning attributed to work and employment." *Chronic Illness 10*, 4, 273–290.

Vehling, S. and Mehnert, A. (2014) "Symptom burden, loss of dignity, and demoralization in patients with cancer: A mediation model." *Psycho-Oncology 23*, 283–290.

Verghese, A. (2011) "Treat the patient, not the CT scan." *New York Times.* Accessed on February 27, 2011 at www.nytimes.com/2011/02/27/opinion/27verghese.html?scp=1&sq=treat%20the%20patient,%20not%20the%20ct%20scan&st=cse.

Vest, N. (2003) *Tending the Holy: Spiritual Direction Across Traditions.* Harrisburg, PA: Morehouse.

Vickers, M. H. (2000) "Stigma, work, and 'unseen' illness: A case and notes to enhance understanding." *Illness, Crisis and Loss 8*, 2, 131–151.

Vijayasingham, L. (2018) "Work right to right work: An automythology of chronic illness and work." *Chronic Illness 14*, 1, 42–53.

Villines, Z. (2017) "What is the best type of meditation?" Medical News Today. Accessed on December 22, 2017 at www.medicalnewstoday.com/articles/320392.php.

Vitorino, L. M., Soares, R. C. E. S., Santos, A. E. O., Lucchetti, A. L. G., *et al.* (2018) "The positive and negative impact of spiritual religious coping on quality of life and depression in dialysis patients." *Journal of Holistic Nursing 36*, 4, 332–340.

Voltzenlogel, V., Ernst, A., de Sèze, J., Brassat, D., and Manning, L. (2016) "Giving meaning to illness: An investigation of self-defining memories in patients with relapsing-remitting multiple sclerosis patients." *Consciousness and Cognition 45*, 200–209.

Wachholtz, A. B. and Keefe, F. J. (2006) "What physicians should know about spirituality and chronic pain." *Southern Medical Journal 99*, 10, 1174–1175.

Wachholtz, A. B., Pearce, M. J., and Koenig, H. G. (2007) "Exploring the relationship between spirituality, coping, and pain." *Journal of Behavioral Medicine 30*, 311–318.

Wang, Y.-C. and Lin, C.-C. (2016) "Spiritual well-being may reduce the negative impacts of cancer symptoms on the quality of life and the desire for hastened death in terminally ill cancer patients." *Cancer Nursing 39*, 4, E43–E50.

Webster, B. (2018) "Distinguishing primary and secondary loss." The Center for the Grief Journey. Accessed on December 7, 2018 at https://griefjourney.com/startjourney/for-the-grieving-person/articles-for-the-grieving-person/distinguishing-primary-and-secondary-loss.

Wendell, S. (1996) *The Rejected Body: Feminist Philosophical Reflections on Disability.* New York, NY: Routledge.

White, G. (2006) *Talking about Spirituality in Health Care Practice.* London: Jessica Kingsley Publishers.

White, M. and Epston, D. (1990) *Narrative Means to Therapeutic Ends.* New York, NY: W. W. Norton & Company.

Whiteman, H. (2014) "Ashamed after a doctor's visit? It could be due to self-contempt." Medical News Today. Accessed on January 19, 2014 at www.medicalnewstoday.com/articles/271361.php.

Whittemore, R. and Dixon, J. (2008) "Chronic illness: The process of integration." *Journal of Clinical Nursing 17*, 7b, 177–187.

Wick, E. (2015) "How I kept living when my body turned on me: I was diagnosed with rheumatoid arthritis when I was 24. Now every day is a battle with myself." BuzzFeed. Accessed on April 7, 2015 at www.buzzfeed.com/emilywick/how-to-keep-living-when-your-body-turns-on-you.

Widera, E. W. and Block, S. D. (2012) "Managing grief and depression at the end of life." *American Family Physician 86*, 3, 259–264.

Wigglesworth, C. (2013) "Empathy precedes compassion." HuffPost. Accessed on March 6, 2013 at www.huffingtonpost.com/cindy-wigglesworth/empathy_b_2796460.html.

Wijesinghe, S. and Parshall, M. B. (2016) "Impermanence and sense of coherence: Lessons learned from the adaptive behaviors of Sri Lankan Buddhist nuns with a chronic illness." *Journal of Transcultural Nursing 27*, 2, 157–165.

Williams, G. (1984) "The genesis of chronic illness: Narrative re-construction." *Sociology of Health and Illness 6*, 175–200.

Williams, J. (2018) "Tell us 5 things about your book: The many costs and confusions of chronic illness." *New York Times.* Accessed on July 8, 2018 at www.nytimes.com/2018/07/08/books/sick-porochista-khakpour-interview.html?emc=edit_bk_20180709&nl=book-review&nlid=6857157520180709&te=1.

Williams, J. and Koocher, G. P. (1998) "Addressing loss of control in chronic illness: Theory and practice." *Psychotherapy 35*, 3, 325–335.

Williams, K. L., Morrison, V., and Robinson, C. A. (2014) "Exploring caregiving experiences: Caregiver coping and making sense of illness." *Aging and Mental Health 18*, 5, 600–609.

Willig, C. (2009) "'Unlike a rock, a tree, a horse or an angel': Reflections on the struggle of meaning through writing during the process of cancer diagnosis." *Journal of Health Psychology 14*, 2, 181–189.

Wilson, K. G., Chochinov, H. M., Mcpherson, C. J., Skirko, M. G., *et al.* (2007) "Desire for euthanasia or physician-assisted suicide in palliative cancer care." *Health Psychology 26*, 3, 314–323.

Wittenberg-Lyles, E., Demris, G., Oliver, D. P., and Burt, S. (2011) "Reciprocal suffering: Caregiver concerns during hospice care." *Journal of Pain and Symptom Management 41*, 2, 383–393.

Wittink, M. N., Joo, J. H., Lewis, L. M., and Barg, F. K. (2009) "Populations at risk: Losing faith and using faith: Older African Americans discuss spirituality, religious activities, and depression." *Journal of General Internal Medicine 24*, 3, 402–407.

Wolfson, P. (2003) *Moonrise: One Family, Genetic Identity and Muscular Dystrophy*. New York, NY: St. Martin's Press.

Wolinsky, H. (2018) "Losing the 'therapeutic gaze.'" MedPage Today. Accessed on March 8, 2018 at www.medpagetoday.com/special-reports/apatientsjourney/71630.

Wong, B. (2019) "The problem with the phrase 'beat cancer.'" HuffPost. Accessed on March 4, 2019 at www.huffpost.com/entry/beat-cancer-phrase_l_5c7479e3e4b03a10c230c8a7.

Wong-McDonald, A. and Gorsuch, R. (2000) "Surrender to God: An additional coping style?" *Journal of Psychology and Theology 28*, 2, 149–161.

Worden, J. W. (2002) *Grief Counseling and Grief Therapy: A Handbook for the Mental Health Practitioner*. New York, NY: Springer.

Worzer, W. E., Kishino, N. D., and Gatchel, R. J. (2009) "Primary, secondary, and tertiary losses in chronic pain patients." *Psychological Injury and Law 2*, 215–224.

Yaden, D. B., Eichstaedt, J. C., Schwartz, H. A., Kern, M. L., *et al.* (2016) "The language of ineffability: Linguistic analysis of mystical experiences." *Psychology of Religion and Spirituality 8*, 3, 244–252.

Yalom, I. D. (1980) *Existential Psychotherapy*. New York, NY: Basic Books.

Yodchai, K., Dunning, T., Savage, S., and Hutchinson, A. M. (2017) "The role of religion and spirituality in coping with kidney disease and haemodialysis in Thailand." *Scandinavian Journal of Caring Sciences 31*, 359–367.

Zeligman, M., Varney, M., Grad, R. I., and Huffstead, M. (2018) "Post-traumatic growth in individuals with chronic illness: The role of social support and meaning making." *Journal of Counseling and Development 96*, 53–63.

Zhang, H., Shan, W., and Jiang, A. (2013) "The meaning of life and health experience for the Chinese elderly with chronic illness: A qualitative study from positive health philosophy." *International Journal of Nursing Practice 20*, 530–539.

Zhang, S. (2018) "Treating the patient's body is not synonymous with treating the patient." KevinMD. Accessed on December 16, 2018 at www.kevinmd.com/blog/2018/12/treating-the-patients-body-is-not-synonymous-with-treating-the-patient.html.

Ziebarth, D. J. (2016) "Wholistic health care: Evolutionary conceptual analysis." *Journal of Religion and Health 55*, 5, 1800–1823.

Zinnbauer, B. J., Pargament, K. I., Cole, B., Rye, M. S., *et al.* (1997) "Religion and spirituality: Unfuzzying the fuzzy." *Journal for the Scientific Study of Religion 36*, 4, 549–564.

Subject Index

Author Index

Aber, R. A. 79, 99
Abercrombie, B. 110
Abu-Raiya, H. 14, 30, 31, 87, 98
Aburub, A. S. 98
Adams, H. 116
Adams, K. 47, 126, 127
Adams, P. J. 52, 79, 103, 147
Adelman, R. D. 90
Afifi, R. 56
Agrimson, L. B. 51, 103
Ahaddour, C. 56
Ahmadi, F. 114
Ahmadmehrabi, S. 87
Alradaydeh, M. 87
Alexander, E. 116
Allen, R. G. 79, 105
Alling, F. A. 126, 137
Ambrosio, L. 146, 153
Anderson, H. 15n3, 29, 139, 198
Anderson, J. M. 44, 75
Anderson, M. 103, 108, 113, 153
Anh-Huong, N. 110
Ankrom, S. 86
Ano, G. G. 106, 107
Antonio, E. 36
Anxiety Canada 86
Applebaum, A. J. 91
Appleby, A. 15
Arabiat, D. H. 56, 56n1, 58, 103
Araten-Bergman, T. 57, 58, 147
Årestedt, L. 152, 157
Arnold, R. 26
Arora, K. R. 15, 19, 36, 39n9,
    61, 112, 128, 135, 155
Asnani, M. 103, 108, 113, 153

Asprem, E. 30
Association of Religion Data Archives 25
Attig, T. 53
Avert 60

Back, A. L. 26, 35, 131, 133
Badaracco, C. H. 15, 59
Baider, L. 27, 48
Balboni, M. J. 14, 15, 79, 98,
    99, 105, 108, 151
Balboni, T. A. 14, 15, 79, 98,
    99, 105, 108, 151
Baldacchino, D. R. 28, 114, 115, 116
Baldwin, M. 40, 156
Barnard, L. K. 134
Barrett, J. 42, 43, 79
Barton, K. S. 36
Bauer, R. 116
Baum, L. F. 20
Beardsley, C. 34
Beaulieu, J. 113
Beck, J. 59
Beck, M. 56
Beesley, V. L. 153
Bell, C. 138
Bell, I. R. 126
Benson, H. 62
Benzein, E. 152
Berger, A. S. 56
Bernard, M. 53
Bernhard, T. 74, 90, 91, 100, 153
Berry, J. 113, 139
Betcher, S. V. 55
Bibler, T. M. 25